International Trade and Finance

Publisher's Note
Two further volumes of ESSAYS IN HONOUR OF JAN TINBERGEN, also edited by Willy Sellekaerts, are published simultaneously: ECONOMIC DEVELOPMENT AND PLANNING and ECONOMETRICS AND ECONOMIC THEORY.

Jan Tinbergen

International Trade and Finance

Essays in Honour of Jan Tinbergen
Edited by
Willy Sellekaerts

 International Arts and Sciences Press, Inc.
White Plains, New York

Published in Great Britain by
The Macmillan Press Ltd.

First U.S. edition published in 1974 by
International Arts and Sciences Press, Inc.
901 North Broadway, White Plains, New York 10603

Library of Congress Catalog Card Number: 73-92710

International Standard Book Number: 0-87332-054-9

Printed in Great Britain

Contents

Preface

In 1969 Ragnar Frisch and Jan Tinbergen were selected to share the first Nobel Prize in Economics. As former students of Professor Tinbergen my wife and I decided to honour him by compiling and editing a collection of previously unpublished articles, written by leading economists. In order to create a lasting monument to Jan Tinbergen we decided to use the royalties from the volume to create a scholarship fund from which outstanding Dutch students in economics will receive financial assistance during their first year of study in the North American university of their choice. Further details will later be arranged with the Netherlands School of Economics in Rotterdam.

Several North American and European economists were invited to write a paper, preferably focusing on Tinbergen's pathbreaking work in international trade, economic development and planning, econometrics and economic theory. Most invited economists readily accepted the invitation. I thank all the contributors for their continuous interest and spontaneous co-operation during the two years between the mailing of the invitations and the completion of the manuscript.

Although a Nobel Prizewinner does not need to be introduced to the scholars of his discipline, I decided to include in this collection of essays a paper written by Bent Hansen, in which he not only skilfully appraises Professor Tinbergen's contributions to economics, but also pictures Tinbergen the man as a humanitarian idealist, a worthy candidate for the Nobel Peace Prize. I thank the *Swedish Journal of Economics*, and in particular Peter Bohm, for giving me permission to reprint Bent Hansen's paper. As an appendix to each of the three volumes of this Festschrift, a *selected* bibliography of Jan Tinbergen's contributions to economics has been included.

In addition to the contributors, many persons have helped to make the publication of this collection of essays in honour of Jan Tinbergen possible. I thank Professor Dole Anderson, Director of the Institute for International Business and Economic Development of Michigan State University, who supported my idea and made the facilities of the Institute available to invite the contributors. The Faculty of Social Sciences of the University of Ottawa also contributed to the success of this volume. I thank Patrick Meany of The Macmillan Company of Canada for his assistance in the publication of the Festschrift. Above all, my wife, Brigitte made the publication of this Festschrift feasible, by providing invaluable technical and editorial assistance.

WILLY SELLEKAERTS

Ottawa,
November 1971

Introduction

JAN TINBERGEN

An Appraisal of his Contributions to Economics*

By BENT HANSEN

PROFESSOR Jan Tinbergen was born on 12 April 1903. He graduated from Leiden University where he also obtained his doctoral degree. From 1929 to 1945 he was, with certain interruptions, an official of the Netherlands' Central Bureau of Statistics. As from 1933 he has also been a professor of economics at the Netherlands School of Economics at Rotterdam. During the years 1936 to 1938 he served on the staff of the League of Nations at Geneva. At the end of World War II, in 1945, he was appointed Director of the newly created Central Planning Bureau of the Netherlands. He resigned from this position in 1955 and has since then – besides teaching and research – served as an adviser and consultant to numerous governments and international organisations. As from 1966 he is the Chairman of the United Nation's Committee for Development Planning. A considerable number of universities have awarded him honorary degrees.

The message that Professors Ragnar Frisch and Jan Tinbergen were selected to share the first Nobel Prize in Economics was received by the profession with great satisfaction. Few

* Reprinted with the permission of the *Swedish Journal of Economics*. The original reference: Hansen, Bent, 'Jan Tinbergen: An Appraisal of his Contributions to Economics', *Swedish Journal of Economics*, LXXI (1969) 325–36.

contemporary economists are respected as they are. Few, if any, can look back to a stream of pathbreaking contributions to economics comparable to those achieved by these two men. And their work has been so closely related that it was only natural that they should share the prize.

Thus the choice of the Swedish Academy of Science was both wise and correct. It was a happy choice, too, because both Ragnar Frisch and Jan Tinbergen increasingly have turned their attention towards development policy, searching for feasible solutions to the economic policy problems of the poor countries and it is in this capacity that they are best known nowadays outside the profession. It will always remain a matter of subjective judgement what exactly constitutes a great contribution to economics and, more generally, to science. But it would certainly be most natural for the Academy to consider not only the extension of knowledge for knowledge's own sake, but also its applied aspects, its potential benefits to mankind. At a time when funds for civil development aid tend to dry up and developed countries self-righteously begin to 'lose patience' with their earlier possessions and turn their back to the Third World mess, it is gratifying to see the problems of the poor countries recognised – if not explicitly then certainly by implications – as *the* important scientific problem of economics rather than turnpikes, double-switching and other esoteric matters. Frisch and Tinbergen have both contributed to the pure theory of economics and its applications, for developed as well as under-developed economies. The whole range of economists, from the celebrities in the ivory towers and think-tanks of the rich countries to the anonymous people doing the dirty development work in the poor countries, may therefore all of them rightly feel that 'our men' have been chosen for this unique honour. But nobody will probably feel this more strongly and with more justification than the latter category. This makes the choice of the Academy particularly satisfactory.

1. *Tinbergen's stages of development*
It is convenient to divide Tinbergen's activities and contributions to economics into three groups which also happen to represent consecutive periods of his career (see above). During

each period he made pioneering contributions to economics and exerted a profound and lasting influence within the field to which he devoted his attention and energy. During each period he helped to set economics on a new track. Each time his contributions opened up new vistas for both economic theory and economic policy. His work paralleled to some extent that of Ragnar Frisch. They were always in close contact and influenced each other on several occasions. In the sequel we shall therefore meet Frisch's name several times.

The *first* period includes the years from the end of the twenties to World War II. This was the period when Professor Tinbergen together with a few other economists and statisticians created econometrics as a science. During the war years Tinbergen was by and large isolated from international contacts, but he used this time in preparing himself for the *second* period, the decade 1945 to 1955 when he, as the Director of the Central Planning Bureau, laid the foundation for modern short-term economic policies. The *third* period, beginning in the middle fifties and, hopefully, continuing many years ahead, Tinbergen has devoted almost exclusively to the methods and practice of planning for long-term development, in particular of under-developed countries, and international economic cooperation.

2. *The establishment of econometrics as a science*
Ragnar Frisch, Jan Tinbergen and Irving Fischer took, in 1930, the initiative in the creation of The Econometric Society. According to the Society's constitution it is 'an international society for the advancement of economic theory in its relation to statistics and mathematics'. Its main objective should 'be to promote studies that aim at a unification of the theoretical–quantitative approach and the empirical–quantitative approach to economic problems and that are penetrated by constructive and rigorous thinking similar to that which has come to dominate in the natural sciences'. The Econometric Society became immediately a success; it obviously satisfied a deeply-felt need. It has served as a stimulating centre of quantitative economic research. I have quoted the words of the constitution of The Econometric Society rather extensively not only because they describe the nature of the direction into which Tinbergen

and the other founders of the Society wanted to develop economics, but also because they characterise so well Tinbergen's own scientific work.

In addition to this organisational achievement Tinbergen made some of the most fundamental early contributions to econometrics. Among them I want in particular to stress the discovery of the so-called cobweb theorem and the related contributions to dynamic theory, and the attempts of statistical testing of business-cycle theories.

In uncontrolled, agricultural markets it is usual to find that prices and quantities fluctuate in opposite directions. This pattern of behaviour is difficult to explain in terms of ordinary demand and supply theory without making rather artificial assumptions of repeated shifts in the demand and/or supply curves. In a celebrated article, 'Bestimmung und Deutung von Angebotskurven: Ein Beispiel,' *Zeitschrif für National ökonomie*, 1930, Tinbergen (simultaneously with, but independent of, two other economists, Hanau and Ricci) pointed out that this phenomenon could be explained on the assumption of fixed demand and supply curves, provided that supply (production) reacts to prices with a time lag of one year. This mechanism is now known as the 'cobweb theorem'. Quite apart from increasing the understanding of price formation in agricultural markets, this innovation in the theory of an isolated market had profound repercussions on economic theory in general. Economic theory at that time ran almost exclusively in static terms. Genuine dynamic economic theory describing a process over time was not entirely unknown; Wicksell's and Robertson's monetary theories are the outstanding examples. But there had been few attempts to formalise dynamic theories; Moore is an example. The cobweb theorem thus became a starting point for modern dynamic theory with the use of difference equations as a characteristic feature. Tinbergen himself applied this mathematical technique to the business cycle problem as early as 1931 in an article on the shipbuilding cycle. By the end of the thirties it had become a standard method of dynamic analysis in economics.

Professor Tinbergen's second great contribution to econometrics was his pioneering work on statistical testing of business-cycle theories. It resulted in the two volumes, *A*

Method and its Application to Investment Activity, and *Business Cycles in the United States of America, 1919–1932*, both published in 1939 by the League of Nations, Geneva. He had already in 1936 ventured upon a model for the Dutch economy, see below, and in 1937 he discussed the question more generally in *An Econometric Approach to Business Cycle Problems*, Paris 1937; the following year he applied his methods in a classical article 'Statistical Evidence on the Acceleration Principle,' *Economica* 1938. But it is the above-mentioned two volumes which stand out as the undisputed monument of early empirical macroeconomic model building and theory testing.

Against the background of the devastating effects of the Great Depression, the League of Nations had, in the middle of the thirties, asked Professor Gottfried Harberler to submit a theoretical study of the business cycle and investigate the differences between various contemporary theories. As a second stage in this research project Tinbergen was then asked 'to confront these various theories with historical facts – to subject them, in so far as those facts can be quantitatively expressed, to statistical analysis'.

In the first volume Tinbergen explained his method and gave three examples of its application. The method was classical multiple regression analysis combined with Frisch's confluence analysis. Tinbergen's contribution was not in statistical methodology, but in the application of existing statistical methods to macroeconomic problems. The methods applied were crude compared with present-day techniques, and the available primary data were highly unsatisfactory for the purpose. Nevertheless, Tinbergen's study of investments yielded results which only recent research has been able to challenge. He showed that whereas residential building is strongly influenced by market rates of interest, the basic determinant of investments in railway rolling stock is the rate of profits. He found little empirical evidence to support the acceleration principle which in contemporary business cycle theory played a predominant role in the discussion of investments. Tinbergen formulated an alternative 'profit principle' which via L. R. Klein became a widely accepted investment theory among econometricians.

In the second volume Jan Tinbergen set up a complete macro model for the United States economy in the form of a system of 48 difference equations, definitional relations, etc. Already the size of the model was a novelty and its details contained a wealth of untraditional ideas concerning economic macro relations. It represented a decisive break with the past in two respects. Old-fashioned business cycle theory had always tended to think in terms of the various phases of the cycle and to search for the 'cause' of each one of these phases. In line with his own early work on the business cycle, Tinbergen demonstrated how the cycle could and should be considered a unified, single phenomenon to be explained by the properties of a complete dynamic model. There was no longer a question of the 'cause' of the business cycle and old-fashioned business cycle theory could at most serve as building blocks for such a complete model. Secondly, he demonstrated the possibility of describing an economy in quantitative terms in such a way that not only may developments of the past be better understood, but also that forecasts of future developments may be made and policies calculated which modify future developments in a desired direction.

It is no exaggeration to say that these two volumes opened up a completely new branch of economics: empirical macro-economics. Keynes' scornful comments branding Tinbergen's work as 'alchemy' fell flat to the ground. Tinbergen's original model for the United States belongs now to history. Economic macro theory has been greatly improved and primary statistical data have been made available in an abundance which nobody could dream about in the thirties. Great progress has, moreover, been made in establishing adequate statistical methods for handling the estimation problems which arise in connection with models of this type. But all these developments were partly triggered off by Tinbergen's pioneering work, and we shall always be in debt to him for initiating this branch of economics.

It has already been mentioned that Jan Tinbergen presented a model for the Dutch economy in 1936. This model is not well known. It was originally published in Dutch and an English translation was not made available until 1959 (in *Selected Papers*, Amsterdam 1959). It deserves to be mentioned, however, not only because it seems to have been the prototype for the later models of the Central Planning Bureau, but also because it is surprisingly modern. The model consists of 24 equations and it explains dynamically both price and volume developments. Money wage changes are explained by a neat Phillips-relation! The rate of change of the money wage rate is a linear function of the rate of change of consumer prices lagged one period, and the level of employment. Prices are thereafter explained by a number of mark-up equations. Consumption is explained (independently of Keynes) by a relatively sophisticated consumption function, and investments are made dependent upon profits. The foreign trade equations, export and import functions, have little to learn from present-day econometric models. World demand and competitiveness determine the volume of exports, while domestic demands and competitiveness determine the various kinds of imports. The main objection to the model, in particular from a policy-making point of view, is that government expenditure and taxation are not integrated properly in the model.

The aim of the 1936 model was partly to discover the dynamic properties of the Dutch economy and partly to construct a basis for economic policy decisions. Tinbergen studied the effects over time of a series of policy measures (the dynamic multipliers in post-Keynesian parlance) but did not at this time formulate the multi-target problem the solution of which should become one of his great postwar achievements.

3. *The foundation of quantitative short-term economic policy planning*

When Professor Tinbergen accepted the directorship of the new Central Planning Bureau he gave macroeconomic model building a new twist. Whilst his pupils and followers, in particular Lawrence R. Klein, for a long time continued to work on the problem originally posed by Tinbergen in his League of Nations work, that is, to explain past developments and test conflicting theories, Tinbergen himself shifted the main emphasis to policy making. His aim was now to build models which would permit reliable forecasts of short-term developments and rational calculation of the policy measures needed for fulfilling given policy targets. As mentioned above, Tinbergen had already tried his hand at this kind of problem in 1936 when he discussed the problem of counteracting the economic consequences of the great depression for the Netherlands by means of econometric methods. A few other countries worked on the same problem, Sweden was one of them, but it goes without saying that nowhere were these efforts pursued so systematically and with so much vigour and progress as in Tinbergen's Central Planning Bureau. It is difficult to pin down exactly what were Tinbergen's personal contributions to 'the Dutch model' and the other achievements of the Central Planning Bureau; its publications are usually anonymous government documents. We have already mentioned, however, that the planning bureau's models seem to have grown out of the 1936 model, and there is plenty of testimony of the pervasive influence he had on all the work done by the bureau. It is in the nature of things that progress in economic prediction must be a slow process extending over many years, a major reason being that until recently prediction has taken place on an annual basis. Nevertheless, already when Tinbergen left the bureau in 1955 it was clear that it had succeeded in building up a model with better predictive capacities than anything else at that time. And, although many of the methods which he originally designed had to be modified and improved upon, partly in response to the experience of other countries, there can be no disagreement about the leading and pioneering role played by Tinbergen's efforts. Most governments in Western countries sponsor now work on these lines. From the very beginning, the Dutch model served as a basis for advice to the government concerning the formulation of the macro-policies of the Netherlands.

Alongside this painstaking work, Tinbergen worked on the theoretical problem of policy making, and in 1952 he made a new breakthrough when he published *The Theory of Economic Policy*, followed in 1954 by *Centralisation and Decentralisation in Economic Policy*, which created a basis for rational thinking and quantitative calculation in economic policy.

In the field of economic policy the tradition had always been to consider various types of economic policy separately and discuss them in relation to particular targets. Fiscal policy, monetary policy, foreign exchange policy, labour market policy, etc., fell apart into so many different policies; policy targets related to the price level, employment, the balance of payments, income distribution, etc., were often dealt with in isolation, subject to one or another of the above-mentioned policies. Even when actual developments forced economists to consider several targets simultaneously, such as the problem of keeping the price level stable during full employment, no method existed for tackling such multi-target problems systematically. Inspired by a memorandum submitted by Ragnar Frisch to the United Nations in 1949 ('Price-Wage-Tax-Subsidy Policies as Instruments in Maintaining Optimal Employment'), Tinbergen gave a precise formulation of the multi-target problem and showed how its solution depended upon the simultaneous, coordinated use of a sufficient number of appropriately chosen instruments. He dealt with both the case of absolute targets and the case of maximising a given social preference function, and solved a number of problems related to the efficiency of policy instruments, centralisation and decentralisation of policy decisions, and other matters. His discussion was confined to so-called quantitative changes in the economy whereas problems related to changes in the economic system as such were left aside. Other authors have continued and extended Professor Tinbergen's basic work which today is considered the obvious starting point for any discussion on general macroeconomic policy problems, although it is a curious fact that it took about fifteen years for the Anglo-Saxon economists to recognise the importance of the Tinbergen theory of economic policy.

It is both interesting and illuminating to compare Tinbergen's theory of economic policy with the so-called modern welfare economics on which the Anglo-Saxon academic economists concentrated during the forties and fifties. The latter was mainly concerned with Pareto-optimal situations in science fiction societies of perfect competition and was developed into an extremely elegant and technically refined body of theorising; it has, however, proved itself rather sterile and difficult to apply to practical policy problems. Tinbergen's theory of economic policy is quite simple, but it is concerned with the actual macro-policy targets of politicians in actually existing economies, and has proved powerful and applicable to current policy problems. This is a characteristic feature of all the scientific work of Tinbergen. He has never been very much interested in esoteric theorising for theory's own sake. His preoccupation has always been quantification and empirical application – an obvious thing in the natural sciences but not in economics – and as soon as a method 'works' empirically he does not waste time on further theoretical refinements, obviously believing that marginal returns are rapidly falling. The *tour de force* which econometrics has taken after his early application of simple least squares methods via complicated statistical methods and back again to improved least squares methods has, therefore, seen little of active participation from the side of Tinbergen. For him the basic economic problems to be tackled have been so many and so large that frontal attacks on a broad scale by means of crude methods look much more rewarding than intensive studies of small isolated problems by means of highly refined methods. In the childhood of the automobile the French engineer Panhard once commented upon the newly invented manual (un-synchronised) gearbox: 'It is brutal, but it works.' Although brutality is the last thing one would associate with Tinbergen, Panhard's comment certainly applies to Tinbergen's economic methods.

In addition to his theoretical studies on economic policy, Professor Tinbergen has also worked on practical problems in line with the principles laid down by the theory. A large number of quantitative policy problems were presented and solved in the volume, *Economic Policy; Principles and Design*, Amsterdam 1956. Many of these problems derived from his work with concrete Dutch policy problems in his capacity as advisor to his government.

4. *Planning for development and economic cooperation*
By the middle of the fifties Professor Tinbergen shifted his field of interest more and more to the problems of economic co-operation and development. His interest in economic co-operation was closely related to the creation of the Benelux and the European Common Market, but with respect to develop-ment it was in particular the problems of poor countries which attracted his attention. These were, of course, the burning issues of the postwar period, but certainly Professor Tinbergen was also led in this direction by his idealistic views on mankind and his deep devotion to humanitarian activities. He has always felt that in working on development problems in poor countries

and devoting his life to improving economic conditions in such countries he would help to repair some of the evils of colonial oppression and pay off some of the debts of the old colonial powers – including his own country.

Tinbergen's scientific contributions to the theory and practices of long-term economic planning for growth are typically Tinbergian in the sense that he has been looking for simple, crude methods that 'work' under the primitive conditions of policy-making in underdeveloped countries. Here again the contrast to contemporary work by mathematical economists, in particular in the United States, is striking. Although he is himself an excellent mathematician, Tinbergen has taken little part in the discussion of topics like optimal growth paths, turnpike theorems and dynamic efficiency. Being essentially an extension of modern welfare theory these theoretical refinements have so far had little practical importance for development planning. Tinbergen's long-term planning models have been designed on the basic assumptions that only a minimum of statistical information is available, and that the skill of planners, administrators and politicians is limited. His contributions are scattered over several books and a large number of memoranda and papers submitted to governments and international organisations, and some of his ideas exist mainly as oral tradition. Three main types of models can, however, be distinguished.

The *first* model can be characterised as 'planning by stages'. A simple macro model of the Keynes and Harrod-Domar type is first used to determine the total investment and savings requirements for the planning period considered. After this follows a sectoral stage where the total volume of investments is distributed by sectors through applications of a small input–output model and sectoral capital–output coefficients. This stage may, depending upon the special circumstances, be followed by a regional stage. The final stage consists of the choice of concrete investment projects within each sector according to investment criteria which depends upon the policy targets of the country. Under favourable circumstances planning can thus follow a recursive chain, but if necessary iteration may lead to a consistent solution. This is probably still the most widely used model for planning in underdeveloped countries.

Its obvious drawbacks are that it does not ensure efficiency in the economic system; and that it does not plan for the implementation in terms of instruments to be used. An otherwise consistent plan may not be possible simply because the necessary instruments (tax and credit policies, for instance) are not available at the given level of development. Moreover, it is not always easy to reach a consistent solution, in particular with respect to foreign trade.

The *second* type of model takes better care of the last mentioned difficulties. Since a growing number of underdeveloped countries now are equipped with computer facilities it becomes possible to work with larger systems of simultaneous equations. Tinbergen has, therefore, designed models where the first and the second stage in the first model are lumped together and where policy instruments are incorporated more explicitly in the solution. This type of model bears close resemblance to the so-called repercussion models upon which Ragnar Frisch worked during the fifties and sixties and is a combination of Harrod-Domar, Keynes and Leontief input–output models. Still, however, this model type does not imply any kind of optimisation with respect to choice of commodities to be produced and/or traded, choice of technique, etc.

The *third* type of model, the so-called semi–input–output method, was designed to overcome all these deficiencies. It differs radically from the other approaches by starting out from the individual projects and simply letting the macro-plan emerge as the sum of micro-plans. The idea here is first of all to let project appraisal be based on shadow prices, and in order to work with observable shadow prices the model centres on the international sectors and international commodity prices, and thus brings the problem of competitiveness at international prices into the planning process right from the beginning. By means of a truncated input–output model, based on engineering data, each investment project in international sectors is converted into an investment block containing the original project and all the necessary complementary investments in domestic sectors. These investment blocks form the basis for investment appraisal. Through concentrating on the investment projects in the international sectors it forces the underdeveloped countries to face the problem of concrete investment projects squarely, and to think in terms of competitiveness in foreign trade, at the same time as it requires a minimum of data about existing conditions in the country.

The semi–input–output method is probably Tinbergen's most ingenious contribution to planning. On the theoretical level it does, however, run into some troubles not only with respect to national sectors where observable shadow prices do not exist, but also with respect to the demand management policies necessary to balance the economy. Attempts to apply the method have run into practical difficulties in determining the international prices needed for the investment block appraisals. The concept of international prices is not a simple one as soon as we leave the basic raw materials and agricultural products and turn to manufactured and semimanufactured goods.

These practical difficulties should not, of course, be taken as an argument against the method as such. Any method of planning which aims at efficiency in production must undertake appraisals of all available investment projects, and for such appraisals appropriate price information is needed. They do, however, have a bearing upon the whole idea of planning for efficiency in resource allocation in underdeveloped countries. Given the production frontier of the country – quite apart from scarcity of capital, shortage of competent engineers and lack of information about technical possibilities may make the frontier lie far inside that of the developed countries – a country may simply not have the specialists (in marketing) needed for finding the optimal point on its frontier. Lack of technical knowledge and inefficiency within the given technical knowledge are both of them characteristics of underdevelopment. To be sure, T. W. Schultz has argued that peasants in underdeveloped countries are highly efficient within their primitive knowledge. He is probably right in that, and his argument extends presumably to all traditional sectors. But it does not apply to development beyond traditional methods in traditional sectors, and this is what matters in development planning.

It goes without saying that what has been said in the last paragraph does not imply that developing countries should pay no attention to the problem of efficiency. On the contrary, there is by far too much unnecessary inefficiency in developing countries which could be removed and thus greatly help to promote growth. But it does imply that one should be careful in condemning such countries for inefficiency, and it raises the question of which planning methods (everything taken into account) are the most efficient ones: the brutal methods that work, or the refined ones that do not work.

This leads us back to the appraisal of Tinbergen's planning methods and his efforts for promoting planning all over the Third World. It is by no means unusual to meet people who maintain that so far, planning by underdeveloped countries in general, and Tinbergen's methods in particular, on balance have done more harm than good. For several reasons this judgement is both unfair and wrong.

People who condemn planning by underdeveloped countries take very often as their basis of comparison an ideal state where both planners and politicians are perfect. This comparison is unfair and overlooks that a basic problem in development policies is exactly that planners and politicians generally are underdeveloped, too. Moreover, governments in underdeveloped countries are usually weak and politically incapable of taking vigorous, rational measures. The relatively disappointing performances of the Third World during the Development Decade have been caused much more by bad internal policies and implementation than by bad planning or external difficulties. Without people like Tinbergen, and their patient, indefatigable efforts things would, however, have been even worse than they are. Those people and their methods should not be blamed for the follies and imperfections of governments and politicians in underdeveloped countries.

Moreover, Tinbergen's crudest model, the stage method, has in most cases been applied to entirely undeveloped or highly underdeveloped countries. In such countries there are often striking natural advantages which have never been exploited, and planners do not need refined optimisation models to understand that such natural advantages should be exploited. It takes only the back of an envelope to figure out that the Euphrates Dam in Syria is a sound economic proposition, and nobody could ever be in doubt that oil drilling was the right thing to embark upon in Abu Dhabi. Some infrastructure is a *conditio sine qua non* for development. If raw materials are available it would be strange if cement, fertilisers and similar products with very high transport costs were not socially profitable. Even without explicit optimisation procedures the possibilities for going seriously wrong at this level of development may therefore be relatively small. The real problems arise when all obvious natural advantages have been exhausted and the most urgent infrastructure is erected. This is the stage of development where advantages have to be created. Even if market forces are strong and the animal spirits of private entrepreneurs are high we may still need planning to take care of externalities. And where private initiative is dormant or ruled out for institutional or ideological reasons the government will have to continue being the primus motor of development. Both the East, the West and the Third World are still waiting for somebody to discover the method which will work at this level of development. Although it certainly is a limitation of Tinbergen's crude planning methods that they apply best, or, perhaps only to highly underdeveloped areas, it should on the other hand be recognised that these are exactly the areas that have been most urgently in need of planning and where the methods actually have been applied.

5. *Other contributions*
Since the thirties Tinbergen has contributed to the solution of many problems other than those now discussed. He has always taken part in the current international debate and has worked on issues such as national accounting, imperfect competition, stability in economic systems, nonlinearities in cyclical models, international factor price equalisation, the theory of interest, international commodity agreements, the empirical determination of demand, supply, and substitution elasticities, problems of education and growth, tariff unions, balance of payments problems, optimum problems in savings and choice of techniques, just to present an unsystematic sample of topics. Since these contributions, brilliant though they very often are, cannot be said to have the quality of outstanding innovation, I mention them here only in passing.

6. *Conclusions*
It must have been quite a problem to select the first Nobel Prize Laureate(s) in Economics. During the last forty years economics

have made great progress and are today the only one of the so-called social sciences that begin to deserve the name of a science. A number of contemporary economists have contributed significantly to this development and could have been selected with the full approval of the profession. It would, however, even amongst this group be difficult to find a more worthy candidate than Jan Tinbergen. From the survey given here it appears that on no less than six occasions has he brought economics a large step forward. Thus,

(i) he was a pioneer in modern economic dynamics; (ii) he helped to establish econometrics; (iii) he is the founder of empirical macroeconomics; (iv) he contributed decisively to create the modern techniques of economic forecasting and prediction; (v) he is the founder of the modern theory of economic policy; (vi) he has contributed significantly to modern development planning in backward countries.

Tinbergen is a truly Schumpeterian figure in economics. A man who has triggered off developments in many different directions.

It remains only to be said, that the humanitarian idealism which Nobel wanted to reward has no representative in our profession so fine and noble as Jan Tinbergen. As much as he is respected in the privileged world, he is beloved by the underprivileged, the underdogs. Always at their service, always on their side, always working on improving their conditions, Tinbergen would be an equally worthy candidate for the Nobel Peace Prize.

1   The Economics of Reciprocity: Theory and Evidence on Bilateral Trading Arrangements

By RICHARD E. CAVES*

MOST modern research on the theory of price discrimination in general equilibrium has sprung from the interest of countries in forming customs unions or free-trade areas. Yet these two forms of integration far from exhaust the kinds of preferential agreements that are observed in real life. The theorists have been conscious that their analyses potentially apply to a much wider set of arrangements – witness the titles of the two leading contemporary treatises [18], [38]. But they have not used their apparatus to explore all the positive and normative questions raised by some of these other types of discriminatory arrangements. Nor, perforce, has the general-equilibrium theory of discrimination been applied to these questions in practice.

The first section of this paper seeks to restate and extend parts of the theory of preferential trading, emphasising its relation to the simple theory of monopolistic discrimination. The second and third apply it respectively to two superficially disparate types of trading arrangements: bilateral trading agreements of the types used by less-developed economies; and 'reciprocity' deals between manufacturing firms, each of which produces an output that serves as an input to the other's production process. The similarity of these arrangements to each other has gone largely unnoticed,[1] and the application to them of the general-equilibrium theory of discrimination has been at best incomplete. I shall not contend that this theory provides a unique and sufficient explanation of either set of

---

* Harvard University.
[1] Compare [16, pp. 73–74].

arrangements – others will be noted – but that it is consistent with substantial amounts of evidence that we possess concerning their occurrence and effects.

1. The Theory of Reciprocal Trading Arrangements

Suppose that m entities barter n commodities among themselves, and that some subsets of entities form clubs and agree to trade some set of commodities among themselves at price ratios which differ from those prevailing between club members and the remaining traders. The general-equilibrium theory of preferential trading deals with arrangements taking this form. A club that we call a customs union covers all n commodities and normally commits its members to internal free trade (common internal opportunity-cost ratios for each member trading entity and among club members). The members adopt a common set of distortions between internal opportunity cost ratios and the external relative prices prevailing among the remaining traders; a free-trade area differs only in the absence of this latter step. A preferential trading area could clearly involve less than the full n traded commodities, or less than complete unification of internal opportunity-cost ratios among club members, or both. Indeed, the actual trading arrangements to be considered below share just these characteristics, usually covering two traders, two commodities (or at most a limited number), and leaving some divergence of the club's price ratio from the internal opportunity costs of its members.

Superficially, the theory of preferential trading as developed by Vanek [38] and Kemp [18] nicely matches this pattern of limited preferential arrangements. In order to achieve simplicity within a context of general equilibrium, it employs the minimum of three countries – two club members and the outside world – trading two commodities. It encompasses both small preferences – what Kemp calls a trading club – and complete free trade within the club. Numerous useful results have been derived concerning the conditions for gain to the club members, the distribution of gains (net of any compensation) among them, the resulting change in the welfare of excluded traders, the effect of unification of the club members' external tariff, and the like.

This theoretical model nicely matches the empirical cases to be investigated below, and it provides a seemingly apt analytical framework of discrimination in general equilibrium. Nonetheless, the theory of preferential trading has placed strikingly little emphasis on purposive welfare-maximising behaviour by a trader forming a preferential arrangement. The following would seem to be central questions:

(*a*) When trading entity A selects a potential partner B for forming a trading club, what traits does he seek in B that will maximise his gains from preferential trading?

(*b*) What distortion of the club's price ratio from that prevailing in the outside world maximises gains for the club (or its dominant member)?

Yet the first has received attention only in special contexts;[2] the second has been given a clear answer, but the answer has not been put to use ordering the taxonomy of cases governing the distribution of gains and losses from preferential trading. I shall first develop the simplest possible model of the discriminating monopolist in general equilibrium and then proceed with several theoretical cases chosen to supply findings useful in my subsequent review of bilateral trading arrangements and business reciprocity arrangements.

1.1 *Theory of discriminating monopoly in general equilibrium*

Reciprocal arrangements by definition involve the consent of two parties, whereas the simple theory of price discrimination[3] deals with unilateral action by a single seller able to divide his market. Yet no strong distinction should be made between them, since the willingness of customers to continue after a simple monopoly price is converted into a discriminatory price structure constitutes (in partial equilibrium) an acceptance of a bilateral trading arrangement as superior to the available alternatives. Furthermore, a discriminating monopolist could conceivably enter into an agreement with a favoured buyer to divide the increment of profits as a bribe, say, for declining to

---

[2] Primarily in papers investigating the consequences of social preferences regarding the mix of activities in which the nation's factor stock is employed, e.g. a desire for 'industry' *per se*. See [7] and [17, especially pp. 279–281]. But its applicability is clearly wider than this.

[3] The classic source is Robinson [25, chap. 15].

resell to the disfavoured customer. Thus it is clear that the considerations underlying simple price discrimination can support an attempt to explain barter-type trading arrangements in a setting where each trader in general is large enough to possess some monopoly/monopsony power in the markets for some commodities.[4]

As Henderson [16a] has shown, partial-equilibrium price discrimination is easily translated into general ebuilibrium with two commodities by the use of reciprocal demand curves, which I assume to be derived from the trade-indifference curves developed by Meade [22]. They thus reflect each entity's willingness to trade at any given price ratio after optimal internal adjustment of production and consumption is made.[5] In Figure 1.1, potential monopolist A exports commodity 2 and imports commodity 1 in its trade with both B and C, whose individual reciprocal-demand curves are illustrated (*OB* and *OC*). If B and C can be confronted with different terms of trade, implying that they cannot exchange commodities 1 and 2 costlessly between themselves,[6] A can select an offer which optimises his trading position with each of them separately. A is required to set prices which equate his internal marginal rates of substitution in production and consumption to his marginal rate of substitution through trade with each party. In terms of offer-curve geometry, this means equating the slopes of an appropriately chosen point on A's highest attainable trade-indifference curve and points on B's and C's offer curves.

The solution can be shown by constructing for A the 'total revenue' curve that indicates the maximum amount of commodity 1 that A can secure through monopolistic discrimination in the sale of any given amount of commodity 2. This is

[4] It is also clear that this line of investigation loses interest in circumstances where market power must be assumed absent.

[5] It is perhaps not obvious under what conditions this apparatus is applicable to the multiproduct business enterprise. I shall consider this matter in Section 3.

[6] In fact, with three countries trading two undifferentiated commodities in the absence of transport costs, one would expect no trading link to exist in competitive equilibrium between one pair of them. If B also exported 2 to C and imported 1, B would implicitly be re-exporting the commodities that it imports from both A and C. To preclude resale in the case of price discrimination of course requires an additional assumption.

equivalent to adding the two offer curves by cumulating small segments of each in order of their maximum slopes, defined as quantities of commodity 1 offered per unit of commodity 2. The process is, of course, analogous to the horizontal aggregation of marginal-revenue curves employed in the partial-equilibrium solution. Once a point has been reached on the steeper (*OC*) offer curve that equals the slope of B's curve at the origin, this aggregation can be done by sliding C's origin along the *OB* curve, keeping the shifting origin at a point whose slope equals the slope of C's curve at the point tracing out the real-total-revenue function (*OMT*). Thus the slope of C's curve at *M*, a point on the envelope function, equals the slope of B's curve at *O'*. Where one of A's trade-indifference curves is tangent to the envelope at *M*, the marginal conditions for maximising A's gains from trade would be satisfied by charging B and C the prices indicated by slopes *OO'* and *O'M* respectively. The higher price is charged to the buyer enjoying the greater average intramarginal surplus.[7]

Note that this envelope total-revenue function will in general lie outside of a collective B–C offer curve aggregated in the way that would describe the trading opportunities if A were to behave either as a pure competitor or a simple monopolist.[8] This is analogous to the distinction between the demand and average-revenue curves made in the partial-equilibrium theory of discriminating monopoly.

A could effect this differential by discriminatory export or import taxes equal to the difference between the slope of a tangent at *M* and the slopes of *OO'* and *O'M* for B and C respectively. This case thus provides answers to the two questions raised in regard to maximising A's gains from trade:

[7] Because the elasticity of an offer curve as generally drawn changes throughout its length, and because position ('intensity of demand') matters as well as elasticity, it is not formally appropriate to describe the disfavoured buyer as possessing the less elastic demand. I shall nonetheless use this expression below as shorthand for the concept of a buyer whose demand for small quantities is 'intense' but whose elasticity of reciprocal demand falls relatively fast as his volume of imports increases. Inelastic stretches of the offer curves are, of course, irrelevant.

[8] This aggregation is shown by Becker [5]. The whole analysis could equally well be carried out in terms of consumption-possibility loci for A [4].

A should choose B as its partner in a trading club and should grant B a preference equal to the difference between slopes OO'

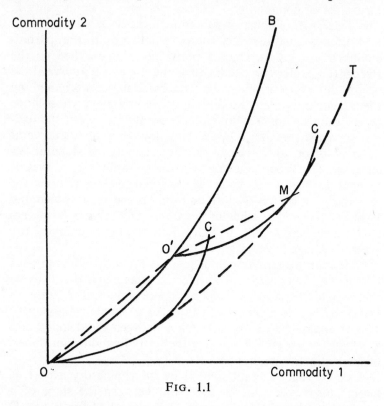

FIG. 1.1

and $O'M$. If B's offer curve is tariff-ridden and B grants A a preference in return, Figure 1.1 still correctly describes the situation *ex post*, with B's concession (resulting in an outward shift of OB from an initial position not shown) taken into account. Ignoring any tariff concession by B, it is clear that B would gain from the adoption of discrimination by A; given the assumption of constant or diminishing returns in A's production structure, B's terms of trade must have improved from an initial non-discriminatory value lying between OO' and $O'M$, permitting B to reach a higher trade-indifference curve at O'. Likewise, A benefits by moving to a trade-indifference curve tangent at M from one that was tangent to a collective B–C offer curve lying uniformly inside *OMT*. A does not benefit, strictly speaking, from the preferential terms of trade offered to B, but rather from the adoption of price discrimination overall. C loses through deterioration of its terms of trade.

Note that the employment of bilateral agreements is incidental to A's unilateral maximisation of welfare through discrimination. That is, what the argument shows is the scope for mutually acceptable trading agreements as vehicles for achieving discrimination. Why such a vehicle is chosen becomes an important but secondary question.[9] It could serve to commit B to preclude resale or otherwise augment A's gains from favouring B; B could bribe a politically reluctant A to undertake discrimination; and so forth. An agreement between A and C is conceivable, but only to formalise C's defeat for lack of a trading alternative. The real question raised by an agreement between A and C, however, is that of the all-or-nothing offer.

1.2 *The role of the all-or-nothing offer*

The all-or-nothing offer, a simple extension of the theory of discriminating monopoly developed in Section 1.1, could readily be embodied in an agreement on the exchange of limited numbers of commodities, as is suggested by references to 'bulk trading' and 'coercive reciprocity' in the trading experience reviewed below. Baldwin [4] has shown how a trading entity capable of inflicting an all-or-nothing offer on a partner can calculate the maximum barter offer that can be forced, at any given terms of trade, and derive therefrom a reciprocal demand curve for the partner showing the set of maximum all-or-nothing offers that would just lie on the margin of acceptability. It can be thought of as a means of extracting the best gross barter terms of trade or the maximum volume of imports attainable for any given quantity of exports.

In general, the same traits make a trader more vulnerable to an all-or-nothing offer as make him a candidate for being the disfavoured partner in simple price discrimination. Figure 1

---

[9] Some writers on business reciprocity (especially [3, 14]) have raised the question of why barter agreements should be used when the discriminating monopolist can maximise by simply rigging the money price of any product in which he has the requisite market power.

can be taken as showing the process of determining optimal all-or-nothing offers to two trading partners if we suppose that *OB* and *OC* at the outset represent all-or-nothing offer curves. A trading agreement would be central to imposing an all-or-nothing offer on any partner, but its payout would be greater with one who would be disfavoured in a move from simple monopoly to discriminating monopoly. This contrasts to the case of discrimination without an all-or-nothing offer, where a bilateral trading agreement seems most useful to deal with the favoured trader.

At the limit, all-or-nothing offers would improve A's welfare (as against any alternative trading systems) and leave B and C indifferent as against no trade at all. Beyond this it is neither simple nor, for present purposes, useful to go on comparing the all-or-nothing offer to alternative trading situations.

1.3 *Selection of trading partner and distribution of benefits*
The literature on preferential trading has not assumed the discriminating monopolist's rationality in the choice of partners. The presence or absence of this rationality, however, serves usefully to classify the possible distributions of gains and losses from preferential arrangements that it predicts. I wish to develop this point and also to show how the more myopic approach taken by customs-union theory usefully points to the criteria that a rational trader would use in picking a 'good' partner for an agreement.

Figure 1.2[10] describes the same trading situation as Figure 1.1 but does not depict the offer curves faced by A and, instead, concentrates on the divergences for A and B between internal opportunity costs and external price ratios (all taxes or subsidies causing these distortions are assumed to be financed by lump-sum transfers). *OT* is the *initial* world price ratio at which A trades with B and C. Trade is restricted by both A and B, so that their internal opportunity-cost ratios are relatively unfavourable to their respective export goods. This is illustrated by the slopes of tangents at P_A and P_B to trade-indifference curves of A and B respectively. Note that A's initial trade with C is shown by the

[10] Figures 2 and 3 employ the same basic devices and notation as a number of those presented by Kemp [18], whose exposition provides the most convenient point of contact with the literature.

vector $P_B P_A$, indicating the excess of A's offer of two for one over B's offer of one for two at OT. Now A and B form a trading club that involves a *small* cut of their trade restrictions in favour of each other. A's original restrictions remain in relation to its trade with C, however. If the preference causes *no* change in A's terms of trade with C (C's offer curve is

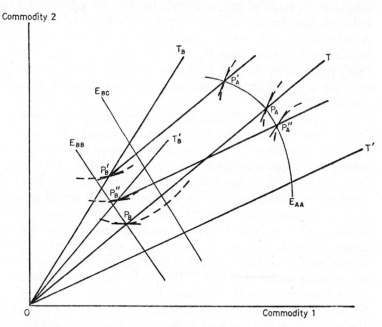

FIG. 1.2

perfectly elastic), it is clear that A will lose from the exchange of preferences. If A continues to trade with C to some extent, A's internal opportunity-cost ratio remains locked to terms of trade OT, and the effect of the preferential reduction in A's tariff is to let B trade at prices, indicated by OT_B, that are somewhat more favourable than OT. Trade between A and B is now shown by vector OP'_B. Point P'_B serves as a base for A's trading vector with C, this trade continuing at the original terms OT. Trade with C carries A to a position of equilibrium at P'_A, placing A on a lower trade-indifference curve than before, B on a higher one, and leaving C's welfare unaffected.

Clearly, this result is consistent with Section 1.1; offering a preference to one trading partner in a 'competitive' market cannot be a profitable unilateral act for the donor. A could benefit from this manouvre, without destroying B's gains, only if the terms of trade OT improve. This requires, of course, that the discrimination favouring B shrinks A's trade with C *and* results in improved terms of trade. Should the preference improve A's external terms of trade to OT , B's gains would be reduced. The preference now improves B's terms of trade with A only to OT'_B; B's trading equilibrium at P''_B still results in a higher welfare level than P_B. But A's trading vector with C, $P''_B P''_A$ (parallel to the new final terms of trade OT'), permits A to enjoy a higher level of welfare at P''_A rather than a lowered one at P'_A.[11]

The conclusions of the preceding two paragraphs are standard in the literature [18, chap. 2; 38, chap. 2]. What I wish to point out is those traits of B's trade-indifference map which make it a relatively attractive entity to be tapped by A for membership in a trading club. A 'myopic criterion' that A might naturally employ is the extent to which a preference for B would expand A–B trade and thereby shrink the volume and improve the terms of A's trade with C. The relevant traits are shown by the Engel curves E_{ij} where i is the country whose Engel curve is shown and j is the country whose prices (initial internal opportunity costs) give rise to the particular curve. Thus E_{BB} is B's Engel curve at B's own initial prices. Also shown is E_{BC}, B's Engel curve at initial world or external prices (I assume for expository convenience that C is a free trader). A preference granted by A to B tends to raise B's income and push B's internal prices toward the initial external terms of trade OT. Figure 2 makes clear that the resulting expansion of A–B trade will be greater the higher is B's income elasticity of demand for imports (the steeper is E_{BB}) and the higher is the marginal rate of substitution in B (the farther does E_{BC} lie from E_{BB} along OT).[12] A's own preference map (slope of E_{AA}) of course also affects the outcome.

---

[11] There is nothing to preclude the preference improving the terms of trade sufficiently for A that B's benefits from the preference are more than offset by the loss on its basic terms of trade: P''_B lies below P_B.

[12] It is worth recalling that these are trade-indifference curves. They incorporate substitution in production and, without necessarily violating

So far I have neglected the possibility of compensation. A *sufficiently* large improvement in A's terms of trade could leave B worse off, but it would always pay A to bribe B to enter into the arrangement, leaving B on or above the indifference curve at P_B and A at a position preferred to P_A. Other significant roles for compensation will be noted below.

1.4 *Optimal rate of preference and possibilities for compensation*

Section 1.1 indicated the optimal preference for the favoured trading partner from the viewpoint of the discriminating monopolist. That analysis neglected the possibilities of compensation being paid as part of the reciprocal bargain, and took only passing notice of the possible consequences of trade restrictions by the passive partner. Both factors influence the possibilities of mutually beneficial reciprocal arrangements. In contrast to the case of the discriminating monopolist, the theory of customs unions shows that the arrangement maximising the *joint* welfare of A and B as trading-club members is internal free trade coupled with a common 'optimum tariff' against the outside world [18, chap. 8].[13] This solution differs from the result of discriminating monopoly pricing by A in B's favour, and a bribe from B to A would generally be both profitable for B and necessary to induce A to move to the solution that maximises their joint welfare.[14]

As in Section 1.3, however, some useful predictions seem to emerge from more myopic cases in which A's and B's trading club raises their joint welfare without necessarily maximising it.

stability conditions, can encompass increasing returns [22, chap. 5]. Thus, the distance between E_{BB} and E_{BC} along OT might be substantially augmented by a range of increasing returns in B's production-possibility function. (This would raise the chances of a reversal in the pattern of trade between A and B, a possibility not considered here.)

[13] In terms of Figure 1.2, this would require, in the case where the external terms of trade are variable, that the slopes of A's and B's trade-indifference curves be equal at P''_A and P''_B, wherefore B's trade-indifference curve would be tangent to vector OT'_B at P''_B; and that the difference in slopes between P''_A and OT' corresponds to the optimum tariff. That is, the common slope at P''_B and P''_A should equal the slope of C's offer curve at the point of equilibrium. Figure 2 as drawn depicts cases in which A and B have failed to exhaust the possibilities of mutually beneficial preferences.

[14] These conclusions relate to the earlier discussion of compensation and tariff-ridden offer curves by Scitovsky, Johnson and others.

Specifically, I shall explore the arrangement that maximises the gain from preferential trading when actions by the club have no effect on the external terms of trade.[15] This gain is conceptually independent of the gain from improving the external terms of trade, since we can define the optimum rate of internal prefer- ence *relative* to the external terms of trade, and thus determine it for those terms which would correspond to the optimum tariff or, alternatively, for any other value of the external terms of trade. The case where the external terms are given pertains not only to circumstances where A and B are relatively small traders. It also serves most usefully to illustrate the case where the prices of goods 1 and 2, and thus the external terms of trade, are fixed by imperfectly collusive arrangements involving A, B, and other parties. The preferential arrangement between A and B in that case becomes a device for one of them to chisel on his collusive agreement without, he hopes, provoking an adverse shift in the market price of his export.

In Figure 1.3 the external terms of trade are given at OT; OP_B again represents initial A–B trade, and P_BP_A is A's trading vector with C. In this case no discrimination in favour of B is profitable for A, and a small preference for B would, as before, raise B's welfare while reducing A's. Suppose, however, that B undertakes to bribe A to offer such a preference. Given A's external tariff (and the fixed distortion that it introduces between A's internal opportunity-cost ratio and world prices or C's internal ratio), we can identify the optimum rate of prefer- ence for B in A's tariff as the one which would maximise A's welfare subject to the condition that the bribe paid by B just exhausts B's gains from the preference. (That is, B's bribe is the maximum it would pay to secure a given preference.)

As Figure 1.3 shows, this optimum rate of preference would be the one that just offsets the distortion introduced by B's own tariff and aligns B's internal prices with those prevailing in the outside world (OT, or C's internal opportunity-cost ratio). E_{BC} is B's Engel curve at these external prices, and the rate of preference just defined would leave B's trading point somewhere

---

[15] I shall assume throughout that changes in production and consump- tion in B, when a non-incremental preference changes internal prices, never suffice to extinguish or reverse A's trade with C. Kemp [18] thoroughly explores the conditions under which such changes occur.

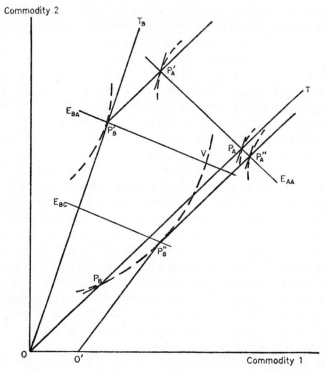

FIG. 1.3

on this line. The maximum that B would pay to A for this preference would be OO' of commodity 1. After this bribe is paid, A trades with B from O' to P_B'', the vector $O'P_B''$ offering to B external prices that lie between world prices (OT) and A's internal prices (slope at P_A). (The size of the bribe is determined by the size of the preference needed to align B's internal prices with world prices OT.) At P_B'' B is left on the same trade-indifference curve as at P_B – its welfare just failing to be improved by the preference. A also trades with C at unchanged external prices along $P_B''P_A''$; given these prices it is clear that no rate of preference, leaving B at some other point on its original trade-indifference curve, would permit A so large a gain in welfare. In short, even without gains from discriminating monopoly, a preferential arrangement could be mutually beneficial to the extent that it offsets inefficient tariff protection by one of the partners. Further gains would be available to the club if A also moves to an optimum external tariff, which with fixed external terms of trade would be zero.

Figure 1.3 also allows us to show (following Kemp [18, chap. 4]) that for A and B to go all the way to internal free trade may be inefficient when the external tariff is not optimised. Free trade permits B to trade at A's internal prices along the vector OT_B, whose slope is equal to that at P_A. Trade between A and B would be carried to P'_B, leaving B better off than at P_B; A trades with C at the unchanged external terms of trade along $P'_B P'_A$ and, in the absence of compensation, emerges worse off at P'_A. The question is, could B bribe A to form a free-trade area and thereby improve A's welfare while leaving B no worse off? In the Figure as drawn, the answer is no. At A's internal prices, the maximum bribe that B would pay carries it to V, the inter- section of its original trade-indifference curve with the relevant Engel curve E_{BA}. Although this bribe exceeds OO', it would not allow A a net improvement in welfare; A would trade from V along a vector parallel to OT, winding up at a point on E_{AA} that is inferior to P_A.[16] Thus we see that bribes might go either way; A might bribe B to co-operate in discrimination that would improve A's terms of trade (Section 1.3), or alternatively B might bribe A for help in an admittedly circuitous exercise in offsetting the welfare cost of B's own tariff.

In the cases considered in this section, as in Section 1.1, an agreement is not necessary to every preferential arrangement that will raise the welfare of one trader without worsening that of the favoured partner. It becomes necessary when compensa- tion must be paid, and it clearly may be useful in all cases for various incidental purposes. It can help to disguise discrimina- tion, a likely requirement if one or both trading partners take part in imperfect collusive agreements to keep the prices of their export goods above the level of internal opportunity costs. In Figure 1.3, for example, consider the total transaction between A and B involved in reaching trading point P''_B – a bribe by B of OO' followed by trade to P''_B. Taking the exchange as a whole, it appears that B has been afflicted with worse terms of

[16] A free-trade area is not necessarily without net benefit; point V could equally well lie below OT, permitting A to trade to a superior position. The result depends on the shape of B's trade-indifference curve.

trade (a line from O to P_B'' would be flatter than OT), yet with a slight reduction in the bribe, B would become better off. As with simple monopolistic discrimination, the possibilities of disguise through reciprocal agreements are further expanded if we note that compensation for some other debt might be thrown into the same package.

1.5 *Predictions from theory of preferential trading*

Besides showing what preferential agreements would be chosen by optimising trading entities, this section has sought to predict the empirical occurrence and weigh the significance of several types of discriminatory arrangements. In framing a study of actual trading agreements, theory will ideally allow us to work backward from the structural traits, form, and content of the agreement to its economic significance. The inventory basically contains three possible types of agreement. Section 1.1 showed the potential uses of agreements to implement monopolistic discrimination, especially as a device for disguising the treatment given to the favoured buyer, securing his co-operation in preventing resale, or perhaps extracting a bribe for the favouritism. The agreement embodying an all-or-nothing offer, noted in Section 1.2, would differ in worsening rather than improving the terms of trade of the 'passive' partner, although either type of agreement should result in an expansion of bilateral trade.

Discriminatory reciprocal trading agreements can also result from the efforts of traders to improve their market positions in the face of constraining collusive agreements on price or other restraints on trade that deter gainful independent action by the trader (Section 1.4). Unlike the types of agreements effecting monopolistic discrimination, this class depends on an initial situation of disequilibrium going deeper than the failure to exploit all profitable discrimination. There is hope of distinguishing this type of 'competitive discrimination'[17] on the basis of its necessary relation to these initial conditions. Making this distinction is important for a correct normative evaluation

---

[17] This label is only partly satisfactory and hence will be kept in quotation marks. Its sense is that: (*a*) monopoly power for the club members as a bloc is not necessary; (*b*) discrimination can result from defections from collusive or monopolistic agreements.

of trading agreements. As specialists in industrial organisation have long recognised, although a clear case exists against monopolistic forms of discrimination, 'competitive discrimination' may possess redeeming virtues if it serves as a wedge to erode a collusively maintained price or undermine other inefficiencies.

2. Trade Agreements of Developing Countries

Bilateral trading agreements have been used extensively by the developing countries during the past two decades, both among themselves and with the centrally planned economies.[18] These agreements are far from homogeneous in form, running from specific agreements on the exchange of particular commodities (sometimes with compensation or planned imbalance) to general shopping lists that involve on the surface no more than 'a simple expression of mutual friendship and interest' [36, pp. 86–87]. These barter arrangements shade into other types of bilateral dealings among countries, such as the outright state-trading operations of the centrally planned economies and the agreements used by the industrial nations after the Second World War to permit the balanced bilateral expansion of trade in the face of extreme shortages of international reserves.

My procedure will be to suggest a number of hypotheses based on the theoretical analysis of preferential trading and to note how fully the available evidence on these trading agreements seems to confirm them. My aim will be to establish or reject *some* role for the model of discrimination in explaining these agreements, and not to exclude competing hypotheses. The hypothetical alternatives are numerous. Trading agreements could serve as devices for reducing uncertainty, as ways to reduce fluctuations in international reserves and thus reduce

---

[18] The only systematic survey information seems to be that collected by the UNO Economic Commission for Africa. It uncovered around three hundred agreements drawn between 1955 and 1963, a large minority of them with other African countries, the bulk of the rest with the centrally planned economies. Bilateral trade under these agreements accounts for something approaching a fifth of Africa's total trade [32, pp. 3–11]. Virtually all African countries have concluded at least one such agreement [33, pp. 15–16].

the need for reserves, or as ways of accommodating the administrative necessities of the centrally planned economies. Ideally, empirical evidence could be gathered that would weigh the explanatory force of these hypotheses against the discrimination model. Unfortunately, what is readily available proves quite inadequate for that purpose; the limited descriptive sources lack much of the pertinent information, and only India's experience has been analysed at all extensively [1] [9] [10] [26].

2.1 *Implementing a preferential agreement*

For a trading agreement to give rise to a discriminatory transaction, it must either stipulate the quantities of goods to be exchanged or substitute some institution for the competitive market to settle the terms of the barter. But this does not seem the typical case. All surveys seem to agree that arrangements of the 'shopping list' variety are in the majority.[19] This lack of extensive preplanning is also shown in the wide dispersion of actual trade levels *ex post* around the targets stipulated in the agreements [23, pp. 77–86]. Even the 'shopping list' agreement could give rise to discrimination, however, if it set up some device that permits non-market transactions or balances to develop. One such device is the use of a state-trading institution by the less-developed country. This is clearly not uncommon, either as a general tool of policy or as an agency to implement trading agreements.[20] Another is the periodic review of the state of bilateral balance of trade under the agreement. A central clearing arrangement is frequently used, and the negotiations over bilateral clearing balances obviously could control the terms of the gross barter transaction.

2.2 *Terms of trade under preferential agreements*

For a trading arrangement to result in discrimination, it must lead to terms of trade (net of lump-sum compensation, and measured outside of tariff walls) that differ from those prevailing with non-members of the club. As Sections 1.1, 1.2 and 1.4 show, assessing the *sign* of the difference requires further information about which party is (the more effectively)

[19] See [23, pp. 67–70; 33, p. 15; 36, pp. 86–87].
[20] See [9, p. 62; 34; 35, p. 27].

sequestered from market alternatives and whether an all-or-nothing offer is in force.

Certainly, there is convincing evidence that *some* less-developed countries take deteriorated terms of trade under *some* bilateral arrangements in order to segment the markets for their primary products, and indeed this is one of the publicly stated objectives of these agreements.[21] Sometimes a tariff preference is explicitly involved, although the terms of the General Agreement on Tariffs and Trade discourage this practice [32, p. 47; 33, p. 17]. Some agreements made by the developing countries, especially with the centrally planned economies, seem to yield after the event poorer terms than multilateral trading, although one cannot tell whether this situation was tacitly foreseen by the contracting parties or instead represents an unanticipated result.[22] Still, many analyses suggest that the bulk of transactions under bilateral agreements take place at world market prices, and that even the trade flows handled by state trading corporations may be marked up by similar percentages both ways, so that no significant net distortion results. India's experience, which has been examined in some detail [1; 9; 10; 26, chap. 2, pp. 287–288], is consistent with no net distortions. Furthermore, the significance of discrimination under bilateral arrangements becomes obscure in those cases where the parties both suffer overvalued exchange rates; what appears to be discrimination with particular commodity markets might not be when assessed at a correct shadow price for convertible foreign currency.[23] One can conclude from this evidence only that the terms under some bilateral arrangements are consistent with the implementing of monopolistic discrimination.

2.3 *Discrimination and resale*

For a trading agreement to involve discrimination at least one trader must be able to segment the market for his exports.

[21] See [32, pp. 21, 36–37; 33, pp. 15–16; 35, pp. 28–29].

[22] See [23, pp. 43–44; 32, pp. 61–64; 39, pp. 100–101].

[23] In confirmation of this, bilateral arrangements among countries with inconvertible currencies sometimes exclude trade in commodities with extensive export markets in convertible-currency areas. See [12, p. 349; 30, p. 52; 39, p. 98].

That is, some trait of the product, its characteristics of use, or the structure of transport costs must impose significant restraints on its resale by the favoured buyer. Alternatively, the terms of the agreement may involve a prohibition on resale.

Bilateral trading agreements typically cover primary products or occasionally simple manufactures, not easily susceptible of market segmentation. Thus one would expect evidence of difficulties in preventing resale if discrimination is occurring. Developing countries have complained periodically of resale of their primary products on multilateral markets by the centrally planned economies, confirming the use of agreements by the former group to effect discrimination (Section 2.2). Furthermore, some agreements in fact do preclude re-exports unless specific permission is secured.[24] Since the agreements in question are among nations with inconvertible currencies, they might be serving as an offset to disequilibrium exchange rates.

2.4 *Demand elasticity and choice of partner*

It was noted that the trading partner likely to be favoured by discrimination through a bilateral trading agreement would tend to be one with high income and substitution elasticities for one's export product (Section 1.3). The height of these parameters is a relative matter, of course. Profitable discrimination requires not only that they differ, but also that the exporter bulks large enough as a supplier of the goods in question that these differences can be monopolistically exploited.

Although these predictions could be tested in some detail, I shall settle for reporting impressions from the evidence at hand. The developing countries in most cases enter into trading agreements covering only their principal exports. The nations most active in forging these arrangements seem to be the larger ones, whose exports of individual products are thus more likely to comprise a significant share of world production. Scattered evidence, including a detailed analysis for India, suggests that the relatively low-income countries selected as club members are likely to have higher income elasticities for primary products than the industrial nations. A weaker probabilistic argument

[24] For evidence on these points see [13, pp. 331–332; 23, pp. 40–41, 54–59; 30, pp. 52–54; 32, p. 61; 33, p. 15].

along this line can be made for their price elasticities. The trading of simple manufactures under bilateral agreements by countries such as United Arab Republic seems consistent with this prediction.[25]

2.5 *Preferential trading and debtors' bargaining power*

Practices in the settlement of net balances under bilateral trading agreements are quite various, but debts are not typically cleared up through the transfer of convertible currencies. Furthermore, swing credits are usually extended, so that the club members focus their joint attention on the net balance only at infrequent intervals. Given these practices, theory suggests weakly that a trading partner selected as a buyer whose demand will respond sensitively to a price concession will enjoy some bargaining power when the question arises of settling debit balances that he has built up. (The same holds true no matter what the benefit accruing to the creditor; this prediction supports the discrimination hypothesis only in that the expansion of the creditor's sales matches his hypothetical motive for joining the club.)

Examples are rather common of bilateral creditors making generous concessions when they negotiate terms for clearing up outstanding balances. The debtor's exports may be valued significantly above world prices, or the creditor may settle for commodities in excess of its import quotas or of substandard quality that renders them difficult to sell or utilise.[26]

2.6 *Adverse demand shifts and resort to bilateral trading*

It was argued in Section 1.4 that a preferential trading arrangement can become particularly attractive when external terms of trade are inefficiently out of line with an entity's internal opportunity costs. This would be the case both for small traders restricting their commerce, although unable to improve their terms of trade thereby, and participants in imperfectly collusive price-fixing arrangements who can benefit from selective price concessions even without raising the price to disfavoured buyers. The latter line of argument in particular predicts that interest in preferential trading arrangements would rise when demand for

---

[25] See [9, pp. 58–60] on India, [32, pp. 51–55] on U.A.R.
[26] See [12, pp. 358–359; 30, p. 52; 39, pp. 100–101].

a particular principal export declines, unless prices are fully flexible.

Many observers note that bilateral trading arrangements arise when countries are facing either deteriorating terms of trade or Balance of Payments difficulties from reductions in the demand for their exports. The worsening terms of trade experienced by many developing countries after the Korean War offered a strong incentive to seek out bilateral arrangements, and they spread rapidly at that time [12, p. 361; 32, pp. 46, 63–64]. Devaluation by an export competitor has caused resort bilateral agreements [32, pp. 30, 41]. The evidence also suggests that distorted price structures encourage the use of agreements when selective price reductions are more attractive than general ones [30, p. 85; 12, pp. 349, 352]. If trading arrangements are used to offset fluctuating sales in multilateral markets, one would expect that trade flows under bilateral agreements would not necessarily be stable themselves, but that they would contribute to the stability of a country's total trade. This result has been noted by those remarking on the failure of bilateral agreements themselves to generate a stable flow of trade [9, pp. 64–65; 35, p. 28].

This evidence does not necessarily point to 'competitive discrimination' undertaken to offset inefficient distortions of trade if we allow that preferential arrangements might result from 'satisficing' behaviour. That is, monopolistic discrimination might be sought only in response to a downturn in the gain from simple monopoly. The uncertainties and administrative costs of bilateral arrangements also might cause countries to pursue them seriously only when their terms of trade worsen, even if discrimination would have been profitable prior to the adverse development. The primacy of 'competitive discrimination' would be shown, however, if we find that countries negotiate bilateral arrangements in response to those concluded by other countries. This defensive behaviour has been occasionally noted [26, p. 194; 30, p. 80].

2.7 *Preferential arrangements and volume of trade*

It is well known that movement of a seller from simple monopoly to a profit-increasing position of discriminating monopoly does not necessarily increase the total quantity sold.

Nonetheless, the agreement with the favoured buyer taken alone should result in an increased volume of trade. Furthermore, since a shift of the terms of trade against the disfavoured buyer seldom seems to coincide with the adoption of a preferential arrangement, one would expect the preference also to result in the short run in increased internal prices and total production of the commodities exported under the agreement.

Once more, causal support exists for both predictions. Very large expansions of bilateral trade following agreements are often noted, although in developing countries this growth could also result because official efforts are necessary to bestir the forging of commercial links. An examination of India's experience confirms the increase of internal prices of exportables associated with the expansion of trade under bilateral arrangements [1; 10; 26, chap. 9].

2.8 *Compensation and extraneous transfers*

If a purpose of trading agreements is to effect clandestine price discrimination, it is possible that bribes might be negotiated as part of the arrangement (Sections 1.3, 1.4). Likewise, there may be advantages in lumping extraneous transfers into the agreements in order to assist in disguising their discriminatory significance.

The information available on trading agreements is too thin to allow developing and testing predictions about the direction of compensation. Still, it is worth noting the evidence that these agreements frequently serve as vehicles for planned transfers or compensations that may or may not be extraneous to the trading agreement. Agreements are used as vehicles for the transfer of foreign aid from the centrally planned economies and between France and her former colonies. The repayment of long-term credits in commodities may be part of an agreement, or alternatively the device may be used to tie foreign aid. Such extraneous matters may be involved as co-operation in air transport and the use of port facilities.[27] Although these instances are consistent with the use of trading agreements for discriminatory purposes, they cannot be said to provide positive evidence.

[27] For evidence see [23, pp. 19–24; 26, chap. 3; 32, pp. 9–10, 16–17, 47–48; 33, pp. 17–18].

2.9 *Summary and evaluation*

Some evidence supports each of a number of predictions about bilateral trading agreements used by the developing countries, drawn from the general-equilibrium theory of preferential arrangements. It is too weak to assert the primacy of this motive behind the agreements, although in a few cases it seems to out-perform other explanations of these agreements where they supply contradictory predictions.[28] I can only offer the usual hope that more detailed information will someday permit the competing explanations to be unravelled more thoroughly. The theory of preferential trading in fact predicts discrimination of several different sorts – monopolistic action with or without all-or-nothing offers, and 'competitive discrimination' to offset inefficient trade interferences or cheat on collusive prices. The evidence here supports the existence of both competitive and monopolistic discrimination without permitting even a qualitative judgement on their respective significance. Little if any evidence confirms the prevalence of the all-or-nothing offer, however much attention it has received in the general literature on state trading.

3. Business Reciprocity Arrangements

Reciprocity arrangements have been common among large business enterprises in certain United States industries at least since the 1920s. They involve a trading agreement between two firms, each of which purchases an input that is an output of the other.[29] As with international trading agreements, the evidence available on the occurrence and effects of business reciprocity is far less than one would wish. Businesses are under less

[28] Agreements with the centrally planned economies are sometimes seen as a method for stabilising the volume and terms of trade of the developing countries. As it is usually put, this argument pertains just to bilateral trade and not to the developing countries' total trade. Thus, one often finds expressions of dismay that this bilateral trade by itself seems anything but stable. On the other hand (Section 2.6), the preference theory predicts with some success that bilaterals would be employed to stabilise total and not bilateral trade.

[29] Agreements involving more than two firms appear not at all uncommon. A may sell B and buy from C, who is also B's customer. For examples, see [29, p. 84]. One survey found 44 per cent of firms engaging in more complex reciprocity arrangements [20, p. 301].

obligation than governments to make their activities known, and the possible illegality of these dealings under the antitrust laws has not helped to loosen executive tongues. Most reciprocity arrangements appear to be informal, as when firm A urges its own purchases of good 1 from B as a reason why B should buy 2 from A, or when A dangles its willingness to start purchasing 1 from B in order to protect or expand its sales of 2.

From the general form of these agreements, it seems clear that they *might* serve to embody the forms of barter discrimination identified in Section 1. The threat to withdraw extant purchases carries the ring of the all-or-nothing offer, and (as we shall see) the model of 'competitive discrimination' (Section 1.4) corresponds closely to the principal explanatory hypothesis evolved by writers on business reciprocity. The relation of the trading entity described by the expository machinery used in Section 1 to the business firm, however, may require explanation. The correspondence is direct if we think of the firm as a multiproduct enterprise purchasing intermediate goods but not necessarily requiring them in fixed proportions to its outputs. It is helpful (though not necessary) to assume that the firm can produce at some cost each of the inputs that it purchases externally (in observed positions of equilibrium). The firm should face declining excess-demand curves for the products it trades, so that its isorevenue contours will possess the same general properties as indifference curves. Divergences arise between internal opportunity costs and external terms of trade because of the use of this market power, which permits firms to impose effectively export taxes on goods they sell; prices diverge from marginal production costs for the output, the input goods, or both. The firm's activities are thus assimilated to the model of trading entities except in regard to determining the scale of production in the sense of total value added. Unlike the national economy, we abjure thinking of the firm as equipped with a fixed endowment of primary factors of production. Since questions of scale enter only incidentally into the hypotheses about reciprocal trading, that non-congruity will cause no trouble.

As in the case of international trading agreements, various explanations for business reciprocity have been offered. The practice is generally agreed to be irrelevant in purely competitive product markets, where at most reciprocity could apply

mutual esteem as a device for solving the inessential indeterminacy of bilateral pairing among large numbers of traders.
The reduction of uncertainty could (once more) supply an
explanation. The most popular model, however, accords with
the theory of 'competitive discrimination.'[30] Assume that the
sellers of products 1 and 2 each belong to imperfect collusive
arrangements that aim to maintain the money prices of the
respective products they sell. The relative market price of the
two products will then be fixed. If the price lies above marginal
cost for the product of which each firm is a net seller, the
individual seller will potentially benefit from any device that
expands his sales without threatening to shatter the collusive
agreement or induce retaliation. (This gain does not depend on
the complete success of collusion in maximising joint profits
for the selling group as a whole, although it increases with the
margin between price and marginal cost.) The exercise of
reciprocity, according to the literature, provides one such device
for expanding sales. If one of the firm's existing suppliers of
good 1 is a reciprocity candidate, the threat to transfer purchases
would suffice to make him switch his demand for good 2, and
indeed possibly to pay a premium for it. If neither firm is selling
to the other at the time reciprocity is arranged, an even wider
range of price ratios (lying between their two internal opportunity-cost ratios) and including the market price ratio permit
mutually profitable trade.[31]

Relating these oligopolistic circumstances to the case of
simple monopolistic discrimination and developing its policy
implications will both prove difficult exercises. On the one hand,
discrimination may occur; on the other, clandestine chiselling
on the collusive agreement could lead to a more efficient
general level of prices than if reciprocity were disallowed.

I turn now to the evidence about business reciprocity as a type
of general-equilibrium price discrimination. All the caveats

---

[30] For expositions, see [3; 14; 29; 37, chap. 6].

[31] The cases identified in the two preceding sentences can be related
to price ratios indicated in Figure 3. If A is already buying commodity 1
exclusively from B, the range of price ratios permitting mutually profitable
reciprocity lies between OT and P_B. These conclusions do not depend on
whether the firm produces some of its requirements of the input it buys;
if such production takes place, marginal cost should equal the input's
initial market price.

from Section 2 will apply: the evidence is decidedly patchwork and it does not serve to discriminate between competing hypotheses.

3.1 *Industry characteristics, firm size and incidence of reciprocity*

If the general equilibrium model of preferential trading plays an important role in explaining business reciprocity, the distribution of reciprocity should vary from industry to industry in association with the traits that make it both possible and profitable. The first of these, obviously enough, is that firms both sell a significant portion of their output as intermediate goods to other firms and buy substantial portions of intermediate inputs; without this condition no reciprocity is possible. It should also be true that seller concentration is reasonably high, so that either discriminating monopoly becomes possible or collusive arrangements are likely to maintain prices significantly above marginal costs. Finally, since reciprocity arrangements no doubt involve fixed costs to the firms that are independent of the volume of business affected, one would expect more bilateral dealings in industries where firms are of large absolute size.

Table 1.1 presents results from what appears to be the only remotely systematic survey of a thousand purchasing agents in what appears to be a fairly representative sample of industries [28]. The industry categories are too broadly drawn to supply more than general indications, but the portion of respondents classifying reciprocity as an important factor in buyer-seller relations matches perfectly against the predicted traits of reciprocity potential and level of seller concentration. The process industries and iron and steel clearly possess a good deal of reciprocity potential, and in the United States most of their subsectors have relatively high levels of seller concentration. Industries such as non-metallic products and construction materials possess moderately high reciprocity potential (columns 5 and 6)[32] but significantly lower seller concentration in many

---

[32] In evaluating the information in columns 3–6 it is probably appropriate to add the 'don't know' observations to reported values near zero. Qualitative evidence on the pervasiveness of reciprocity makes one doubt that reciprocity potential in excess of 10 per cent could often go unnoticed except in an atomistic industry, and industries of highly competitive structure seem under represented in the sample.

subsectors, and thus show an unsurprising lower incidence of reciprocity (column 1).

Table 1.1 also indicates the role of absolute size in explaining the occurrence of reciprocity. The explanatory power of size

TABLE 1.1. *Extent and Importance of Business Reciprocity Agreements, by Industry and Size of Firm, Based on Survey of Purchasing Agents*

Industry or size of firm (sales)	Reciprocity 'a factor' in buyer-seller relations (%) (1)	Reciprocity increased due to excess capacity (%) (2)	Proportion of sales made to suppliers		
			Don't know (%) (3)	0–10 (%) (4)	10–30 (%) (5)	over 30 (%) (6)
Miscellaneous non-metal-lic products	68	50	17	60	13	10
Chemicals, petroleum, other pro-cess indus-tries	100	63	16	32	41	11
Iron and steel	100	69	7	23	30	40
Services	45	28	27	42	19	12
Metal fabri-cators	56	37	9	79	7	5
Construction materials	55	31	6	83	11	0
Electrical	44	41	6	78	12	4
Consumer goods	36	15	27	70	3	0
All industries, by volume of sales ($million):						
less than 10	46	20	8	78	10	4
10–50	62	37	6	68	22	4
over 50	78	52	30	28	22	20
All respon-dents	51	35	8	74	12	6

Source: Calculated from *Purchasing*, LI, (20 November 1961) 76-77.

no doubt derives from several sources. One is the transaction costs of reciprocity, mentioned above. This would operate without any other differences between large and small firms. The table shows, however, that reciprocity potential is signifi-cantly greater for large firms: 42 per cent of purchasing agents in firms selling goods worth over $50 million annually believe that over 10 per cent of sales are made to suppliers, whereas the figure is only 26 per cent for medium-size firms. Finally, numerous studies of market structure show that absolute size and seller concentration (relative size) are highly correlated, so the influence of concentration is also reflected. Other surveys confirm the importance of reciprocity to the large firm; for instance, 60 per cent of the firms on *Fortune's* list of the five hundred largest non-financial corporations employ 'trade-relations men,' the current euphemism for those charged with arranging reciprocity deals [21, p. 180].

3.2 *Excess capacity and persistence of reciprocity*

For a number of reasons mentioned in Section 2.6, a reduction in demand for a trader's output might promote a search for reciprocity arrangements. If the maintenance of sticky collusive market prices is an important condition for reciprocity, as the standard view suggests, falling demand should be reflected in excess capacity and a decline in marginal cost relative to market price. Thus an increase in the resort to reciprocity would be expected during recessions. On the other hand, some observers have marked excess capacity as a necessary condition for reciprocity, implying that it would show little persistence with the return of good times.

The evidence shows clearly that reciprocity tends to increase during recessions. It first drew attention during the depression of the 1930s [11, 20]. The survey summarised in Table 1.1 [28] took place just after the minor recession of 1960–61, and the percentages of respondents noting an increase during the recession (column 2) are not only high but also correlated with the portion viewing reciprocity as a significantly persistent factor. Another survey of purchasing agents [8] found that 43 per cent of them noted an increase in reciprocity during the early 1960s, 26 per cent in the relatively prosperous 1952–1959 period, only 17 per cent during the highly prosperous years 1946–1951. At least one observer suggests that industries with high fixed costs, where excess capacity would tend to widen the gap between price and short-run marginal cost more markedly, are notable for their volume of reciprocal dealings [2, p. 117].

But the amount of reciprocity could fluctuate with excess

capacity while resting on a large permanent base, and this also seems to be the case. In no period since the Second World War have many observers found reciprocity to be levelling off [8, p. 10], and it has been called 'a traditional way of life' in some industries [22, p. 180]. Firms' organisational arrangements for furthering reciprocity are clearly not meant to serve only in foul weather [27, p. 29]. Descriptions of individual reciprocity arrangements show them to be long-lived, and industries' trading patterns sometimes grow ridden with them so that firms obligate themselves to divide up their purchases in complex relation to the distribution of their sales.[33]

3.3 *Reciprocity and constrained pricing*

The link between reciprocity and high seller concentration confirms the relation of reciprocity to discrimination in a general way, but fails to distinguish between the 'monopolistic' and 'competitive' cases (Sections 1.1, 1.2, 1.4). The latter turns on imperfect collusion, the former on the power to discriminate; both tend to rise as we move across the spectrum of industries toward those with higher concentration. The probable significance of 'competitive discrimination' would rise if some evidence associates the practice specifically with defections from collusive prices. Some such evidence does exist.

Price is likely to be most rigid where its minimum value is set by public authority, as in the case of public utilities and common-carrier transportation in the United States. Furthermore, discrimination in the form of selective price-cutting is normally illegal in these sectors. They should, then, be strong prospects for systematic and sustained reciprocity. This prediction is amply confirmed. During the 1930s it was found that purchasing by the United States railroads was riddled with reciprocity, and it paid large buyers of transportation services (such as meat packers) to purchase companies manufacturing railway equipment just for their reciprocity potential.[34] Local public utilities apparently also practice reciprocity heavily [20, pp. 299–300],

---

[33] See [19; 28, p. 71; 29; 37].

[34] For descriptions, see [29, 37], and also *Reciprocity in Purchasing and Routing*, 188 I.C.C. (1932) 417; and *Waugh Equipment Co.*, 15 F.T.C., (1931) 232.

although their near-monopoly position (compared to railroads) may lend it a different significance. Finally, among unregulated industries selling intermediate or producer goods, one gets the general impression that reciprocity is more common, the more standardised are the goods in question [2, 28]. The high cross-elasticities of demand between competing sellers of such goods inflate their interest in various sorts of collusive pricing arrangements. Reciprocity is likely to prove an attractive way to chisel in these cases because direct price discrimination is hard to conceal, and also potentially vulnerable to legal attack (under the Robinson–Patman Act) even if rivals are unable to retaliate effectively [3, p. 1027].

3.4 *Terms of trade under reciprocal arrangements*

The theory of preferential trading shows that mutually acceptable terms of trade may often lie within limits of some width. If reciprocity were due only to collusive pricing practices, as the standard explanation suggests, reciprocal exchanges would take place solely at market prices and would be free of elements of monopolistic discrimination in this sense. On the other hand, firms might also use reciprocity against disfavoured partners to improve their terms of trade (Section 1.2). This would be possible where the potential partner lacks a way to sustain his current sales at a comparably reduced net profit by any alternative strategy (e.g. a price cut).

The quality of the evidence available on the terms of reciprocity deals is lamentably poor, since businessmen are naturally reluctant to testify on the point. The standard protestation is that reciprocal transactions take place only at market prices, and in the one survey dealing with this point only 18 per cent of managers canvassed would admit using reciprocity to extract prices higher than their competitors' [20, p. 301]. Neutral observers, however, are often sceptical about the degree of adherence to market price. The purchaser's specifications for a given product are not independent of the identity of the seller who may supply it. 'The buyer often makes the low man – he can determine who is going to come in with the low bid, just by making special demands' [21, p. 192]. The amount of ancillary service provided by a seller and aspects of the quality of his product can be varied, even if nominal price is that of 'the market'.[35]

A strong piece of indirect evidence of this forcing of penalty prices via reciprocity is the universal dislike of the practice voiced by purchasing agents, whose proximate objective is to minimise input costs to the firm.[36] If firms possessed monopoly/monopsony power as traders in general equilibrium, discriminatory reciprocity should prove as attractive to them – when the firm is on the winning end – as to the salesmen. On the other hand, if reciprocal trading tends heavily to depend on imperfectly collusive pricing, the sales department will always appear to garner the gains from the firm's favourable reciprocity deals, the purchasing agent to suffer the cost of unfavourable ones inflicted on the firm.

Care must be taken in identifying the gainers and losers from reciprocity. When firm A inflicts reciprocity on firm B, one of its current suppliers, by threatening to divert purchases, the best that B can hope for is to maintain its prior terms of trade, merely by switching its purchases to A. Where the firms have not been trading with each other, however, and both sell in imperfectly collusive markets, the difference between A's internal opportunity–costs and market prices also becomes territory in which the bargain might settle.[31] The firm that initiates the transaction then might appear to be the loser, in terms of market prices, with apparent financial losses (if any) in purchasing more than offset by gains on sales. My general impression is that firms pursue reciprocity mainly along the first of these two routes – rummaging through lists of their current suppliers in search of reciprocity potential.[37]

3.5 *Reciprocity, mergers and diversification*
An indication (though not a measure) of the distortion that reciprocity can create in patterns of economic activity is the

---

[35] For evidence see [2, p. 122; 20; 29]. Also, some weight can perhaps be given to the *a priori* argument that if B was not purchasing from A at market prices and now does so under 'reciprocity' pressure, the former arrangement must in general have given B better terms of trade in *some* fashion.

[36] See [2, pp. 119–122; 15, p. 100].

[37] The literature on reciprocity suffers from trying to make a false dichotomy between 'coercive reciprocity' and reciprocity involving

diversification that a trading entity might undertake in its mix of products for the purpose of increasing its reciprocity potential. The growth of conglomerate enterprise has had the result, accidental or intended, of greatly increasing possible reciprocal dealings for many firms, and the conglomerate movement has been cited as a reason for the post-war growth of reciprocity.[38] The earlier purchases of railway equipment firms by meat packers were mentioned above. More recently, several mergers attacked by the Federal Trade Commission have involved a large company that makes heavy purchases from other firms acquiring a smaller (and not necessarily successful) company for its reciprocity potential.[39]

3.6 *Business reciprocity, welfare and economic policy*

Reciprocity has been a lively issue in American antitrust policy during the past few years. Mergers have been struck down on the ground of their reciprocity potential where the acquiring firm is a buyer of substantial absolute size in its input markets, and the acquired firm holds a significant share of the market in which it sells.[40] Reciprocity itself does not enjoy a well-defined status at law, but the Antitrust Division has secured consent decrees against several large firms whereby they agree for a period of time to undertake no reciprocity arrangements. In the consent decrees the signatories do not admit their guilt of charges brought under Section 1 of the Sherman Act, so the effect is to create a presumption that systematic reciprocity is illegal without providing any well-defined legal standard.

Because of this situation it seems particularly important to summarise the results of this analysis of the theory and practice of business reciprocity and indicate briefly what sort of economic inefficiency the practice may involve. The evidence

concessions from collusive prices. This results from failure to notice the consequences of imperfect collusion existing in the market for both products, which on the evidence cited here (Sections 3.1–3.3) seems quite likely. Cf. Ferguson [14, pp. 571–573], who admittedly considers what I have called 'competitive reciprocity' to be 'of limited empirical validity'.

[38] For example, [11, p. 851; 21, p. 180].

[39] See [27, p. 28; 29, pp. 78–79; 37, chap. 6].

[40] The volume of commentary on these cases is large. See [6; 14; 16; 37].

suggests that business reciprocity operates primarily as a second-best device for firms engaged in the imperfectly collusive maintenance of their selling prices to effect a preferential price shift. Without any change in collusively maintained prices, it is possible for at least one party to a reciprocal agreement to gain from the expansion of trade on which price exceeds marginal cost. Approximately equal losses will be inflicted on firms from which trade is diverted, so that no net social gain occurs if market prices are unaffected. Where a firm inflicts reciprocity on an existing supplier through an actual or implied threat to withdraw purchases, it gains, the supplier loses, and losses also accrue to the firm(s) from which the supplier's purchases are diverted. A net social loss occurs to the extent that transactions are diverted to a higher-cost supplier. Thus, most reciprocity appears to represent 'competitive discrimination' (Section 1.4) coupled with some use of the all-or-nothing offer (Section 1.2).

In contrast to the trading agreements employed by developing countries, little evidence suggests that business reciprocity is used to effect monopolistic price discrimination (as described in Section 1.1). That is, there is no indication that sellers search out for a reciprocity partner – the sort favoured by a discriminating monopolist – one with (in effect) high price and income-elasticities of demand for the monopolist's export (Section 1.3). There is no evidence of profitable resale or efforts to prevent it (Section 2.3). There is no indication that the expansion of trade through reciprocity assists the active party in effecting discrimination against outside traders, since the usual pattern of the agreement is to improve his terms of trade or leave them unchanged, rather than to worsen them selectively (Section 1.5). The passive party might acquiesce in deteriorated terms of trade, however, with the expectation that he could recoup through discrimination against excluded parties. Whatever its discriminatory significance, 'competitive discrimination' may help to avert general adjustments of collusively restrained market prices that would otherwise occur.

These conclusions can be related briefly to the literature on economic policy toward business reciprocity. There, discussion of the effects of reciprocity has been confused by preoccupation with the effects of 'forestalling' competitors (a matter of some

concern under the antitrust laws, especially the Robinson–
Patman Act, but little *direct* relevance to economic welfare) and
unsuccessful pursuit of the notion that reciprocity somehow
serves to increase the leverage of a monopoly position. As
recent contributions have correctly argued [3, 14], there is no
well-defined sense in which reciprocity directly raises market
power. It can decrease efficiency, by coercion of a supplier to
shift from a cheaper to a dearer source of supply, however, and
it can raise the profitability of a position of market power
already held. More attention might be given to this real cost of
discrimination, especially in view of the evidence that reciprocity
is highly persistent and can distort procurement patterns
throughout an industry. Systematic reciprocity of that sort can
also contribute to barriers to entry in the sense of raising the
incidence of those resulting from any of their conventional
sources.[41] To that extent monopoly power may be *indirectly*
increased. Sporadic reciprocity might serve the desirable
function of other forms of 'price chiselling' in undermining
imperfectly collusive pricing arrangements, but the evidence
reviewed above provides little empirical hope for a justification
along this line. Reciprocity seems typically to be an entrenched
and sustained practice, and even sporadic reciprocity may
provide firms with a substitute for manoeuvres that would be
more likely to undermine collusive prices.[42] The case against
sustained and systematic reciprocity in a concentrated industry,
or against conglomerate mergers that would make such
reciprocity possible,[43] seems reasonably sound.

[41] Thus, given some economies of scale, a potential entrant must expect
to capture some minimum share of the market before attaining minimum
average costs. He will see his chances as reduced if reciprocity precludes
detaching present purchases from their old suppliers, and he is locked into
the 'pessimistic assumption' of the Sylos-Bain model about the reduction
from the ruling price that will be needed to attract extra demand equal
to his minimum efficient output; see [24].

[42] The dilemma of the possible virtues of sporadic price discrimination
versus the vices of persistent discrimination is familiar in the literature of
antitrust.

[43] See [31, pp. 1386–1393].

References

[1] AHUJA, K. 'India's Trade with Eastern Europe – A Comment', *Indian Economic Journal*, IX, (January 1962) 361–5.

[2] AMMER, D. S. 'Realistic Reciprocity', *Harvard Business Review*, XL, (January–February 1962) 116–24.

[3] ANDERSON, J. P. 'Reciprocal Dealing', *Yale Law Journal*, LXXVI, (April 1967) 1020–29.

[4] BALDWIN, R. E. 'Equilibrium in International Trade: a Diagrammatic Analysis', *Quarterly Journal of Economics*, LXII, (November 1948) 748–62.

[5] BECKER, G. S. 'A Note on Multi-Country Trade', *American Economic Review*, XLII, (September 1952) 558–68.

[6] BOCK, B. 'Mergers and Reciprocity', *Conference Board Record*, II, (July 1965) 27–36.

[7] COOPER, C. A. and MASSELL, B. F. 'Toward a General Theory of Customs Unions for Developing Countries', *Journal of Political Economy*, LXXIII, (October 1965) 461–76.

[8] DAUNER, J. R. 'The Attitude of the Purchasing Agent Toward Reciprocity', *Journal of Purchasing*, III, (August 1967) 5–15.

[9] DAVE, S. 'India's Trade Relations with East European Countries, 1952–53 – 1959–60, A Study in Bilateralism', *Indian Economic Journal*, IX, (July 1961) 48–68.

[10] DAVE, S. 'India's Trade with East European Countries – Rejoinder', *Indian Economic Journal*, IX, (April 1962) 479–83.

[11] DEAN, J. 'Economic Aspects of Reciprocity, Competition and Mergers', *Antitrust Bulletin*, VIII, (September–December 1963) 843–52.

[12] DE LOOPER, J. H. C. 'Current Usage of Payments Agreements and Trade Agreements', *I.M.F. Staff Papers*, IV, (August 1955) 339–97.

[13] DE NEUMAN, A. M. ' "Tied" International Trading – the Indonesian Rami Fibre Test Case', *Economic Journal*, LXIV, (June 1954) 324–36.

[14] FERGUSON, J. M. 'Tying Arrangements and Reciprocity:

An Economic Analysis', *Law and Contemporary Problems*, XXX, (summer 1965) 552–80.

[15] FINNEY, F. R. 'Reciprocity and Public Policy', *Antitrust Law and Economics Review*, II, (summer 1969) 97–110.

[16] HALE, G. E. and HALE, R. D. 'Reciprocity under the Antitrust Laws: A Comment', *University of Pennsylvania Law Review*, CXIII, (November 1964) 69–76.

[16a] HENDERSON, A. M. 'A Geometrical Note on Bulk Purchase', *Economica*, XV, (February 1948) 61–9.

[17] JOHNSON, H. G. 'An Economic Theory of Protectionism, Tariff Bargaining, and the Formation of Customs Unions', *Journal of Political Economy*, LXXIII, (June 1965) 256–83.

[18] KEMP, M. C. 'A Contribution to the General Equilibrium Theory of Preferential Trading', *Contributions to Economic Analysis, No. 61*, (Amsterdam: North Holland Publishing Co., 1969).

[19] LEWIS, H. T. 'No Matter What you Call It – It's Still Reciprocity', *Purchasing*, LII, (15 January 1962) 74–5.

[20] LEWIS, H. T. 'The Present Status of Reciprocity as a Sales Policy', *Harvard Business Review*, XVI, (spring 1938) 299–313.

[21] MCCREARY, E. JR, and GUZZARDI, W. JR, 'A Customer is a Company's Best Friend', *Fortune*, LXXI, (June 1965) 180–2.

[22] MEADE, J. E. *A Geometry of International Trade*, (London: George Allen & Unwin, Ltd, 1952).

[23] MIKESELL, R. F. and BEHRMAN, J. N. *Financing Free World Trade with the Sino-Soviet Bloc*, Princeton Studies in International Finance, No. 8, Princeton, N.J., (International Finance Section, Princeton University, 1958).

[24] MODIGLIANI, F. 'New Developments on the Oligopoly Front', *Journal of Political Economy*, LXVI, (June 1958) 215–32.

[25] ROBINSON, J. *The Economics of Imperfect Competition*, (London: Macmillan, 1933).

[26] SEN, S. *India's Bilateral Payments and Trade Agreements, 1947–48 to 1963–64*, (Calcutta: Bookland Private Ltd, 1965).

[27] SIMON, L. S. 'Industrial Reciprocity as a Business

Strategy', *Industrial Management Review*, VII, (spring 1966) 27–39.

[28] SLOANE, L. 'Reciprocity: Where Does the P.A. Stand?', *Purchasing*, LI, (20 November 1961) 70–9.

[29] STOCKING, G. W. and MUELLER, W. F. 'Business Reciprocity and the Size of Firms', *Journal of Business*, XXX, (April 1957) 73–95.

[30] TRUED, M. N. and MIKESELL, R. F. *Postwar Bilateral Payments Agreements*, Princeton Studies in International Finance, No. 4, Princeton, N.J., (International Finance Section, Princeton University, 1955).

[31] TURNER, D. F. 'Conglomerate Mergers and Section 7 of the Clayton Act', *Harvard Law Review*, LXXVIII, (May 1965) 1313–95.

[32] U.N.O. Economic Commission for Africa, *Bilateral Trade and Payments in Africa*, U.N.O. Doc. E/CN 14/STC/24 (1963).

[33] U.N.O. Economic Commission for Africa, *General Review of Activities in Trade and Customs*, U.N.O. Doc. E/CN 14/W.P. 1/3 (1966).

[34] U.N.O. Economic Commission for Asia and the Far East, 'State Trading in Countries of the E.C.A.F.E. Region', *Proceedings of the United Nations Conference on Trade and Development*, New York: United Nations, 1964. Vol. VII, pp. 1–32.

[35] U.N.O. Economic Commission for Asia and the Far East, 'Trade between Developing E.C.A.F.E. Countries and Centrally Planned Economies', *Economic Bulletin for Asia and the Far East*, XV, (June 1964) 16–51.

[36] U.N.O. Economic Commission for Asia and the Far East, 'Trade Liberalization in the E.C.A.F.E. Region', *The Asian Development Bank and Trade Liberalization*, Regional Economic Cooperation Series, No. 2. U.N.O. Doc. E/CN 11/707 (1965).

[37] U.S. Federal Trade Commission, *Economic Report on Corporate Mergers: Staff Report*, in U.S. Senate, Committee on the Judiciary, Subcommittee on Antitrust and Monopoly, *Economic Concentration*, Hearings pursuant to S. Res. 40. Washington: Government Printing Office, 1969. Part 8A.

[38] VANEK, J. *General Equilibrium of International Discrimination: the Case of Customs Unions*. Harvard Economic Studies, Vol. 123 (Cambridge, Mass.: Harvard University Press, 1965).

[39] VERBIT, G. P. *Trade Agreements for Developing Countries* (New York: Columbia University Press, 1969).

2 Elasticity Pessimism, Absorption and Flexible Exchange Rates

RANDALL HINSHAW*

THE remarkable resurgence of interest in flexible exchange rates – which has even invaded circles, such as central banks, where formerly the subject was close to anathema – is doubtless in considerable measure inspired by the now justly famous 'Tinbergen Principle': the rule that, to assure the attainment of policy goals, the makers of policy need as many techniques as they have objectives. According to this criterion, if those in power want full employment *and* price stability *and* a high rate of capital formation *and* international balance without direct controls, they cannot hope to achieve these objectives by relying on only one or two techniques, such as variation in the money supply or in the level of government expenditure. Only by a happy coincidence will all objectives be attained if the number of tools is less than the number of goals and, in the absence of such an unlikely conjuncture, the most that can be achieved is some kind of 'second-best' compromise involving 'trade-offs' between, for example, employment and price stability, or employment and liberal trade policies.

In principle, however, Professor Tinbergen has shown that it is not necessary to settle for second-best solutions, so long as the techniques chosen are, first of all, effective for the particular purposes for which they are used and, second, are sufficient in number. Basically, the appeal of exchange rate flexibility is that it constitutes an additional tool, enabling a country to maintain liberal international policies (freedom from exchange control, import quotas and high tariffs), while successfully pursuing important domestic economic objectives, such as full employment and price stability, by other techniques.

The key question, of course, is whether exchange rate

* Claremont Graduate School.

flexibility is an *effective* policy. That is to say, will flexible exchange rates, when combined with appropriate domestic policies, assure international balance at an optimal, or near-optimal level of trade?[1] The answer clearly depends on international demand elasticities, supply elasticities, income effects and 'absorption' effects; and while the literature on these subjects is vast, certain questions need to be re-examined in view of the greatly increased interest in flexible exchange rates in both academic and official circles.

Most of the points in the ensuing analysis have been made by others, though some, I believe, are new.[2] Whether old or new, they are intended to comprise a coherent (if somewhat individualistic) synthesis, and are presented in the spirit of Professor Tinbergen's strong humanitarian interest in important questions of policy. I shall resist the temptation to plunge into a symbolic treatment, because I wish to be as widely understood as possible and because the points I wish to make can all be made in lucid English. Attention will be centred on the trade account, but in the context of an implicit model which retains as many relevant features of the real world as possible. In particular, I shall avoid any conclusions derived from the two-country, two-commodity analysis so familiar in the pure theory of international trade and, unfortunately, so frequently employed with misleading results in the theory of international adjustment. It will be assumed throughout that we are considering the problems of a single country in a much larger world and that the country is successful in maintaining full employment by domestic measures. The latter assumption means, of course, that in the short run any increase in the

[1] 'Optimal' balance is here distinguished from less-than-optimal balance (balance via controls or high taxes on international payments) and from more-than-optimal balance involving subsidies on either exports, imports, or both. The adjective 'near-optimal' is intended to take account of possible distortions' of the type analysed by Harry G. Johnson, Jagdish Bhagwati, and others.

[2] My intellectual debts to others are obvious. In addition to those cited in the essay, I would like particularly to name Sidney S. Alexander, Gottfried Haberler, Arnold C. Harberger, Sir Roy Harrod, Fritz Machlup, J. E. Meade, Lloyd A. Metzler, Robert A. Mundell, Joan Robinson, and my early mentor and friend, Frank D. Graham, who taught me to be sceptical of much accepted wisdom in international economics. Any deficiencies in the present analysis are, of course, strictly my own.

country's real output is small, being limited by the slow growth of output per man and the growth, if any, in the employed population.

1. Elasticity Pessimism as an Empirical Question

Professor Tinbergen did some of the earliest empirical exploration of price elasticities in international demand, and came to the conclusion reached by other early investigators – including the present writer – that those elasticities, on the basis of interwar data, were often surprisingly low.[3] These investigations had a profoundly disquieting effect, and gave birth to an extensive literature concerned with the issue of 'elasticity pessimism', a term contributed by Fritz Machlup. Some economists questioned the statistical results, giving various reasons why the elasticities might have been underestimated. Other economists accepted the findings, and in some cases jumped to the conclusion that changes in exchange rates would therefore be a poor means of dealing with payments disequilibria. A third position – my own – would be that elasticity pessimism, within certain broad limits, need not imply pessimism with regard to the efficacy of changes in exchange rates, whether such changes are occasional, in response to substantial payments deficits or surpluses, or are continuous, in response to 'mini deficits' or 'mini surpluses'.

On the empirical issue, my position can be briefly stated. Although such writers as Fritz Machlup [6] and Guy H. Orcutt [8] provided ample grounds for scepticism regarding the early estimates of international price elasticities of demand, I remain convinced that for the only country I have studied, the United States, the figure was low for the interwar period.[4] It should be

[3] My work in this field is confined to an early estimate of the price elasticity of the United States demand for imports; the estimate, derived from interwar data, is −0·5—well below unity [2]. Using some of the same data, Tinbergen concluded that, for the United States, 'the most probable results point to elasticities at least as low as those found by Hinshaw.' [10, 88].

[4] Similar results have been obtained from postwar data. In a study based on the period 1951–66, H. S. Houthakker and Stephen P. Magee have derived an import price elasticity for the United States which rounds to the same figure (−0·5) as my estimate [5, 113].

remembered that the period was characterised by high American tariffs on manufactured goods and that, no doubt partly as a result, the great bulk of American imports consisted of a rather short list of industrial raw materials and tropical foodstuffs. For commodities such as these, the careful work of Henry Schultz has provided much evidence that the individual price elasticities of demand were typically well below unity (see [9, chap. XVII]. Moreover, with few exceptions, these primary products were not produced in the United States, so that there was no possibility of substitution between foreign and domestic output; that is to say, the American demand curve for the product was identical with the American import demand curve.

It is important, however, to be clear about what the statistical investigators in this field have attempted to measure. In most of the statistical studies, a country's volume of imports (imports at constant prices) is assumed to be a function of relative import prices (measured by dividing an import index by a domestic price index) and the country's level of real income. On this assumption, price and income elasticities of demand are derived by multiple correlation. In such studies, the estimates of import price elasticities, for what they are worth, are measures of the pure Hicksian 'substitution effect' of a price change, with real income held constant. Thus, as has sometimes been pointed out, the estimated elasticities are 'partial' elasticities in the sense that the Hicksian 'income effect' of a price change is clearly excluded.

This observation has an important bearing on the analysis of exchange rate changes, since much of the literature in this field reaches the gloomy conclusion that the income effect of an exchange rate change is likely to make matters worse – that is, to make the import demand curve, defined as a measure of the pure substitution effect, shift in the wrong direction. With inappropriate monetary and fiscal policies, there is no doubt that the income effect can indeed make matters worse, but in a later section an effort will be made to show that, with proper policies, the *domestic* income effect will promote, rather than impede, international adjustment and will assure any needed change in absorption. First, however, it will be helpful to examine certain basic relationships involving international price elasticities.

2. Import Elasticities Versus Export Elasticities

As Professor Machlup has pointed out, there are various degrees of elasticity pessimism. At one end is the extremely pessimistic view that, in the short run at least, the relevant elasticities are so low that the exchange market is unstable, which means that if the exchange rate is free to move in response to a disturbance of any kind, it will move farther and farther away from an equilibrium position. Thus, if the rate is moving down in response to an emerging deficit, the deficit will get larger and larger as the rate gets lower and lower. Machlup refers to this sad prospect as 'hopeless' elasticity pessimism. Clearly, under such conditions a flexible exchange rate would make no sense.

A less pessimistic position is that the required elasticities are high enough to assure a stable equilibrium, but that a change in the exchange rate will be accompanied by a change, *in the same direction*, in foreign exchange earnings. Those who hold this view conclude that a fall in the exchange rate[5] will typically be accompanied by a fall in foreign exchange receipts, matched by a still greater fall in foreign exchange expenditure. In terms of the Marshall-Lerner condition (subject to all the qualifications which that conclusion requires), the sum of the demand elasticities is greater than unity.

But this is not a very comforting step in the direction of optimism. For, whatever the sum of the elasticities may be, if the demand for a country's exports has a price elasticity below unity, the case for a flexible exchange rate is weak indeed. If a fall in the exchange rate, while restoring equilibrium, is accompanied by a fall in foreign exchange earnings, then it would surely be better to maintain the existing parity (at least for export transactions) and to reduce imports by other means. The superiority of exchange depreciation over import limitation as

[5] Since the present analysis is concerned with flexible exchange rates, the term 'devaluation', implying deliberate change, will be avoided. Instead, the broader term 'fall in the exchange rate' will here be used to include both cases of planned devaluation and cases of exchange depreciation in response to market pressures. In certain varieties of exchange rate flexibility—for example, the 'crawling peg'—the exchange rate changes can be thought of as 'mini-devaluations' or 'mini-revaluations' (upward).

a means of removing a deficit rests on the assumption that depreciation will expand foreign exchange earnings, thereby making possible a more efficient use of domestic resources by avoiding the often immense encouragement to high-cost production afforded by import controls, whether direct or indirect. To put the matter another way, the economic case for flexible exchange rates rests on the assumption, not simply that they promote international balance – for balance can be achieved by import quotas (or import taxes or a separate import exchange rate) – but that they promote balance at an optimal, or near optimal, level of trade.

This means that for a flexible exchange rate to make sense as an adjustment technique, a fall in the exchange rate must be accompanied by a rise in foreign exchange earnings. That is to say, a country's *export* price elasticity (in terms of foreign currency) must be greater than unity – and in the short run. It is no comfort to invoke the familiar proposition that long run elasticities are likely to be higher than short run elasticities, because in the context of flexible exchange rates it is short run elasticities that are relevant.[6]

Here, however, it is essential to emphasise a distinction of great importance – namely, that a world of low *import* price elasticities does not imply a world of low *export* price elasticities. There are strong reasons for believing that export price elasticities are typically greater than unity even if low import price elasticities are common – and, of the two, export price elasticities, for reasons just indicated, are of greater interest in evaluating the case for flexible exchange rates.

Consider, for example, a world in which *every* country has an import demand with an average price elasticity of less than unity, but in which each export commodity is typically produced by several countries. In such a world, if (say) a coffee-producing country under Balance of Payments pressure lets its exchange rate fall, while other exchange rates remain unchanged (or at least fall by a smaller proportion), it is likely to experience

[6] At least in the case of *floating* rates, where there is clearly a danger of what Sir Roy Harrod calls 'intolerable oscillations' in rates if short-run elasticities are low. In the case of the crawling peg, the exchange rate changes, though frequent, are so gradual that longer-run elasticities may also be of considerable relevance.

a sharp rise in foreign exchange earnings even if the world demand for coffee has a very low price elasticity. Foreign coffee buyers, confronted with a lower price, will buy more from the country, switching purchases from other sources. This action may quickly remove any price discrepancy, but only because foreign buyers are buying more, per period, from the country than they did before the fall in the exchange rate.

How much the country's foreign exchange earnings will rise in such a case will depend not only on the foreign elasticity of demand for its output but also on its own elasticity of supply. If its export supply elasticity is zero, the rise in foreign exchange earnings will also be zero, no matter how elastic the foreign demand; but a vertical export supply curve is highly unlikely because, as Professor Haberler and others have shown, the export supply curve of a particular commodity is not to be confused with the country's total supply curve of that commodity, but rather is the difference (if positive)[7] between the domestic supply curve and the domestic demand curve. Thus the export supply function may be quite elastic even if the total domestic supply function has a very low elasticity.[8]

Where the short run export supply curve is horizontal – also a most unlikely situation, though often explicitly or implicitly assumed in oversimplified adjustment theory – the country whose exchange rate has fallen will capture the entire market for commodities produced under such conditions. While the resulting increase in foreign exchange earnings may be great indeed (at least temporarily), the outcome is by no means necessarily optimal. In the first place, it involves a deterioration in the country's terms of trade, since, in domestic currency, the import price level has risen whereas the export price level (for commodities with horizontal supply functions) has remained unchanged. In the second place, such a situation is almost certain to lead to retaliatory action by countries hitherto exporting the same commodities. Indeed, under a flexible-rate

---

[7] If negative, the difference is an import demand curve.

[8] Using the same reasoning, Haberler has shown that a country's import demand function for a commodity is likely to be more elastic than its total demand function for the commodity. This reasoning applies, of course, only where there is domestic production of the item imported—a condition not met for several important United States imports.

regime, the 'retaliation' need not even be deliberate; deprived of exports by the country whose exchange rate has initially fallen, such countries may themselves experience payments difficulties leading automatically to at least some decline in *their* exchange rates. Thus, the desired short run elasticity of export supply is one which is high enough to assure an increase in foreign exchange earnings but not so high as to lead to a serious deterioration in terms of trade or to appreciable declines in the exchange rates of export competing countries. Fortunately, most short run export supply functions surely fall within this broad range.

The general conclusion which emerges from these considerations is that there are solid grounds for expecting the appropriate substitution or 'switching' effects from changes in exchange rates even if import price elasticities of demand are typically low. As most export commodities are produced by several countries, export price elasticities of demand can be expected to be well above unity and thus to assure an increase in foreign exchange earnings, provided the export supply functions fall within the wide range just indicated.

On export price elasticities, the empirical evidence unfortunately is clouded, since, except for the years since 1960, it is impossible to find a period since 1930 not characterised by widespread direct controls on international payments. In their study cited earlier, Houthakker and Magee derive encouragingly high export price elasticities for certain countries, such as the United States $(-1·51)$ and France $(-2·27)$, but low elasticities for other countries, such as the United Kingdom $(-0·44)$ [5, p. 113]. With deep respect for the authors and their efforts, I nevertheless remain sceptical about the reliability of these estimates, since they are obtained from data for the period 1951–66, the first half of which was characterised by heavy, though diminishing, quantitative restrictions on trade in manufactured goods, whereas the second half – at least in Western Europe and the United States – was largely free of import quotas outside the agricultural sector.[9] My guess is that data confined to the years beginning around 1960 would yield

[9] This criticism also applies to all estimates of *import* price elasticities for countries which have made wide use of import quotas during periods covered by statistical studies.

much higher elasticities, but the period is as yet too short to give reliable results. This is a matter on which much useful empirical work can be done in the future – assuming that the world does not retreat into another era of extensive trade controls.

Of course, one way of looking at controls is to view them as having a warping effect on international demand elasticities, effectively transforming possibly very high elasticities into very low ones. This is perhaps the main argument against such controls, and it would be futile to deny that flexible exchange rates are unlikely to work well in a world in which *other* countries typically balance their international accounts by means of quantitative restrictions. But the present world is freer from trade controls than for many years, and it is encouraging to note that, contrary to what would be expected from the low export price elasticity estimated by Houthakker and Magee, the United Kingdom devaluation of November 1967 was promptly followed by a sharp increase in foreign exchange earnings from merchandise exports.[10]

3. Income, Absorption and Flexible Rates

In contemporary literature, the income effect of a change in the exchange rate is usually regarded as counter-productive. The reasoning is simple. If, in response to a payments deficit, the exchange rate falls, one result will be an increase in export income in terms of domestic currency – even if the foreign demand for the country's output (expressed, of course, in foreign currency) has a low price elasticity – and this rise in income (which, via the foreign trade multiplier, may eventually be substantially greater than the increase in exports) will lead to an increase in imports, thereby offsetting at least part of the corrective effect on the Balance of Payments. On this ground, Professor Diaz has written that 'elasticity optimism does not necessarily lead to devaluation optimism' [1, p. 10], and, on the same ground, one might conclude that elasticity pessimism is reinforced, rather than weakened, by contemplating the income effects of exchange rate changes.

[10] On an October 1967 base, the *dollar* value of United Kingdom exports was 114 in December 1967, 122 in January 1968 and 129 in February 1968. By June 1970, the figure had climbed to 171.

But here it is of the utmost importance to distinguish sharply between the level of money income, the level of real income (= real output), the level of absorption uncorrected for price changes, and the level of real absorption (= real expenditure by the domestic sector: consumers, business, and government). Failure to make these distinctions can lead to no end of confusion.

In absorption terminology, a deficit on current account occurs when absorption (expenditure by the domestic sector) exceeds income (= value of output). In real terms, real absorption exceeds real output. To remove the deficit, either real output must increase or real absorption must decline. Under our assumption of full employment, any increment in real output in the short run will be small; consequently, the elimination of a deficit will often require an absolute fall in real absorption.

To reduce real absorption, it is necessary by one means or another to change the relationship between the level of money income, on the one hand, and the general price level, on the other. The 'general price level', as here defined, is simply a weighted average of the price level of 'home goods' (output not entering into international trade) and the 'international price level', which in turn is a weighted average of the import price level and the price level of 'exportables' (goods and services sold both at home and abroad, and weighted by the amount sold at home). An excessive rate of real absorption implies that the level of money income is too high in relation to the general price level (and, in particular, to the international price level), leading to excessive expenditure on imports and on exportables.

A fall in the exchange rate deals with this problem by raising a country's general price level (via its international price level). To put the matter simply, a fall in the exchange rate will induce a fall in real absorption, provided the accompanying rise in the general price level is greater (proportionately) than the rise, if any, in the level of money income.

A fall in the exchange rate will, of course, be accompanied by *some* rise in the general price level.[11] The import price level, in

[11] Except when the fall in the exchange rate is in response to falling prices abroad.

domestic currency, will always rise,[12] and the price level of exportables will also rise unless, as is most unlikely, the short run export supply functions are infinitely elastic.[13] The key question is whether the rise in the general price level will be greater than the rise – if any – in the level of money income. If the price level rise is greater, proportionately, than the money income rise, real expenditure by the domestic sector (real absorption) *must* fall; and since real output under full employment is slowly growing, the current account deficit will also fall – and at a slightly higher rate.

Thus, absorption pessimism or optimism concerning the efficacy of exchange rate variation depends crucially on what happens to the level of money income. This in turn depends on the monetary and fiscal assumptions.[14] Unless these assumptions are clearly spelt out, anything can happen. In the absence of monetary and fiscal restraint, the level of money income accompanying a fall in the exchange rate can rise more sharply than the general price level, in which case real absorption will increase; or the two variables can rise at the same rate, in which case real absorption will remain unchanged.

Of course, a deficit on current account (absorption in excess of income) can continue indefinitely if it is *externally* financed by an equivalent net inflow of capital. In this case, the overall Balance of Payments is in equilibrium, and the impact of the

[12] See Note 11.

[13] This matter has a clear bearing on the effect, if any, of a fall in the exchange rate on the terms of trade. I do not wish to pursue the subject here, as I have stated my position elsewhere [3], [4]. Suffice it to say that I remain persuaded, on both analytical and empirical grounds, that in a many-country, many-commodity world, a change in the terms of trade is neither a necessary part of the adjustment mechanism nor a presumptive lasting effect of an exchange rate change. Of course, an autonomous change in the terms of trade—caused, for example, by a change in tastes—may create payments difficulties leading, under a flexible-rate regime, to a fall in the exchange rate, but in this case the change in terms of trade induces the fall in the exchange rate, rather than the other way around. In such a situation, careless empirical work could easily put the cart before the horse.

[14] The monetary analysis in this section is influenced by, though somewhat different from, the reasoning in Michael Michaely's perceptive article [7].

Balance of Payments on the domestic money supply is neutral (zero). Under these conditions, absorption can exceed income indefinitely, and no corrective action is indicated unless conditions change.

The story is very different if the current account deficit is internally rather than externally financed. If it is financed by an outflow of international monetary reserves (say, gold) rather than by a net inflow of capital, the monetary impact is no longer neutral. In the absence of compensatory action by the monetary authorities, the domestic money supply will decline as long as the Balance of Payments deficit continues. Assuming that economic conditions abroad remain on an even keel, the result will eventually be a return to balance on current account via deflation – a process which may be very painful, since, if money wage rates are inflexible, it may entail large-scale unemployment.

The existence of a chronic deficit on current account that is not externally financed is clear evidence that this automatic adjustment process has been interfered with. Presumably, the central bank – precisely to avoid deflation and unemployment – has offset the loss of reserves per period by an equivalent monetary injection which keeps the domestic money supply from declining. The difficulty with this procedure, of course, is that in the meantime the country is losing gold, and the situation can continue only so long as there is gold to lose.

Once its monetary reserves are dissipated, the country, unless it can borrow from abroad, must either impose controls on international payments which limit payments to receipts, or let the exchange rate decline. The seductiveness of trade controls arises in part from the impression that they are likely to be more *effective* than a lower exchange rate in reducing an external deficit. It is by no means clear that this impression is justified. For while import controls can obviously reduce imports, they also tend to reduce exports. Domestic income, prevented from being spent on imports, may be largely diverted to exportables. Consequently, unless supplemented by controls in other sectors, or by restrictive monetary or fiscal policies, import restriction is likely to be a sluggish method of reducing real absorption. But whether or not import controls offer a viable solution to payments difficulties, they certainly do not offer an optimal solution, since, as a byproduct, they encourage the transfer of productive resources to sheltered high cost industries.

This undesirable side effect is avoided by the alternative approach – a fall in the exchange rate. The danger here is that the fall in the exchange rate will be accompanied by an inappropriate rise in the domestic money supply. Such a rise may occur more or less automatically as a result of increased business borrowing from the commercial banks induced by the rise in the general price level. The rise in the money supply will, of course, require the co-operation of the central bank, but that co-operation will be forthcoming if the central bank decides to keep interest rates from rising by providing the increased reserves desired by the commercial banks. A rise in the money supply may also occur because of an increase in government borrowing from the central bank to finance programmes made more expensive by the higher price level. If a fall in the exchange rate is to work effectively, these inappropriate responses by the central bank and by the government must be resisted or kept within narrow margins.

Ideally, any growth in the money supply should be confined to the slow growth of real output. This means that within any short period of, say, a few weeks, the quantity of money will remain virtually unchanged. Under this condition, a fall in the exchange rate, by raising the general price level, will reduce the aggregate *real* cash balance (and thus will reduce average real cash balances throughout the economy). On the reasonable assumption that consumers, investors and government equate the marginal utility of their real expenditure with the marginal utility of their real cash balances, domestic real expenditure (real absorption) must decline.[15]

[15] On the assumption that the volume of imports is a function of relative import prices (Hicksian substitution effect) and of the level of real income *accruing to the domestic sector* (Hicksian income effect), a fall in the exchange rate under the conditions here described will induce a shift of the import-demand curve *to the left*, yielding a somewhat higher 'total' price elasticity than the 'partial' elasticity reflected in the import-demand curve itself. The degree of shift will depend on the income elasticity of demand expressed in real terms.

As a corollary, any rise in the level of money income will be less, proportionately, than the rise in the general price level. Indeed, the level of money income may not rise at all, as there will be cuts in domestic expenditure – including particularly domestic expenditure on exportables, which will have risen in price both absolutely and in relation to the prices of home goods. The extent to which the general price level needs to rise in relation to the level of money income will depend on how large the excessive absorption (payments deficit)[16] is in relation to total income. In percentage terms, the excessive absorption is usually very low – hardly ever as much as 4 per cent of total income. Thus, where the aim is to remove an external deficit by a fall in the exchange rate, the required rise in the price level will generally be modest – provided, of course, that any rise in the level of money income (beyond the growth of real output) is minimised by monetary and fiscal restraint.

For a country which maintains continuous international balance by means of a flexible exchange rate, the changes in price and absorption levels will be minimal. A 'mini deficit' will induce a 'mini devaluation' leading to a 'mini rise' in the general price level accompanied by a 'mini fall' in real absorption. The opposite will be true of a 'mini surplus', which will induce a 'mini appreciation' leading to a very slight fall in the general price level accompanied by a very slight rise in real absorption.

There are two cases in which international adjustment involves no need for a change in a country's general price level, and both reflect a situation where any monetary or fiscal mistakes are being made, not at home, but abroad. In a world like that of the early 1930s, characterised by falling prices, a country can keep its general price level stable and its international accounts in continuous balance by letting its exchange rate gradually fall. Similarly, in a world which knows how to avoid deflation but which has a strong inflationary trend, a country can keep its price level stable and its international

---

[16] It is the *overall* deficit that is relevant here. Absorption can be excessive even if the current account is in surplus if that surplus is exceeded by a net outflow of capital (or foreign aid).

accounts in balance by letting its exchange rate gradually rise. In these cases, a change in the country's general price level is not needed, since the deflationary or inflationary mistakes are of foreign rather than domestic origin.

Concluding Observations

The principal conclusions of this analysis can be stated in a few brief propositions:

(1) Low *import* price elasticities are consistent with high *export* price elasticities, and it is the latter which are of primary interest in successful international adjustment by means of flexible exchange rates;

(2) elasticity pessimism (on the import side) is consistent with absorption optimism;

(3) even at full employment, absorption optimism is justified for a country with a flexible exchange rate, provided the country's monetary and fiscal policies are successful in maintaining its aggregate money income at the correct level in relation to its general price level (embracing 'home goods', imports and 'exportables');

(4) the case for flexible exchange rates is strongest where any monetary and fiscal mistakes are made, not at home, but abroad. If a country is successful in maintaining full employment and price stability, a flexible rate can be of great assistance in maintaining external balance at an optimal, or near optimal, level of trade. In a world of rising prices, such a country would find its exchange rate gradually moving upward. This upward movement would keep the stable internal price level consistent with the rising price level abroad. Indeed, without a rising exchange rate, the country would have difficulty maintaining a stable general price level, since its international price level, at a fixed exchange rate, would be steadily rising. To maintain a stable price level at a fixed exchange rate would require a *declining* price level of home goods – a far from attractive requirement which, among other things, would make more difficult the maintenance of full employment.

This essay is in no sense an effort to say the last word. In such a complex and controversial field, that would be a foolishly arrogant ambition. In the future, the wisdom of employing flexible exchange rates will depend, not merely on the matters here considered, but on the path followed in the further evolution of international monetary arrangements – in particular, on the degree to which national monetary and fiscal authority is transferred to international institutions.

References

[1] ALEJANDRO, CARLOS F. DIAZ. 'Exchange-Rate Devaluation in a Semi-Industrialized Country: The Experience of Argentina, 1955–1961, (Cambridge, Mass.: M.I.T. Press, 1965).

[2] HINSHAW, RANDALL. 'American Prosperity and the British Balance-of-Payments Problem', *Review of Economics and Statistics*, XXVII, (February 1945) 1–9.

[3] HINSHAW, RANDALL. 'Currency Appreciation as an Anti-Inflationary Device', *Quarterly Journal of Economics*, LXV, (November 1951) 447–62.

[4] HINSHAW, RANDALL. 'The Effect of Devaluation on the Price Level: Further Comment', *Quarterly Journal of Economics*, LXXII, (November 1958) 616–25.

[5] HOUTHAKKER, H. S. and MAGEE, STEPHEN, P. 'Income and Price Elasticities in World Trade', *Review of Economics and Statistics*, LI, (May 1969) 111–25.

[6] MACHLUP, FRITZ. 'Elasticity Pessimism in International Trade', *Economia Internazionale*, II, (1950) 118–41; reprinted in his International Payments, Debts, and Gold: Collected Essays (New York: Charles Scribner's Sons, 1964).

[7] MICHAELY, MICHAEL. 'Relative-Prices and Income-Absorption Approaches to Devaluation: A Partial Reconciliation', *American Economic Review*, L (March 1960) 144–7.

[8] ORCUTT, GUY H. 'Measurement of Price Elasticities in International Trade', *Review of Economics and Statistics*, XXXII, (May 1950) 117–32.

[9] SCHULTZ, HENRY. *The Theory and Measurement of Demand* (Chicago: The University of Chicago Press, 1938).

[10] TINBERGEN, JAN. 'Some Remarks on the Problem of Dollar Scarcity', *Econometrica*, XVII, (July 1949) Supplement, 73–97.

3 Economic Policy in a Small Economy

PETER B. KENEN*

Introduction

GENERAL principles sometimes seem trite once they are properly articulated. Often, indeed, they govern our work long before they are recognised explicitly. Once discovered, however, they unify our understanding of specific instances and grant access to problems that had been intractable. Tinbergen's analysis of economic policy is a major case in point [10]. Like the basic law of supply and demand, the principle was used before it had been formulated, and one prime application was international. As Mill had used the law of supply and demand to show how the terms of trade are determined [5], so Meade had discovered the need for separate instruments equal in number to one's policy targets in his pioneering work on the Balance of Payments [4]. But the formal and general articulation of Tinbergen's 'rule' placed Meade's contribution in broader context.

International economists continue to use Tinbergen's rule. They have, in fact, helped to refine it. Tinbergen showed that those who would achieve a set of quantifiable goals must have at hand a set of policy instruments, each with a distinct effect upon the set of targets, equal in number to the targets. Mundell and others have since shown how to pair the instruments with the targets so that, in the absence of perfect knowledge and policy co-ordination, the instruments can still be manipulated to achieve the targets.[1] They have also sought to show how the proper pairing or assignment of instruments depends upon the

* Walker Professor of Economics and International Finance, Princeton University.
[1] See: [6], [7] and [8].

structure of the economy. With international capital mobility, for example, monetary policy is said to lose some of its effect upon domestic interest rates and, therefore, its 'Keynesian' effect upon domestic activity, but to gain additional command over the Balance of Payments. In these circumstances, monetary policy should be assigned to the maintenance of external balance, while fiscal policy is assigned to the maintenance of internal balance.

Since Mundell's first papers on this subject, there have been a number of important contributions.[2] Some authors have asked how flexible exchange rates modify Mundell's policy prescription [1] [9]. Others have refined the specification of the monetary and fiscal instruments and have studied the dynamic implications of decentralisation, diverging targets and uncertainty.[3] Finally, some have introduced behavioural relationships that limit or extend the instruments' influence.[4]

This paper seeks to do several of these things. It compares the influence of policy instruments under alternative exchange rate regimes. It defines the monetary instrument operationally (as a change in central bank holdings of government securities) and looks separately at changes in tax rates and government spending. It explores the implications of portfolio balance, using demand functions for financial assets and capital goods, and of long-run balance in the government's accounts. To do these things, of course, it simplifies reality in drastic ways. It assumes that the country under study is too small to affect world prices, including the interest rate on its public debt, and excludes every other consequence of size. It pretends that there is no net saving or investment unless there is a change in the *level* of income. It rules out money illusion and, more im-

---

[2] For an excellent survey of the literature, see: [11].

[3] See the papers by Cooper, Jones and Patrick, cited by Whitman: [11].

[4] See the papers by Johnson, McKinnon and Oates and McKinnon, cited by Whitman, and Mathieson [2]. Mathieson's research caused me to begin the work described below, but my model is simpler and different in several respects. His includes a factor market and allows incomplete specialisation in production; it makes explicit provision for excess bank reserves and permits international transfers of private securities. His paper, however, does not study the effects of shifts in the behavioural relationships and does not set forth the implications for the assignment of instruments to targets.

portantly, price rigidities. It simplifies behaviour toward risk (and precludes any change in securities' prices) by treating all debt instruments as demand obligations, trivially different from interest-bearing cash.

It is, therefore, capable of furnishing strong propositions. Monetary policy, for example, has no effect on the domestic economy, even in the absence of capital mobility. Fiscal policy can have perverse effects on the Balance of Payments, whether or not exchange rates are flexible. More generally, the presence or absence of capital mobility and the choice of exchange rate regime make very little difference for the conduct of policy in a small, open economy. Yet the scope for an independent economic policy is somewhat larger than one might suppose. Finally, Mundell's well known assignment – monetary policy to external balance and fiscal policy to internal balance – is not much modified by the analysis.

1. The Model

In a small open economy with no barriers to trade, home currency prices depend on world prices and the exchange rate. Thus

$$p_1 = \bar{p}_1/x \tag{1.1}$$

$$p_2 = \bar{p}_2/x \tag{1.2}$$

where p_1 and p_2 are the home currency prices of two commodities; $\bar{p}_1$ and $\bar{p}_2$ are their world prices; and x is the exchange rate (in units of foreign currency per unit of home currency).[5] When, further, the economy produces one commodity (with constant returns to scale), is fully employed and is perfectly competitive

$$Q_1 = f(K), \quad f'(K) > 0, \quad f''(K) < 0 \tag{1.3}$$

$$p(r + z) = f'(K) \tag{1.4}$$

where Q_1 is output per worker; K is the capital-labour ratio (with capital consisting entirely of imported goods subject to

[5] A complete list of variables, precisely defined, is appended. Note that most stocks and flows are measured *per worker*.

depreciation at a fixed rate, z); p is the price ratio (p_2/p_1); and r is the net rate of return to capital.

Let this first commodity, the home good, be consumed by households, government and banks, and be sold to foreigners

$$Q_1 = Q_{1h} + Q_{1g} + Q_{1b} + Q_{1f} \tag{1.5}$$

with
$$Q_{1h} = h(Y, p), \qquad h_y > 0, \qquad h_p > 0 \tag{1.6}$$

$$Q_{1g} = G \tag{1.7}$$

$$Q_{1b} = (r_g B_b + r_w W)/p_1 \tag{1.8}$$

$$Q_{1f} = p(Q_{2h} + Q_{2k}) + (r_g B_f/p_1) \tag{1.9}$$

Equation (1.6) asserts that the household demand for the home good depends on disposable income per worker, Y, and on relative prices. Equation (1.7) asserts that all government spending, G, is directed to the home good. Equation (1.8) asserts that the banks' gross income from investments is wholly expended on the home good, which is used to produce services for depositors; r_g and r_w are the rates of interest on government and private securities, respectively, while B_b and W are the government and private securities held by commercial banks.[6] Finally, Equation (1.9) says that merchandise exports are equal to merchandise imports by households and producers *plus* interest payments on government debt held by foreigners.[7]

Next, write definitions for disposable income and the demand for imports by households and producers

$$Y = (1 - t)N \tag{1.10}$$

$$N = Q_1 - zpK \tag{1.11}$$

and
$$pQ_{2h} = Y - Q_{1h} - (r_w W/p_1) \tag{1.12}$$

$$Q_{2k} = zK \tag{1.13}$$

[6] The implicit assumption that banks earn no income derives from another assumption, below, that banks have no net worth. Without net worth, they will earn no income under perfect competition.

[7] Note that Equation (1.9) implies continuous balance on current account; foreigners do not buy government securities when the system is at rest.

The first pair of equations says that taxes are levied on net factor incomes (which must equal gross output *less* depreciation).[8] The third says that there is no net saving when disposable income is fixed; household income after taxes is used fully to buy home and foreign goods and to pay interest on private debt. The fourth equation says that there is no net investment in equilibrium; the demand for capital goods is equal to depreciation.

Consider, next, the public sector, consisting of a government that taxes, spends and issues debt and a central bank that holds government securities and foreign exchange reserves. The Government's behaviour yields two equations

$$tN = G + r_g(B - B_c)/p_1 \tag{1.14}$$

$$B = B_c + B_b + B_f \tag{1.15}$$

Tax receipts must cover government spending and debt service payments.[9] Government debt, B, is held by the central bank, commercial banks and the outside world.

The central bank's behaviour is described by one equation

$$B_c + E = R \tag{1.16}$$

where E is the stock of foreign exchange reserves and R is the stock of high-powered money.

All high-powered money is held by commercial banks, in order to satisfy a fixed reserve requirement; there are no excess reserves, nor is there any currency in circulation. Furthermore, the banks have no net worth. Therefore

$$R = qC \tag{1.17}$$

$$R + B_b + W = C \tag{1.18}$$

where C is the stock of demand deposits owned by households and producers and q is the reserve requirement against demand

---

[8] The definition of disposable income in terms of home goods can introduce several distortions: the household demand for imports and the supply of exports depend directly upon Y, and the size of the capital stock depends upon net worth (which depends, in turn, upon disposable income). These distortions, however, do not damage our conclusions, as the price ratio, p, is exogenous in the small country case.

[9] The central bank's interest income is turned back to the Government.

deposits. The banks, then, have only one decision to make – how to allocate $(1 - q)C$ of assets between government and private securities. Let this decision depend upon the relevant interest rates, not upon the size of the bank's portfolios

$$W = v(r_w, r_g)(1 - q)C, \qquad v_w > 0, \qquad v_g < 0 \quad (1.19)$$

where $0 < v < 1$ even when $r_w > r_g$.[10]

The several assumptions made thus far have now to be reflected in the balance sheet for households and producers. As the central bank and foreigners hold no private debt, all such debt must lodge with the commercial banks. The public debt, moreover, is held by banks and foreigners, so that none of it appears in this final balance sheet.[11] Consequently

$$A = p_2 K + C - W \qquad (1.20)$$

where A is net worth per worker. Let households add to their net worth when their incomes rise, even though they do not save from a constant income

$$A = a(Y)p_1 \qquad (1.21)$$

and let $0 < ra' < 1$, in order to guarantee determinate results when the system is displaced. In addition, let the structure of net

---

[10] As the debt instruments comprising B and W are demand obligations and, therefore, equally liquid, one must assume that private debt bears a default risk. Otherwise, B_b would be zero (v would be unity) whenever $r_w > r_g$.

[11] This assumption is not very restrictive. Whether or not households and producers hold government debt, Equations (1.16), (1.18) and (1.20) combine to give

$$A = p_2 K + B + (E - B_f)$$

The net worth of households and producers must equal the stock of capital goods *plus* the government debt *plus* net foreign assets. Furthermore, a different feature of the model practically precludes non-bank holdings of government debt. As its two debt instruments are equally liquid, but private debt bears a default risk, r_w will usually exceed r_g and the private non-bank sector can have no cause to issue debt merely to acquire government securities. It will borrow only to hold cash, needed for transactions, and capital goods, needed for production. (Note, indeed, that the demand for capital goods could itself generate limitless private debt, absent an intrinsic aversion to indebtedness. This could happen whenever $r > r_w$. To exclude this possibility, assume that used capital goods cannot be re-exported or that some uncertainty attaches to their future price. Either way, capital goods will be less liquid than private debt.)

worth depend upon the relevant interest rates, not upon the size of A

$$p_2 K = k(r, r_w)A, k_r > 0, k_w < 0 \tag{1.22}$$

$$C = c(r, r_w)A, c_r < 0, c_w < 0 \tag{1.23}$$

$$W = w(r, r_w)A, w_r > 0, w_w < 0 \tag{1.24}$$

so that $$k + c - w = 1$$

where $(1 - k) = (c - w) > 0$, because $A(c - w) = (R + B_b)$,

and $$k_r + c_r - w_r = 0$$

$$k_w + c_w - w_w = 0$$

Finally, $x = \bar{x}$ with fixed exchange rates, and $E = 0$ with flexible rates, while $r_g = \bar{r}_g$ with perfect capital mobility, and $B_f = 0$ in its absence.

Before exploring the behaviour of this simple economy when it is disturbed, consider several of its peculiarities:

(1) Because the commercial banks have no net worth, their balance sheet (Equation (1.18)) has no price term, and the banks' behaviour is not directly affected by a change in the price level or the exchange rate. They do respond, however, to a change in the stock of foreign exchange reserves; a change in reserves will alter the stock of high-powered money, causing the banks to adjust their deposits and investments. Households and producers, by contrast, have net worth and will therefore respond directly to a change in the price level or the exchange rate. But they are not directly affected by a change in foreign exchange reserves. With fixed exchange rates, then, the commercial banks are the prime movers of the system; they alter the demand for government and private debt. With flexible exchange rates, households and producers are the prime movers of the system; they alter the demand for cash and capital goods and the supply of private debt.[12]

---

[12] There is a similar dichotomy within the public sector: under fixed exchange rates, the central bank is directly affected by any change in the Balance of Payments; every change in E also changes R. Under flexible exchange rates, the Government is directly affected; every change in x alters the real value of government interest payments.

(2) Because the current account (Equation (1.9)) and the government budget (Equation (1.14)) are separately balanced when the system is at rest, and there is no net saving, all balance sheets are stationary in equilibrium. The changes which take place when the system is disturbed – whether by a shift in stocks or flows – are once-for-all adjustments.

(3) Because the government budget is balanced, moreover, the role of fiscal policy is quite circumscribed. Any change in tax rates has to cause a change in real income sufficient to restore total tax receipts, and the Government cannot always alter its spending without causing tax receipts to change by the same amount.[13] Constrained by portfolio balance, fiscal policy becomes a close cousin to monetary policy. Each is a device for altering $(B - B_c)$, government debt in the hands of the public, but each has a different set of side effects. Monetary policy alters the stock of bank reserves. Fiscal policy alters disposable income (and net worth) when it involves a change in tax rates; it alters the supply of home goods for export when it involves a change in government spending.

(4) Because the foreign demand for home goods is infinitely elastic, there can be no deficiency of aggregate demand. Furthermore, factor prices are flexible. In consequence, monetary and fiscal policy can affect total output and income only by changing the size of the capital stock. This paper may be said to deal with the long-run implications of short-run stabilisation policies.

(5) Because the foreign demand for home goods is infinitely elastic, the exchange rate cannot affect directly the trade balance. Export supply and import demand are each affected by relative prices, but these are independent of the exchange rate. A change in the exchange rate can alter the current account only by changing the foreign currency cost of external interest payments or by its indirect effect on the demand for capital goods (resulting from its impact on net

---

[13] There may also be a change in the size of the government debt, occasioned by transitional surpluses or deficits, and a corresponding change in debt service payments. This additional budgetary effect has a vital role below.

worth). These are reasons why the choice of exchange rate regime does not much affect the behaviour of the model.[14]

The system set out here consists of 26 equations and conditions (including those defining the exchange rate regime and denoting the presence or absence of capital mobility), but contains only 24 endogenous variables.[15] Notice, however, that (1.24) is redundant, given (1.21), (1.22) and (1.23), and that (1.5) is redundant, given (1.6) through (1.14).[16] When, further, (1.5) has been deleted, one can also dispense with (1.6) through (1.9), as they serve only to define an argument of (1.5), and one can dispense with (1.12) and (1.13), as they define arguments of (1.9). We are left with 18 equations and the same number of endogenous variables. These, in turn, can be combined into a set of ten. Setting $\bar{p}_1 = 1$

$$N - f(K) + zpK = 0 \tag{2.1}$$

$$q[W + (B - B_f)] - (1 - q)E - B_c = 0 \tag{2.2}$$

$$qW - v(r_w, r_g)(1 - q)(E + B_c) = 0 \tag{2.3}$$

$$A - (p/x)K - E - (B - B_f) = 0 \tag{2.4}$$

$$(p/x)K - k[(f'/p - z), r_w]A = 0 \tag{2.5}$$

$$(E + B_c) - qc[(f'/p - z), r_w]A = 0 \tag{2.6}$$

$$xA - a[(1 - t)N] = 0 \tag{2.7}$$

$$xr_g(B - B_c) + G - tN = 0 \tag{2.8}$$

while

$$x = \bar{x} \quad \text{or} \quad E = 0 \tag{2.9}$$

and

$$r_g = \bar{r}_g \quad \text{or} \quad B_f = 0 \tag{2.10}$$

---

[14] The principal proximate regulators of the current account, in addition to disposable income, are the levels of government spending and the capital stock. An increase of government spending reduces the supply of exports by an equal amount. An increase in the capital stock augments imports equally while it is occurring, then by the increase of replacement demand, $z\ (dK)$, permanently.

[15] These are $p_1, p_2, x, Q_1, Q_{1h}, Q_{1g}, Q_{1b}, Q_{1f}, Q_{2h}, Q_{2k}, K, Y, N, r, r_g, r_w, W, B, B_b, B_f, A, E, R$ and C. The exogenous variables are $\bar{p}_1, \bar{p}_2, p, z, t, q, G$ and B_c.

[16] Put differently, the absence of net saving and investment, together with a balanced budget, implies a balanced current account, making Equation (1.9) redundant.

depending upon the exchange rate regime and the condition of capital markets.

2. Displacement and Adjustment

Suppose, now, that the system of Equations (2.1) through to (2.10) is in equilibrium. A change in any one of its exogenous variables – in central bank holdings of government securities, reserve requirements, the tax rate, government spending, or relative prices – or in any one of its behavioural relationships requires a change in its endogenous variables if equilibrium is to be restored. The balance of this paper is concerned with those changes. It seeks first to identify the requisite changes, then to ask what they imply for the conduct of policy.

To this end, differentiate Equations (2.1) through to (2.10) with respect to all arguments except z, p and q, set $p = x = 1$ initially, eliminate dW, dA and dK by successive substitution, and collect the exogenous arguments

$$\begin{bmatrix} F & A(1-k)r & r & 0 & 0 & r & 0 \\ 0 & 0 & -B_b/R & A(w/v)v_w & A(w/v)v_g & 1 & 0 \\ -U_k/r & A(1-k)k & k & Ak_w & 0 & k & 0 \\ -U_c/r & Ack & c(B_b+K)/R & -Ac_w & 0 & -c & 0 \\ -t & r_g(B-B_c) & 0 & 0 & (B-B_c) & 0 & r_g \end{bmatrix} \begin{bmatrix} dN \\ dx \\ dE \\ dr_w \\ dr_g \\ d(B-B_f) \\ dB \end{bmatrix}$$

$$= \begin{bmatrix} -[ra'N]\,dt \\ [(A/R)(1-k)]\,dB_c \\ 0 \\ -[C/R]\,dB_c + [A]\,dc^* \\ [r_g]\,dB_c + [N]\,dt - dG \end{bmatrix} \quad (3.1)$$

where dc^* represents an autonomous change in the demand for real cash balances; where

$$U_c \equiv c + (Af'')c_r > 0$$
$$U_k \equiv 1 - k - (Af'')k_r > 0$$

and where $\quad F \equiv 1 - r(1-t)a', \quad 0 < F < 1$

assuming $ra' < 1$, as above.[17]

To study the behaviour of this system under fixed exchange rates, set $dx = 0$ and delete the second column of the matrix;

[17] Definitions of such terms as U_c, U_k and F are given in the glossary, appended.

to study its behaviour under flexible rates, set $dE = 0$ and delete the third column. To study the effects of capital mobility, set $dr_g = 0$ and delete the fifth column; in the absence of mobility, set $dB_f = 0$ and combine the sixth and seventh columns. There are, then, four permutations of (3.1), each with five equations, five endogenous variables, and its own determinant:

(1) With fixed exchange rates and perfect mobility, the determinant is

$$J_{ME} = r_g(A^2/R)H_m > 0 \qquad (3.2a)$$

where $H_m \equiv [cU + (1 - k)Z]$, with $U \equiv [(U_k + kF) \times (w/v)v_w - Fk_w] > 0$, and $Z \equiv -[(U_c - cF)k_w + (Uk + kF)c_w] > 0$ (so that $H_m > 0$);

(2) with flexible exchange rates and perfect mobility, the determinant is

$$J_{MX} = r_g(A^2)H_m = R(J_{ME}) > 0 \qquad (3.2b)$$

(3) with fixed exchange rates and no mobility, the determinant is

$$J_{IE} = -(A^2)H_i < 0 \qquad (3.2c)$$

where $H_i \equiv \{(B - B_o)H_m - r_g(w/v)v_g[RZ - A(F + tr/r_g)ck_w]\} > 0$

(4) with flexible exchange rates and no mobility, the determinant is

$$J_{IX} = -(A^2)H_i = R(J_{IE}) < 0 \qquad (3.2d)$$

Notice at once that the choice of exchange rate regime does not much affect the structure of the determinant. For this reason alone, one would not expect it to have much impact on the comparative static changes in the other variables.[18]

[18] Notice, further, that $R(dx/du) = (dE/du)$, or $(dx/du) = [(dE/du)/E](E/R)$, where du is any exogenous disturbance. Whatever the condition of the capital market, the change in the equilibrium exchange rate caused by a disturbance must equal the percentage change in foreign exchange reserves required under fixed rates, multiplied by (E/R). In this context, (E/R) may be taken to measure the 'openness' of the financial system; it compares the stock of foreign exchange reserves to the supply of high-powered money.

3. The Role of Monetary Policy

Most studies of this type concur in one assertion: with fixed exchange rates and perfect mobility, monetary policy cannot control the domestic economy. An open-market purchase of government securities, for example, will not alter interest rates or the stock of money. It will raise the price of government securities, but this will cause foreigners to run down their holdings, and they will continue to do so until the price is driven back to its initial level. At this initial level, moreover, resident holders of government debt (here, the commercial banks) will want to hold as many government securities as they did before the central bank entered the market, so that total foreign sales must ultimately equal the central bank's purchases. Finally, absent any other change in the economy, foreign sales of government securities must generate a deficit in the Balance of Payments and a matching outflow of foreign exchange reserves. The central bank will have swapped foreign exchange reserves for government securities, instead of altering the stock of high-powered money.

The model set out here generates the same result, but makes one more assertion. As expected

$$\left.\begin{aligned} (dr_w/dB_c)_{ME} &= 0 \\ (dN/dB_c)_{ME} &= 0 \\ (dE/dB_c)_{ME} &= -1 \end{aligned}\right\} \tag{3.3}$$

There is no enduring effect on the interest rate or national income, and the change in foreign exchange reserves offsets the change in central bank holdings of government securities. In addition, however

$$\left.\begin{aligned} (dB/dB_c)_{ME} &= 1 \\ (dB_f/dB_c)_{ME} &= 0 \end{aligned}\right\} \tag{3.4}$$

When equilibrium is re-established, the Government's *total* debt must be enlarged (by enough to offset the once-over increase in central bank holdings), and foreign holdings of government securities must be restored to their initial level. By implication, the Government must run a deficit sufficient in size and duration to swell its debt by dB_c, and all of the additional government debt must be lodged with foreigners.[19]

The need for these additional results is readily identified. If there were no increase in the total public debt, Equation (2.8) could not be satisfied, as there have been no changes in x, r, r_g, N, G and t. But the change in debt needed to attain equilibrium may not, in fact, occur. Taken by itself, an open-market purchase reduces the Government's interest payments to the public. It produces a surplus, retiring debt, rather than a deficit, creating debt.[20] In models of this type, with a budget constraint, additional discretionary policy changes may be required to move the economy from one equilibrium position to another.[21]

This model generates another surprise. Other investigators have suggested that the introduction of flexible exchange rates gives domestic influence to monetary policy. The central bank recaptures effective control over the stock of high-powered money, even when capital is perfectly mobile. Here, however, $(dr_w/dB_c)_{MX} = (dN/dB_c)_{MX} = 0$, while $(dx/dB_c)_{MX} = -(1/R)$. There is, again, no change in interest rates or national income, and the percentage change in the exchange rate is equal (with opposite sign) to the percentage change in the stock of high-powered money.[22] This last result is, of course, the reason for the

[19] These additional transactions with foreigners will not cause a further change in foreign exchange reserves, even though they imply a surplus on capital account. With no net saving or investment, any budget deficit implies an identical deficit on current account, and this will offset the capital inflow.

[20] Before any change in its total indebtedness, the Government's interest payments will decline by $xr_g(dB_c)$, causing a corresponding surplus in the government budget and on the current account (the latter because $dB_f = -dB_c$, so that total interest payments and payments to foreigners fall by the same amount). This will shrink the total debt and foreign holdings. The process of debt retirement, moreover, would seem bound to cumulate; as bonds are repaid, interest payments fall further, the budget surplus grows, and debt retirement accelerates.

[21] The Government, for example, could augment temporarily its purchases of goods, running a deficit and issuing debt until $dB = dB_c$. Alternatively, it could raise its purchases permanently, by $xr_g(dB_c)$, thereby to balance its budget (and the current account) without any once-over increase of debt. This second approach is explored in Appendix B, where government spending is made to be endogenous and the total debt becomes exogenous.

[22] Once again, however, additional discretionary measures may be needed: $(dB/dB_c)_{MX} = 1 + (B - B_c)/R > 0$.

others. As the *real* money stock is (C/p_1), or (xR/q), the comparative-static change in the exchange rate leaves that stock unchanged, precluding any other domestic effect.

Consider, finally, the results of open-market operations when capital does not move. Once again, one might expect monetary policy to have important domestic effects. But this is not the case. Under fixed and flexible exchange rates, alike, there are no changes in r_w and N, while $(dE/dB_c)_{IE} = R(dx/dB_c)_{IX} = -1$, as before. Under fixed exchange rates, an open-market purchase of government securities leads, at first, to an increase in the stock of high-powered money, an increase in bank deposits, and a decline in the interest rates on government and private debt. With lower interest rates, however, the demand for capital goods must rise, and the Balance of Payments must move into deficit, expelling foreign exchange reserves and cutting back the stock of high-powered money. Interest rates must turn round.[23] Under flexible exchange rates, the process is similar, but the larger demand for capital goods has its effect on the exchange rate, reducing the real money stock. In either case, a change in the demand for traded goods occasioned by a change in the real money stock can substitute perfectly for a capital flow, erasing that initial change in the real money stock.

4. The Role of Fiscal Policy

In the model studied here, the instruments of fiscal policy – changes in tax rates and government spending – are far from symmetrical. They can be used interchangeably to alter the stock of government debt – to generate a temporary surplus or deficit in the government budget – but they differ importantly in their further effects on the economy. An increase of government spending has as its chief proximate effect a reduction in the supply of exportables (which, by itself, must cause a loss of

[23] Notice, however, that these results depend upon an increase in the total public debt. It is needed to balance the budget and, more importantly, to adjust the stock of debt in the hands of the public. Open-market operations diminish this stock, and the interest rate cannot return to its initial level until the stock has been restored. In a model with endogenous government spending (adjusted to balance the budget) and an exogenous debt, monetary policy has an important domestic effect when capital is immobile (see Appendix B).

foreign exchange reserves or a depreciation of the exchange rate). A decrease of tax rates raises disposable income, causing net saving and investment. The impact of the instruments, moreover, is differently affected by the presence or absence of capital movements.

When capital is perfectly mobile, a permanent increase in government spending will generate an endless disequilibrium. The system will not come to rest. The government budget and current account will each lapse into deficit, and the debt which is created by the government's deficit will be sold to foreigners, producing a capital inflow just large enough to finance the imbalance on current account. There can be no change in foreign exchange reserves or in the exchange rate – no change of the type required to reach an equilibrium. The perpetual disequilibrium, moreover, will be self-enlarging. Rising interest payments will add to the government's deficit and the growth rate of its debt, and the current account will continue to worsen, as all of the additional interest payments will go to foreigners.

When capital is perfectly immobile, the system must come to rest. The change in the stock of government securities occasioned by a change in spending has to alter interest rates. The change in the current account occasioned by that change in spending has to alter reserves or the exchange rate. But the necessary resting place has peculiar properties

$$
\left.
\begin{aligned}
(dr_w/dG)_{IE} &= (dr_w/dG)_{IX} \\
&= [(w/v)v_g/H_i]c(U_k + kF) < 0 \\
(dN/dG)_{IE} &= (dN/dG)_{IX} \\
&= [(w/v)v_g/H_i]rAck_w > 0 \\
(dE/dG)_{IE} &= (dE/dG)_{IX} \\
&= -[(w/v)v_g/H_i]RZ > 0
\end{aligned}
\right\}
\qquad (3.5)
$$

For the system to achieve a new equilibrium, there must be a decline in the interest rate on private securities, a concomitant increase in the capital stock, and an increase in national output and income.[24] The real money stock must grow, so as to enlarge

[24] The increase in the stock of capital must, of course, reflect the decrease in the interest rate *and* the growth of income (which will cause net saving).

the banks' demand for private debt, and this calls for an increase in foreign exchange reserves (to generate additional high-powered money) or currency appreciation (to enhance the value of the nominal money stock). All of these effects serve one simple purpose – to balance the budget by adding to tax revenues. At some point, indeed, the budget must display a surplus, in order to retire debt

$$(dB/dG)_{IE} = [(w/v)v_g/H_i][RZ - cAFk_w] < 0 \qquad (3.6a)$$

and

$$(dB/dG)_{IX} = [(w/v)v_g/H_i][A(1 - k)Z - cAFk_w] < 0 \quad (3.6b)$$

This change, too, is needed to balance the budget in equilibrium.[25]

Changes in the tax rate have similar effects in all four permutations of the model. In each instance, moreover, the system may fail to reach equilibrium unless the new tax rate is 'ratified' by temporary changes in the other instruments of economic policy. Consider, for example, the solution of (3.1) under fixed exchange rates and perfect mobility[26]

$$\left.\begin{array}{l} (dr_w/dt)_{ME} = a'(N/AH_m)k[cU_k - (1 - k)U_c] > 0^{[27]} \\[2mm] (dN/dt)_{ME} = -a'(N/AH_m)rAk\{c(w/v)v_w \\[1mm] \qquad\qquad - [ck_w + (1 - k)c_w]\} < 0 \\[2mm] (dE/dt)_{ME} = -a'(N/AH_m)R[(cU_k \\[1mm] \qquad\qquad + kU_c)(w/v)v_w + T] < 0 \end{array}\right\} \qquad (3.7)$$

One would, of course, expect a reduction of output, as an increase in the tax rate causes dissaving, reducing the stock of capital goods. But one might not forecast the increase of interest rates, or any loss of foreign exchange reserves. Instead,

----

[25] The very strange requirements set out in Equations (3.5) and (3.6) suggest, once more, that government spending should be made endogenous, as in Appendix B, with the government debt exogenous.

[26] For solutions of Equation (3.1) under flexible exchange rates and in the absence of capital mobility, see Appendix A.

[27] Because $[cU_k - (1 - k)U_c] = e_r(r/k)(c/k)(cw_r - wc_r) > 0$.

one might expect a decrease of interest rates (as dissaving will reduce the stock of private debt), along with an increase in foreign exchange reserves (as dissaving will reduce the demand for capital goods). Note, finally, that the government has to run a deficit during the transition; it has again to increase its total indebtedness

$$(dB/dt)_{ME} = (N/r_g H_m)[H_m - t(ra')k\{c(w/v)v_w$$
$$- [ck_w + (1 - k)c_w]\}] > 0\,[28] \quad (3.8)$$

To sum up, fiscal policy has powerful effects on the domestic economy, even when the budget must be brought into balance. In the absence of capital mobility, an increase of spending will add to total income, and a decrease of taxes will have the same effect, whether or not capital is mobile. The choice of exchange rate regime, moreover, has little bearing on the use of these instruments (which are, indeed, equally perverse in their comparative-static effects on reserves and the exchange rate).

5. Notes on the Assignment Problem

As monetary policy has no direct domestic effects in this model, the assignment of instruments to targets would seem straightforward. The central bank should operate to stabilize the Balance of Payments (or the exchange rate), using open-market operations. The Government should operate to stabilize national income (or the capital stock), using the tax rate. It would even seem possible for the Government to operate independently of the central bank. As open-market operations do not affect national income, the Government need not allow for current or prospective interventions by the central bank. (The central bank, however, must allow for changes in tax rates, because they can alter the Balance of Payments. It must know what the Government will do, or lacking that knowledge, must intervene sequentially – to deal with the primary, direct effects of any disturbance, then with the tax-induced income effects.)

[28] Because $[H_m - t(ra')k\{c(w/v)v_w - [ck_w + (1 - k)c_w]\}] = [cU_k(w/v)v_w + (1 - k)T + (1 - ra')k\{c(w/v)v_w - [ck_w + (1 - k)c_w]\}] > 0.$

4

To put these points formally, represent the role of the Government by

$$(dN/du)\,du + (dN/dB_c)\,dB_c + (dN/dt)\,dt^e = 0 \qquad (3.9)$$

where du is any disturbance and dt^e is the requisite change in the tax rate, then represent the role of the central bank by

$$(dE/du)\,du + (dE/dB_c)\,dB_c^e + (dE/dt)\,dt = 0 \qquad (3.10)$$

where dB_c^e is the requisite change in central bank holdings of Government debt.[29] As $(dN/dBc) = 0$ in every case considered here,[30] Equation (3.9) yields

$$dt^e = -[(dN/du)/(dN/dt)]\,du \qquad (3.11)$$

and Equation (3.10) yields

$$dB_c^e = -[(dE/du)\,du + (dE/dt)\,dt](dE/dB_c) \qquad (3.12)$$

or $\quad dB_c^e = -[(dE/du)/(dE/dB_c)]\,du$

$$- [(dE/dt)(dN/du)]/(dN/dt)(dE/dB_c)]\,du \qquad (3.12a)$$

Tax rate changes can and should be geared to the direct domestic effect of any disturbance. Open-market operations can and should be geared to the Balance of Payments effect, but must also neutralise the income effects of fiscal policy.[31]

But fiscal policy may not be quite this independent. There may be need to change the total public debt when the central

---

[29] As $R(dx/du) = (dE/du)$ in every case considered here, Equation (3.10) can also represent the central bank's role under flexible exchange rates.

[30] But not in Appendix B, where $(dN/dB_c) > 0$ in the absence of capital mobility.

[31] Similar equations can be used to show that no other assignment will work. If open-market operations are employed in an effort to stabilize national income:

$$dB_c^e = -[(dN/du)\,du + (dN/dt)\,dt]/(dN/dB_c) \to \infty$$

because $(dN/dB_c) = 0$. Furthermore

$$dt^e = -[(dE/du)\,du + (dE/dB_c)\,dB_c]/(dE/dt) \to \infty$$

because $dB_c^e \to \infty$. The central bank will seek unsuccessfully to stabilize national income; the Government will try in vain to correct the external impact of the central bank's intervention (and will further destabilize national income in the process).

bank intervenes in the market. Consider the effects of an increased demand for real cash balances[32]

$$\left.\begin{array}{l}
(dN/dc^*)_{ME} = r(A/H_m)(1 - k)k_w < 0 \\
(dr_w/dc^*)_{ME} = (1/H_m)(1 - k)(U_k + kF) > 0 \\
(dE/dc^*)_{ME} = (R/H_m)U > 0 \\
(dB/dc^*)_{ME} = r(A/H_m)(1 - k)(t/r_g)k_w < 0
\end{array}\right\} \quad (3.13)$$

The tax rate must be reduced to stabilize income

$$(dt^e/dc^*) = -[(dN/dc^*)/(dN/dt)] < 0^{[33]} \quad (3.14)$$

The central bank must buy government securities

$$(dB_c^e/dc^*) = -[(dE/dc^*) \\
+ (dE/dt)(dt^e/dc^*)]/(dE/dB_c) > 0^{[34]} \quad (3.15)$$

But one must combine the disturbance, the tax reduction and the open-market purchase in order to compute the change in the total public debt needed to attain equilibrium

$$(dB/dc^*)^e = (dB/dc^*) + (dB/dt)(dt^e/dc^*) \\
+ (dB/dB_c)(dB_c^e/dc^*) \quad (3.16)$$

The first two terms of this expression are unambiguously negative, the third is positive, and the sign of $(dB/dc^*)^e$ itself is, in fact, uncertain.[35] A transitional change in public spending may still be required, and the Government must know what the central bank is doing.

Appendix A

Additional results
This appendix tabulates six sets of solutions mentioned briefly in the text: The impact of a change in the tax rate, dt, and of a change in demand for real cash balances, dc^*, with (*a*) perfect

[32] For the corresponding changes under flexible rates and without capital mobility, see Appendix A.
[33] For $(dN/dt)_{ME}$, see Equation (3.7).
[34] For $(dE/dB_c)_{ME}$ and $(dE/dt)_{ME}$, see Equations (3.3) and (3.7).
[35] For $(dB/dt)_{ME}$ and $(dB/dB_c)_{ME}$, see Equations (3.8) and (3.4).

mobility and flexible exchange rates, (*b*) no mobility and fixed exchange rates and (*c*) no mobility and flexible exchange rates. The symbols used here are defined in the text and listed in the glossary that follows Appendix B.

Perfect Mobility and Flexible Exchange Rates

Here, r_w and N change as they do under fixed exchange rates

$$(dr_w/dt)_{MX} = (dr_w/dt)_{ME} > 0$$
and
$$(dr_w/dc^*)_{MX} = (dr_w/dc^*)_{ME} > 0$$
$$(dN/dt)_{MX} = (dN/dt)_{ME} < 0$$
and
$$(dN/dc^*)_{MX} = (dN/dc^*)_{ME} < 0$$

Furthermore

$$R(dx/dt)_{MX} = (dE/dt)_{ME} < 0$$
and
$$R(dx/dc^*)_{MX} = (dE/dc^*)_{ME} > 0$$

Finally

$$(dB/dt)_{MX} = (dB/dt)_{ME} + a'(N/AH_m)$$
$$\times (B - B_c)[(cU_k + kU_c)(w/v)v_w + T] > 0$$
$$(dB/dc^*)_{MX} = (dB/dc^*)_{ME} - (1/H_m)(B - B_c)U < 0$$

No Mobility and Fixed Exchange Rates

With a change in tax rates

$$H_i(dr_w/dt)_{IE} = H_m(B - B_c)(dr_w/dt)_{ME} - N(w/v)v_g$$
$$\times \{c[U_k + (1 - ra')k] + r_g a'(V/A)\} > 0\dagger$$
$$H_i(dN/dt)_{IE} = H_m(B - B_c)(dN/dt)_{ME} - rN(w/v)v_g\{Ack_w$$
$$+ r_g a'[(A - R)ck_w + Rkc_w]\} < 0$$
$$H_i(dE/dt)_{IE} = H_m(B - B_c)(dE/dt)_{ME}$$
$$+ RN(w/v)v_g[(1 - ra')T'$$
$$+ (r + r_g)a'T] < 0$$
$$H_i(dB/dt)_{IE} = H_m(B - B_c)[d(B - B_f)/dt]_{ME}$$
$$+ N(w/v)v_g\{(1 - ra')[(A - R)ck_w$$
$$+ Rkc_w] - Ra'T\} \gtrless 0\ddagger$$

$\dagger$ Where $V \equiv [(A - R)cU_k - RkU_c] = \{cB_b + (r/k)e_r[B_b(ck_r - kc_r) + K(cw_r - wc_r)]\} > 0.$
$\ddagger$ Where $[d(B - B_f)/dt]_{ME} = -a'(N/AH_m)[V(w/v)v_w + B_bT] < 0.$

With a change in demand for real cash balances

$$H_i(dr_w/dc^*)_{IE} = H_m(B - B_c)(dr_w/dc^*)_{ME}$$
$$- r_g R(w/v)v_g(U_k + kF) > 0$$

$$H_i(dN/dc^*)_{IE} = H_m(B - B_c)(dN/dc^*)_{ME}$$
$$- r_g R(w/v)v_g(rA)k_w < 0$$

$$H_i(dE/dc^*)_{IE} = H_m(B - B_c)(dE/dc^*)_{ME}$$
$$+ r_g R(w/v)v_g[F + tr/r_g]Ak_w > 0$$

$$H_i(dB/dc^*)_{IE} = H_m(B - B_c)[d(B - B_f)/dc^*]_{ME}$$
$$- R(w/v)v_g(rA)tk_w \gtrless 0\dagger$$

No Mobility and Flexible Exchange Rates

Once again, r_w and N change as they do under fixed rates

$$(dr_w/dt)_{IX} = (dr_w/dt)_{IE} > 0$$

and
$$(dr_w/dc^*)_{IX} = (dr_w/dc^*)_{IE} > 0$$

$$(dN/dt)_{IX} = (dN/dt)_{IE} < 0$$

and
$$(dN/dc^*)_{IX} = (dN/dc^*)_{IE} < 0$$

As before, moreover

$$R(dx/dt)_{IX} = (dE/dt)_{IE} < 0$$

and
$$R(dx/dc^*)_{IX} = (dE/dc^*)_{IE} > 0$$

Finally

$$(dB/dt)_{IX} = (dB/dt)_{IE} - (B_b/R)(dE/dt)_{IE}$$
$$= -(N/H_i)[(B - B_c)a'k[cU_k - (1 - k)U_c]$$
$$\times (w/v)v_w + (w/v)v_g\{[A(1 - k) + r_g a'B_b]$$
$$\times T - Ak(1 - ra')[ck_w + (1 - k)c_w]\}] \gtrless 0$$

$$(dB/dc^*)_{IX} = (dB/dc^*)_{IE} - (B_b/R)(dE/dc^*)_{IE}$$
$$= -(AB_b/H_i)\{(1 - k)(U + Fk)$$
$$+ (w/v)v_g[r_g F + tr(1 - k)(A/B_b)]k_w\} < 0$$

$\dagger$ Where $[d(B - B_f)/dc^*]_{ME} = -(1/H_m)[RU + AF(1 - k)k_w] \gtrless 0$.

Appendix B

An alternative formulation

At several points, the text suggests that fiscal and monetary policies may be viewed as different methods for altering $(B - B_c)$, the stock of public debt held by banks and foreigners. It also suggests that the restoration of equilibrium after a disturbance may require transitional, discretionary changes in government spending to adjust the stock of debt. To pursue this same theme, rewrite Equation (1.7) of the text as

$$S = Q_{1g} + xr_g(B - B_c)$$

where S is public spending on home goods *and* debt service. Rewriting Equation (2.8) consistently, then differentiating, Equation (3.1) becomes

$$
\begin{bmatrix}
F & A(1-k) & R & 0 & 0 & 1 & 0 \\
0 & 0 & -B_b & (w/v)v_w & (w/v)v_g & 1 & 0 \\
-(U_k + Fk) & 0 & 0 & k_w & 0 & 0 & 0 \\
-U_c & Ack & c(B_b + K) & -c_w & 0 & -c & 0 \\
-tr & 0 & 0 & 0 & 0 & 0 & 1
\end{bmatrix}
\begin{bmatrix}
dN/r \\
dx \\
dE/R \\
(A)\,dr_w \\
(A)\,dr_g \\
-dB_f \\
dS
\end{bmatrix}
$$

$$
=
\begin{bmatrix}
-[a'N]\,dt - dB \\
[(A/R)(1-k)]\,dB_c - dB \\
[ka'N]\,dt \\
-[C/R]\,dB_c + [c]\,dB + [A]\,dc^* \\
[N]\,dt
\end{bmatrix}
$$

Here, changes in the total debt are exogenous, while changes in government spending are endogenous.†

To study subsystems with fixed rates, set $dx = 0$ and delete the second column of the matrix; with flexible rates, set $dE = 0$ and delete the third column. With capital mobility, set $dr_g = 0$ and delete the fifth column; in its absence, set $dB_f = 0$ and delete the sixth column.

---

† Notice, however, that changes in S will not be automatic; the fiscal authority must regulate S with a view to achieving the desired stock of debt. Notice, further, that $dS = 0$ may not imply inaction. It may still be necessary to change spending temporarily (in order to modify B) or to shift between spending on goods and debt service payments (in order to stabilize total spending).

Perfect Mobility and Fixed Exchange Rates

The determinant of this subsystem is $J^S_{ME} = AH_m > 0$. With a change in demand for real cash balances

$$(dN/dc^*)^S_{ME} = r(A/H_m)(1 - k)k_w < 0$$

$$(dr_w/dc^*)^S_{ME} = (1/H_m)(1 - k)(U_k + kF) > 0$$

$$(dE/dc^*)^S_{ME} = (R/H_m)U > 0$$

$$(dB_f/dc^*)^S_{ME} = (R/H_m)[U + (A/R)F(1 - k)k_w] \gtrless 0$$

$$(dS/dc^*)^S_{ME} = t(dN/dc^*)^S_{ME} < 0$$

With a change in central bank holdings of government securities

$$(dN/dB_c)^S_{ME} = (dr_w/dB_c)^S_{ME} = (dS/dB_c)^S_{ME} = 0$$

$$(dE/dB_c)^S_{ME} = (dB_f/dB_c)^S_{ME} = -1$$

With a change in tax rates

$$(dN/dt)^S_{ME} = -ra'(N/H_m)k\{c(w/v)v_w$$
$$- [ck_w + (1 - k)c_w]\} < 0$$

$$(dr_w/dt)^S_{ME} = a'(N/AH_m)k$$
$$\times [cU_k - (1 - k)U_c] > 0\dagger$$

$$(dE/dt)^S_{ME} = -a'(N/AH_m)R[(cU_k + kU_c)$$
$$\times (w/v)v_w + T] < 0$$

$$(dB_f/dt)^S_{ME} = a'(N/AH_m)[V(v/w)v_w + B_bT] > 0$$

$$(dS/dt)^S_{ME} = (N/H_m)[H_m - t(ra')k\{c(w/v)v_w$$
$$- [ck_w + (1 - k)c_w]\}] > 0\ddagger$$

And with a change in total debt

$$(dN/dB)^S_{ME} = (dr_w/dB)^S_{ME} = (dE/dB)^S_{ME} = (dS/dB)^S_{ME} = 0$$

$$(dB_f/dB)^S_{ME} = 1$$

$\dagger$ Because $[cU_k - (1 - k)U_c] = e_r(r/k)(c/k)(cw_r - wc_r) > 0$.
$\ddagger$ Because $[H_m - t(ra')k\{\cdots\}] = [cU_k(w/v)v_w + (1 - k)T + (1 - ra')k\{c(w/v)v_w - [ck_w + (1 - k)c_w]\}] > 0$.

Perfect Mobility and Flexible Exchange Rates

Here, the determinant is $J_{MX}^S = J_{ME}^S > 0$. As in the text, moreover, N and r_w change as they do with fixed exchange rates. For example

$$(dN/dc^*)_{MX}^S = (dN/dc^*)_{ME}^S < 0$$

and $$(dN/dt)_{MX}^S = (dN/dt)_{ME}^S < 0$$

$$(dN/dB_c)_{MX}^S = (dN/dB_c)_{ME}^S = 0$$

and $$(dN/dS)_{MX}^S = (dN/dS)_{ME}^S = 0$$

In addition $$R(dx/dc^*)_{MX}^S = (dE/dc^*)_{ME}^S$$

and the same regularity holds with changes in B_c, t and B. Finally

$$(dB_f/dc^*)_{MX}^S = (dB_f/dc^*)_{ME}^S + (B_b/H_m)U > 0$$

$$(dB_f/dB_c)_{MX}^S = (dB_f/dB_b)_{ME}^S - (B_b/R) < 0$$

$$(dB_f/dt)_{MX}^S = (dB_f/dt)_{ME}^S - a'(NB_b/AH_m)$$
$$\times [(cU_k + kU_c)(w/v)v_w + T] > 0$$

$$(dB_f/dB)_{MX}^S = (dB_f/dB)_{ME}^S = 1$$

while

$$(dS/dc^*)_{MX}^S = (dS/dc^*)_{ME}^S - (B - B_c)(U/H_m) < 0$$

$$(dS/dB_c)_{MX}^S = (dS/dB_c)_{ME}^S + (B - B_c)/R > 0$$

$$(dS/dt)_{MX}^S = (dS/dt)_{ME}^S + (B - B_c)a'(N/AH_m)$$
$$\times [(cU_k + kU_c)(w/v)v_w + T] > 0$$

$$(dS/dB)_{MX}^S = (dS/dB)_{ME}^S = 0$$

To summarise, the outcome with perfect mobility is not much different from what it was in the text. Shifts in demand for real cash balances, open-market operations and changes in the tax rate have identical effects on N, r_w, E and x; the effects on B_f are equal (with opposite sign) to the effects on $(B - B_f)$; and the effects on S are similar to those on B (because changes in S and in r_gB serve the same budget balancing function). Exogenous changes in the public debt have effects quite similar to those of open-market operations (but do not lead to any change in E or x because they are accomplished by temporary changes in the budget that are fully reflected in the current account). The introduction of flexible exchange rates has little significant effect.

No Mobility and Fixed Exchange Rates

The determinant of this subsystem is $J_{IE}^S = [R(w/v)v_g]H_s < 0$, where $H_s \equiv Z - c(A/R)Fk_w > 0$. With a change in demand for real cash balances

$$(dN/dc^*)_{IE}^S = r(A/H_s)k_w < 0$$

$$(dr_w/dc^*)_{IE}^S = (1/H_s)(U_k + kF) > 0$$

$$(dE/dc^*)_{IE}^S = -(A/H_s)Fk_w > 0$$

$$(dS/dc^*)_{IE}^S = t(dN/dc^*)_{IE}^S < 0$$

With a change in central bank holdings of government securities

$$(dN/dB_c)_{IE}^S = -r(C/RH_s)k_w > 0$$

$$(dr_w/dB_c)_{IE}^S = -(C/ARH_s)(U_k + kF) < 0$$

$$(dE/dB_c)_{IE}^S = (C/RH_s)Fk_w < 0$$

$$(dS/dB_c)_{IE}^S = t(dN/dB_c)_{IE}^S > 0$$

With a change in tax rates

$$(dN/dt)_{IE}^S = ra'(N/RH_s)[c(A - R)k_w + Rkc_w] < 0$$

$$(dr_w/dt)_{IE}^S = a'(N/AH_s)V > 0$$

$$(dE/dt)_{IE}^S = -a'(N/H_s)T < 0$$

$$(dS/dt)_{IE}^S = (N/H_s)[(1 - ra')T' + ra'T$$
$$- (1 - ra')(A/R)ck_w] > 0$$

And with a change in total debt

$$(dN/dB)_{IE}^S = -(dN/dB_c)_{IE}^S, \qquad (dr_w/dB)_{IE}^S = -(dr_w/dB_c)_{IE}^S,$$

$$(dS/dB)_{IE}^S = -(dS/dB_c)_{IE}^S, \qquad (dE/dB)_{IE}^S = -(Z/H_s) < 0$$

The effects of a change in demand for real cash balances are not much different from the ones obtained with perfect mobility (and, therefore, quite similar to those in the text). So, too, are the effects of a change in tax rates. But open-market operations have major new effects: because the central bank can alter the stock of government debt held by the commercial banks (and the Government is not obliged to offset the change, merely to balance its budget), an open-market purchase of government securities reduces the interest rate and raises the national income. It still leads to a loss of foreign exchange reserves, but not of the same size as the open-market purchase. An increase of the total debt has the predictable, opposite effects on r_w and N, but it, too, causes a reduction in foreign exchange reserves (because an increase in the debt requires a transitional budget deficit and, therefore, a deficit in the Balance of Payments).

No Mobility and Flexible Exchange Rates

Here, the determinant is $J_{IX}^S = A[(w/v)v_g]H_x < 0$, where $H_x = [(1 - k)Z - cFk_w] > 0$ (so that $J_{IX}^S = J_{IE}^S + B_b[(w/v)v_g]Z$). As one might expect, then, the changes in N and r_w are similar to those obtained with fixed exchange rates. For example

$$(dN/dc^*)_{IX}^S = (H_s/H_x)(1 - k)(dN/dc^*)_{IE}^S < 0$$

$$(dN/dB_c)_{IX}^S = (H_s/H_x)(1 - k)(dN/dB_c)_{IE}^S > 0$$

$$(dN/dt)_{IX}^S = ra'(N/H_x)k[ck_w + (1 - k)c_w] < 0\dagger$$

$$(dN/dB)_{IE}^S = -[R/A(1 - k)](dN/dB_c)_{IX}^S < 0$$

Furthermore

$$(dx/dc^*)_{IX}^S = (H_s/AH_x)(dE/dc^*)_{IE}^S$$

and the same regularity holds with changes in B_c, t and B. Finally

$$(dS/dc^*)_{IX}^S = t(dN/dc^*)_{IX}^S$$

and there are analogous relationships with changes in B_c and B, while

$$(dS/dt)_{IX}^S = (N/H_x)\{(1 - k)T - k(1 - ra')$$
$$\times [ck_w + (1 - k)c_w]\} > 0$$

$\dagger$ Correspondingly, $(dr_w/dt)_{IX}^S = a'(N/AH_x)k[cU_k - (1 - k)U_c] > 0$.

Definitions

p_1, p_2	The home currency prices of the home and foreign goods, respectively.
$\bar{p}_1, \bar{p}_2$	The foreign currency prices of the home and foreign goods (exogenous).
p	The price ratio p_2/p_1 (exogenous).
x	The exchange rate in units of foreign currency per unit of home currency.
K	Capital goods per worker in units of the foreign good.
z	The proportional rate of depreciation (exogenous).
Q_1	Output per worker of the home good.
Q_{1h}	Household purchases per worker of the home good.
Q_{1g}	Government purchases per worker of the home good.
Q_{1b}	Bank purchases per worker of the home good, used to produce banking services.
Q_{1f}	Foreign purchases per worker of the home good (merchandise exports).
Q_{2h}	Household purchases per worker of the foreign good (a component of merchandise imports).
Q_{2k}	Producer purchases per worker of the foreign good, used to adjust the capital stock (a component of merchandise imports).
G	Government expenditure per worker in units of the home good (exogenous).
Y	Disposable income per worker in units of the home good.
N	Pre-tax income per worker in units of the home good.
r	The net return on capital.
r_g	The market interest rate on government securities.
r_w	The market interest rate on private securities.
B	The stock per worker of government securities, being demand obligations.
B_c	The stock per worker of government securities held by the central bank (exogenous).
B_b	The stock per worker of government securities held by the commercial banks.
B_f	The stock per worker of government securities held by foreigners.

W	The stock per worker of private securities, being demand obligations.
R	The liabilities per worker of the central bank (or high-powered money) serving as commercial bank reserves.
E	The stock per worker of foreign exchange held by the central bank.
C	The stock per worker of demand deposits held by household and producers.
A	The net worth (accumulated savings) per worker of households and producers.
q	The required ratio of commercial bank reserves to demand deposits (exogenous).
t	The proportional tax rate on pre-tax income per worker (exogenous).

Glossary of Principal Symbols

(All terms are defined to be positive)

e_r	$-(K/r)f''$
U_c	$c + (Af'')c_r$, or $[c - e_r(r/k)c_r]$
U_k	$1 - k - (Af'')k_r$, or $[(c - w) + e_r(r/k)k_r]$
F	$1 - r(1 - t)a'$
U	$(U_k + kF)(w/v)v_w - Fk_w$
T	$-(U_ck_w + U_kc_w)$
T'	$-[(U_c - c)k_w + (U_k + k)c_w]$
Z	$-[(U_c - cF)k_w + (U_k + kF)c_w]$
H_m	$cU + (1 - k)Z$
H_i	$(B - B_c)H_m - r_g(w/v)v_g[RZ - A(F + tr/r_g)ck_w]$
H_s	$Z - c(A/R)Fk_w$
H_x	$(1 - k)Z - cFk_w$
V	$[(A - R)cU_k - RkU_c]$, or
	$\{cB_b + (r/k)e_r[B_b(ck_r - kc_r) + K(cw_r - wc_r)]\}$

References

[1] KRUEGER, A. O., 'The Impact of Alternative Government Policies under Varying Exchange Rates', *Quarterly Journal of Economics*, LXXIX, (May 1965) 195–208.

[2] MATHIESON, D., *Portfolio Balance in International Finance*. Unpublished Ph.D. Dissertation; Stanford University, 1970.

[3] MCKINNON, R. I. and OATES, W. E., 'The Implications of International Economic Integration for Monetary, Fiscal and Exchange Rate Policy', *Princeton Studies in International Finance*, No. 16, March, 1966.

[4] MEADE, JAMES E., *The Theory of International Economic Policy*, Vol. I. London, New York: Oxford University Press, 1951.

[5] MILL, JOHN S., *Essays on Some Unsettled Questions in Political Economy*. London: Longmans, Green, Reader & Dyer, 1874. (Reprinted 1968 by A. M. Kelley, New York.)

[6] MUNDELL, R. A., 'The Appropriate Use of Monetary and Fiscal Policy for Internal and External Stability', I.M.F. *Staff Papers*, IX, (March 1962) 70–79.

[7] MUNDELL, R. A., 'Capital Mobility and Stabilization Policy under Fixed and Flexible Exchange Rates', *Canadian Journal of Economics and Political Science*, XXIX, (November 1963) 475–485.

[8] MUNDELL, R. A., 'The Monetary Dynamics of International Adjustment under Fixed and Flexible Exchange Rates', *Quarterly Journal of Economics*, LXXIV, (May 1960) 227–257.

[9] SOHMEN, EGON, 'Fiscal and Monetary Policies under Alternative Exchange Rate Systems', *Quarterly Journal of Economics*, LXXXI, (August 1968) 515–523.

[10] TINBERGEN, JAN, *On the Theory of Economic Policy*, Amsterdam: Elsevier, North Holland, 1952.

[11] WHITMAN, M. VON NEUMANN, 'Policies for Internal and External Balance', *Princeton Special Papers in International Economics*, No. 9, December 1970.

4 Economic Integration Via External Markets and Factors

C. P. KINDLEBERGER*

1

IN a previous paper, I compared the definitions and concepts of economic integration of Tinbergen, Balassa and Myrdal [1]. To Tinbergen, integration meant free trade, to Balassa, the absence of governmental discrimination, to Myrdal, factor-price equalisation.[1] There is something to be said for each definition, and something against it. Free trade provides factor-price equalisation, of course, under certain assumptions regarding competition, absence of transport costs, numbers of goods and factors, etc. In the real world these conditions are seldom met, and freedom to trade cannot provide integration between two countries which are so distant from one another that they barely trade at all. The absence of governmental discrimination subsumes free trade, but goes beyond it to permit factor movements. With free trade under certain limited assumptions, or with free movement of all factors, or some combination of the two, factor-price equalisation could be achieved, and the Balassa definition would be covered by the Myrdal. But it need not be. If governments do not discriminate against factors by nationality, the factors may themselves do so. The European Common Market permits free movement of labour, but Germans prefer to work in Germany and Frenchmen in France. In addition to discrimination by the factors themselves, there are transactions costs or costs of transfer, analogous to transport costs for goods, which may prevent sufficient mobility of factors to give factor-price equalisation.

* Massachusetts Institute of Technology.
[1] See [4], [9], [1] and [8].

Absence of governmental and even of private discrimination in the location of factors is unlikely to be sufficient to produce a single market for factors between countries, and hence one price. The Myrdal definition is more general and a standard. Economic integration in the sense of factor-price equalisation can be approached or retreated from. It is seldom achieved.

The Myrdal definition is not only more general, but subsumes the Tinbergen and Balassa definitions as special cases. It also extends out to social and political integration. 'Equal pay for equal work' is a social slogan of women as well as a criterion for judging whether men and women are integrated into the same market or function as non-competing groups.

If one contemplates the experience with economic integration in Europe of the last decade, however, it is evident that a considerable movement toward factor-price equalisation has been brought about with outside factors – Eurodollars, American corporations and Mediterranean labour. Equally, it is possible theoretically for two countries to achieve factor-price equalisation by trading not with each other but with third markets. An interesting question is whether it is appropriate to call such factor-price equalisation through external markets or external factors 'economic integration' in a meaningful sense, when there is no direct contact of goods or factors between the countries. In Section 2, we discuss the process of factor-price equalisation through external markets and factors. In Section 3 the issue of whether this is integration in the ordinary sense of the word is assessed.

2

It may be useful to distinguish between external factors, operating inside two countries involved in the integration process, and external markets for goods or factors. Under the first category come, say, United States corporations with subsidiaries in the various members of the European Common Market, and Mediterranean labour already working in the Common Market. In the second can be found the Eurodollar and Eurobond market for capital, the flow of new workers from the Mediterranean, and external markets for goods. The distinction is not of great importance, but in the first instance,

foreign factors already located in Europe choose not to discriminate between countries on the basis of nationality and are
attracted to the least-cost, highest-return occupation as they
move about Europe. In the second case, the basic economic
decision is made between some country in Europe and an
outside market for factors or goods; a choice of one over
another European location is made, and presumably on the
basis of economic rather than nationality considerations, but
that choice is incidental to the major decision to move between
non-Europe and some European country. In the first instance
there is trade or factor movement between European countries;
in the second, only trade or factor movements between Europe
and the outside world, with no trade or factor movements
between the separate countries themselves.

The reason that Mediterranean labour and United States
corporations are prepared not to make distinctions between
member countries of the Common Market is that they are, as a
rule, both equally strange. So long as the Greek worker is out
of Greece, it is likely to make no difference to him whether he
is in France or Germany. He is thus prepared to go where he
can earn the higher return, and a change in relative wages will
produce a movement of Greek workers at the margin which
will tend to keep wages equal. It is assumed that there is a high
threshold which must be overcome before a worker will leave
the country in which he has been brought up. This prevents
German workers from going to France, assuming that wages
are somewhat higher in France than in Germany, or French
workers from going to Germany under the opposite circum-
stance. Once Greek workers are out of Greece, however, the
threshold has been overcome and it presumably makes little
difference whether a worker is in one country rather than
another.

This statement exaggerates, of course. Spanish, Portugese and
South Italian workers prefer to work in France to Germany
because it is a Latin country, and the language, if not under-
standable, sounds less harsh. Foreign workers prefer Switzerland to Scandinavia because it is nearer to the Mediterranean
and easier and cheaper to reach for holidays. It will make an
important difference to an individual foreign worker whether
the country and especially the city in which he contemplates

working has a colony of his compatriots. Foreign workers travel in channels from colony to colony, rather than spread themselves evenly in space in response to wage differentials. While they do not, like French and German workers, discriminate between the countries as such, they make a variety of lesser distinctions which modify their mobility and hence their capacity to equalise wages.

It is of interest to note that most countries in Europe have considerable traffic in border workers, especially those who live in Belgium and work in the Netherlands or France. This ancient practice of international commuting is explicable in terms of the familiarity of those who live along borders with conditions on both sides, and readiness to respond to economic stimuli within a limited range, provided that the worker can return to his own culture each evening, or in some cases each weekend. There are limits to such border work, imposed partly by law, and partly by the social horizons of workers who live at a distance from the borders. It should be possible to study border commuting and its impact on wage gradients on each side of a border by econometric methods, and to see how the impact of the higher (lower) wage area declines with distance from the frontier.[2]

Only a small number of foreign workers need be mobile between France and Germany to equalise wages under conditions where French and German workers themselves, apart from a limited number along the border, discriminate between the two markets. What proportion depends of course on the elasticities of excess demand for labour in the high-wage country, and of excess supply for labour in the low-wage country. The lower these elasticities, the smaller the volume of movement necessary to produce wage equality. In the real world, of course, there are hundreds of markets for different kinds of labour, and Mediterranean workers tend to produce primarily equality of wage for common labour, or for workers in dirty occupations such as sweepers, miners, railroad workers, construction, farm labour, etc. Over time, as foreign workers get attracted to and recruited for better jobs, such as those in assembly lines in factories, they begin to produce convergence in other occupations than low-grade labour.

[2] See [2].

It is probable that the major effect of external labour on Common Market wage rates is felt less through the movement of labour already working there than through the differential effects on recruitment of new labour. While the transactions costs of foreign workers in moving from one country to another in the Common Market are much less than those of native workers, since they have little emotional attachment to one or another locality, these costs are not zero. If a new recruit is indifferent in terms of culture, distance from home, and the number of workers already in the various markets, he can be attracted to one or another market solely through comparative wage rates, adjusted for differences in living conditions. With a large number of foreign workers in middle and Northern Europe, and substantial gross recruitment for replacement, movement from one country to another need not be large. The same effect can be achieved through variation in the attraction of the separate national markets to new recruits to replace those whose contracts are expiring and who are returning home.

The same distinction must be made for foreign corporations: between new entrants, attracted to one and another location by economic considerations, and established firms with capacity to shift operations among markets in response to economic incentives. Both tend to keep factor prices in line more than the operations of German and French corporations in each others' markets. In a discussion of international business concerns I made a distinction between 'domestic corporations with foreign operations', the 'multinational corporation' and the 'international corporation'.[3] The first feels at home in a single country, and strange everywhere else; the second tries to be a good citizen of every country in which it operates, to grow at the rate of growth of the country, and not to contemplate closing down corporations in a particular national location to move them to another country; the third is indifferent to national location, concerned only to maximise returns for the enterprise as a whole. In the present context, French and German corporations that feel fully at home only in France and Germany, respectively, fall into the category of 'domestic corporations with foreign operations', and discriminate sharply between the

---

[3] See [3], 179ff. It should be noted that other writers use similar terminology with other meanings.

domestic market and any foreign one, even within the European Economic Community, whereas American corporations which are prepared to shift operations from one market to another, depending upon where costs are lower or returns higher, serve as examples in the European context of truly 'international' firms. They may not be indifferent as between the United States and Europe, but once they get to Europe, they care little whether they are located in one country of the Common Market or another, apart from the economic advantages or disadvantages of the location.

The second category of multinational corporation which tries to be a good citizen of each country in which it is located forms an intermediate case, but one more like domestic corporations than international. Assume that a United States corporation got started in each member country of the Common Market (except Luxembourg) before the Treaty of Rome when markets for goods were separated by tariffs, and the tariffs are then removed. Presumably, free trade presents a new collection of costs and prices which calls for a different pattern of investment, production and distribution of outputs. A multinational corporation will ignore it; an international corporation will reorganise its operations, allowing its investment in high-cost locations to run down, and building up output in low-cost countries.

As in the case of labour, the presence of foreign factors disinclined to adjust to parametric changes may be of reduced significance if there is a steady flow of new factors from abroad. With foreign firms, there is nothing comparable to the gross flow of Mediterranean labour which permits reallocations or a turnover even when total labour in Europe is fixed and no worker moves from one Common Market country to another. But additional firms undertake new investment in Europe, and existing firms add to their investment with resources brought from the United States. Fifteen years after the Treaty of Rome, which produced a shift in the horizon of United States firms and attracted attention to existing opportunities, the process of opening up European subsidiaries for the first time has slowed down drastically. New investment by existing firms continued. The press recently made much of the protracted decision of the Ford Motor Company over whether a new facility should be built in Bordeaux or Alsace. It was of some interest that in earlier cases the French authorities were constrained in making conditions for the establishment of foreign firms in France by the possibility, often realised in practice, that such firms would go to other countries in the Common Market. In this instance, two sections of France were bidding by subsidies to attract a firm which had already decided to go to France. But it is hardly possible to contemplate such subsidies offered to a Belgian, Dutch, Italian or German firm to leave its existing location in its own country and to move to France.

There are few examples of United States firms which drastically re-ordered their production arrangements in response to the establishment of the Common Market. The International Business Machines Company (I.B.M.) is said to be one. In discussing it one can deal only in rumour and hearsay, rather than hard evidence, but it had been widely understood that, prior to the Common Market, I.B.M. produced specialised parts for its computers in most countries of Europe, but a complete array of parts for particular machines in none, as a means of protecting against nationalisation: a country which took over an I.B.M. plant would find itself with production of a few parts only, and dependent for complete machines on imports of components from I.B.M. facilities in other countries. Or the same pattern of production could have been adopted to achieve scale economies in production. The Ford plants at Antwerp and Cologne specialise in production of particular parts, and exchange them across the Belgian-German border to get long runs. (It was once stated that with the coming of the Belgian Ford plant into full operation, Belgian exports and imports both rose more than 25 per cent in a single year representing exchanges of parts between Ford of Cologne and Ford of Antwerp). With the coming of the Common Market, I.B.M. is stated to have altered its production to the extent of halting assembling of a full line of its products in each country, achieving scale economies in assembly as well as in parts production. If this be the case, it represents the sort of adjustment which one expects of foreign factors but not of domestic ones.

Transnational mergers are beginning in Europe. Agfa-Gevaert in photographic supplies was for a long time the only major example, but has lately been followed by others – Dunlop-Pirelli in tyres, Fiat-Citroën in automobiles, being the outstanding ones. Neither internationally merged firms, nor the major international firms with a strong base in a Common Market country such as Philips Electric, Royal Dutch Shell or Unilever, seem as free to reallocate resources from one country to another as a company owned and directed from outside. The desire of multi-national firms to be a good citizen wherever they are located may limit the reallocation in practice. Despite the Common Market, new foreign firms may be moved by such slogans as 'To sell in France, produce in France'. Or foreign firms in establishing new subsidiaries in the Common Market may to some extent have followed the leaders into existing locations, rather than settled on plant sites on solid engineering and economic considerations. But there can hardly be doubt that on balance the presence of a large number of United States firms in Europe at the time of the establishment of the Common Market, and the addition of many more since, have contributed to the integration of the Community, i.e. to raising wages in low-cost areas and reducing capital costs where they were highest. The external factor, such as corporate enterprise, may discriminate on non-economic grounds between countries where they are established, and even in setting up new enterprises, but it is apt to discriminate, thus far in the integration process, much less than local corporate enterprise.

In addition to labour and corporate enterprise, a third external factor is capital. Foreign corporate enterprise does produce some reallocation of capital among the countries of Europe through drawing depreciation allowances and profits out of one country for investment in another. It may even borrow domestic savings in one country for investment in another, particularly if such enterprise is a foreign bank with branches in the various Common Market countries.[4] The major force making for convergence of interest rates in Europe has been the external market for capital represented by the Euro-dollar and Eurodollar bond markets. Prior to the development

[4] This is done only by the most sophisticated 'international corporations' which are prepared to embrace the exchange risks involved. Most foreign corporations borrow local currency only for local needs without regard to cost (i.e. interest rates).

of these Eurodollar markets, of course, the same function was performed to a lesser extent by the New York money and capital market.

There is no direct movement from one European country to another as was possible and to some extent took place with Mediterranean labour and United States owned corporations. Rates of interest at short and long term are equalised, if at all, by movements between the separate countries of the Common Market and the Eurodollar money and capital markets, but not between one another.

In the initial stages, the Eurodollar and Eurodollar bond markets were used primarily by subsidiaries of United States corporations in Europe. Gradually, however, they were followed by leading European based companies. This is another example of foreign factors pointing the way to integration among European countries, but this time by means of external markets. The proportion of European based companies using Eurodollar facilities started small and has been increasing. There remain numbers of companies too small, too little known and too limited in their operations to qualify as credit worthy on the international capital market. The analogy in the United States between those firms outside New York which borrow in Wall Street, and those which are restricted to local lenders is exact. But the use of a new market constitutes a learning process. The international firms lead the way. They are followed by the largest and best-known national firms. After time, the position settles down with some national companies known to be qualified for use of the international market, and some excluded by lack of creditworthiness. As the latter grow in size, more and more of them qualify. For the remainder there are transactions costs, or costs of information, which limit their access.

Whether the process is likely to go far enough to equalise interest rates in, say, France and Germany, with capital moving between them and the Eurodollar markets but not between France and Germany themselves, is hard to say. It was clearly going that far when the various European countries interfered with the process in the interest of maintaining independent monetary policies. In the fall of 1970, both Germany and France tried to resist the reduction in interest rates which came about because of increased money supplies in the United States which lowered interest rates there; repayment by United States banks of debts to Eurodollar institutions; a reduction of Eurodollar rates; and increased German and French borrowing in the Eurodollar market. They were unable to. If they had lowered their interest rates concomitantly with the reductions in the United States, it seems likely that there would have been less continental borrowing in the Eurodollar market and hence lesser increases in German and French reserves from this source. The repayment of Eurodollar obligations by United States banks may or may not have taken place, depending upon the relative pulls, with interest rates broadly the same, between the desire of United States bankers to liquidate their debts and their interest in maintaining a source of credit against which reserves were not required, i.e. the May 1969 level of bank borrowing from Europe.

French and German interest rates could, of course, be helped to converge through the Eurodollar market without United States monetary policy being involved, if United States banks discriminated between lending and borrowing opportunities in Europe and the United States. Suppose that normally interest rates in Dallas and San Francisco are equalised, or kept in a structural equilibrium which differs somewhat from equality, for a given class of large borrower, through movements between New York and Dallas on the one hand, and San Francisco and New York on the other, with no borrowing and lending taking place between Dallas and San Francisco. It could happen that interest rates would tighten or loosen for particular classes of borrowers in New York without affecting the terms at which San Francisco and Dallas firms trade in New York, and hence without affecting the interest rate structures of the two regional markets. Competition makes such an outcome unlikely, however. With enough large borrowers with inter-regional (or international) credit worthiness, competition is likely to result in altering the rates of subsidiary markets, but probably not their relation to each other, whenever the primary market undergoes a parametric change.

Factor-price equalisation in Europe through foreign factors and foreign markets has been enhanced by Mediterranean labour, United States corporations and the Eurodollar money and capital markets. Whether export of goods in third markets does produce factor-price equalisation is debatable, but it is a theoretical possibility. Take identical countries, equidistant from a large market (or with equal or negligible costs of transport) and selling and buying the same range of goods in it. With the strong assumptions of the factor-price equalisation theorem, factor prices can be equalised between them with no factor movements and without the necessity for trade between them. The assumptions required can, in fact, be weaker than in the textbook two-country case, since the addition of the outside market makes it possible to allow for transport costs, so long as they are equal as between the two countries. Moreover, it is intuitively evident that Denmark and New Zealand are unable to sell any butter to each other, but that both are selling butter on the British market, and have their factor prices held in line through the third market.

The role of third markets in trade is familiar in economic literature primarily in connection with the adjustment process. Machlup and Meade have discussed the possibilities,[5] and the role of the British market in settling the Franco-Prussian indemnity provides an historical example [5, p. 328]. Perhaps Japan and Germany selling small automobiles in the United States can affect each other's factor prices, though hardly to the point of equalisation.

3

The possibility of factor-price equalisation through external factors and external markets poses the question whether under these circumstances, factor-price equalisation constitutes economic integration. Take external markets first. Assume large scale capital movements between Paris and New York and Frankfurt and New York which result in identity of interest rates between the two pairs of markets and, since each pair has a market in common, between Paris and Frankfurt. This may well mean that New York and Paris are integrated with New York and Frankfurt. They do not convey to me that Paris and Frankfurt are integrated. Things equal to the same things are equal to each other. True. But parts of the same thing

---

[5] See [6], Appendix B and [7], Part IV.

are not parts of each other. The law of one price says that in one market there will be one price, but the definition is not reversible – that with one price there is one market.

Integration means oneness. Each hand can be an integral part of the body, but this does not mean that the two hands are integrated.

Where external factors move back and forth between countries of Europe, whether Mediterranean labour or United States enterprise, the position is different. In this case, where there is traffic or trade or connection between two markets sufficient to produce factor-price equalisation, I am disposed to regard that as integration, despite the 'foreignness' of the equalising agents. In these cases there may be sufficient movement to equalise factor prices in Europe but without sufficient movement to equalise factors between the separate countries of Europe and the outside market. The definition of integration thus becomes factor-price equalisation based on direct movements between countries. This excludes the case where both prices are equalised through an outside market, e.g. have factor prices equalised to it and thus to each other. The wider integration does not necessarily imply the integration of the parts. *A fortiori* it excludes the case where each European country achieves a fortuitous factor-price equalisation by failing to equalise with an outside economic entity in the same directions and to the same extent.

These notions may seem empty, but they are relevant to the issue of the 1970s. Europe wants economic integration in a sense that implies some separation from the outside world, i.e. more internal trade, and more internal factor movement – presumably of native factors and not those of foreign origin. Factor-price equalisation in which the separate countries of Europe achieved factor-price equalisation with the United States or with southern Europe in labour is not the same thing.

References

[1] BALASSA, BELA. *The Theory of Economic Integration.* Homewood, Illinois: R. D. Irwin, 1961.

[2] GLESJER, HERBERT and DRAMAIS, A. 'A Gravity Model of Independent Flows', forthcoming.

[3] KINDLEBERGER, C. P., *American Business Abroad*, New Haven, Conn.: Yale University Press, 1969.

[4] KINDLEBERGER, C. P., 'European Integration and the Development of a Single Financial Center for Long-Term Capital', *Weltwirtschaftliches Archiv*, XC, (July, 1963) 189–209.

[5] KINDLEBERGER, C. P., *International Economics*, Homewood, Illinois: R. D. Irwin, 4th ed., 1968.

[6] MACHLUP, FRITZ. *International Trade and the National Income Multiplier*, Philadelphia: The Blakiston Company, 1943.

[7] MEADE, JAMES E. *The Theory of International Economic Policy, Vol. I. The Balance of Payments*, New York: Oxford University Press, 1951.

[8] MYRDAL, GUNNAR. *An International Economy, Problems and Prospects*. New York: Harper and Row, 1956.

[9] TINBERGEN, JAN. *International Economic Integration*. (2nd completely revised edition of *International Economic Cooperation*). Elsevier, Amsterdam, 1954.

5 Decreasing Marginal Cost and the Pattern of Trade

ANTHONY Y. C. KOO*

CURRENT trends in the pure theory of trade are mainly concerned with the Heckscher-Ohlin factor endowment analysis. But the literature exploring and refining the H–O model has largely ignored variable returns to scale by assuming a linear homogeneous production function. The notable exception is the work of Kemp [2, pp. 110–129].[1] Kemp, however, limits his exploration to an aspect of decreasing marginal cost, i.e. increasing returns (to scale) where all physical inputs are increased in the same proportion with consequent more than proportional increase in output. But it is well known that decreasing marginal cost may result either from increasing returns to scale or, when some factor is fixed while others are variable, from operation in early portion of stage I of production (where MVP and AVP are rising). His and other writers' omission of the distinction between the two (to be labelled type A for the former and type B for the latter) leaves the problem of increasing returns in international trade theory still at the point of Tinbergen's version of Graham's theory [4] which also falls short in clarifying these two types.

The purpose of the present note is to raise three questions: (a) is increasing marginal product of variable inputs a relevant phenomenon of economic growth?; (b) how do we incorporate it into an analytical model? and (c) what light can the model throw on the pattern of trade of a country whose industry is

---

* Michigan State University.

[1] This single reference is not intended to overlook many contributors to the earlier discussion of increasing returns to scale. The single authoritative source is [1, pp. 160–174].

undergoing the stage of increasing marginal product of the variable inputs?

1

One may argue whether a rational producer would ever operate in a region in which the increasing returns to the variable inputs are associated with the negative marginal product of the fixed input. If market conditions dictated such a small level, so the argument goes, the output would be produced by using fewer units of fixed input. But this argument fails to see that a society may necessarily operate some industries with increasing average product because of low man/land ratio such as transportation and communication industries. In addition, there is the problem of economic growth in developing countries where plant and equipment come in sizes designed to meet the projected market demand rather than the immediate one. In the interval of reaching for the projected market demand, one finds the plant in the stage of increasing marginal product of variable inputs. Naturally, this stage will disappear as soon as the projected market size of output is reached or the useful life of equipment comes to an end, whichever comes first.

Interestingly, a model of decreasing marginal cost describing type B of increasing returns can be built on the Tinbergen's construct. Following Tinbergen, we begin our transformation curve from the underlying cost curves rather than going back to factor endowment. In so doing, we are aware that increasing marginal product of variable inputs (type B) or all inputs (type A) can mean falling marginal costs only in partial equilibrium where the condition of constancy of all factor prices (output price being given externally) is met. Under general equilibrium the above statement may not be valid. When factor supplies are constant, inputs into one industry can rise only at the expense of factors used in other industries. Unless there is only one input in all processes (Tinbergen's assumption) or multiple inputs are used in the same proportion in all processes, the expansion of an industry must bid up the relative price of the factors it uses most intensively. Total money costs increase more rapidly than the quantity of physical factor units employed. This condition holds for both types of increasing returns, but it does not apply with equal force to type B where

the variable inputs do not have to increase in the same proportion as in type A. Thereby, substitution between inputs
become possible.

2

For simplicity but no loss of generality we assume that there
are two goods y_1 and y_2 to be produced and a revenue function

$$F = F(y_1, y_2) \tag{1}$$

On the assumption that we are dealing with a small and open
economy and that the prices of goods are determined externally
or fixed, the total revenue is given by the linear equation
$F = p_1y_1 + p_2y_2$, where p_1 and p_2 are the prices of products
y_1 and y_2 respectively. Consider the problem of maximising (1)
subject to the two functional (resources) constraints[2] on our
freedom to adjust y_1 and y_2.

$$f(y_1, y_2) \leq 0^{[3]} \tag{2}$$

$$g(y_1, y_2) \leq 0$$

where $y_1, y_2 \geq 0$.

The function $f(y_1, y_2) = 0$ in (2) above defines a relation
between y_1 and y_2 (product transformation curve) such as that
indicated by the contour in quadrant 1 of Figure 5.1.[4] For each
y_1 there is a corresponding y_2 given by $f(y_1, y_2) = 0$.

We shall confine ourselves in the text to the simpler case of
one constraint say, $f(y_1, y_2) = 0$, but refer the interested reader
to the Kuhn-Tucker theorem for the necessary mathematical
underpinning and generalisation of our model [3, pp. 189–196].

In Figure 5.1 let y_1 be measured along the positive part of the
horizontal axis and y_2 along the positive part of the vertical
axis. The negative halves of these axes and quadrant 3 are used
to plot the input(s) in physical units [resource(s)] for producing
y_1 and y_2 respectively and will be denoted **a**. The line a_1a_2

---

[2] In Tinbergen's special case, there is only one functional constraint on
our freedom to adjust y_1 and y_2 because he imposes a total resources
limitation a on the productive process of y_1 and y_2.

[3] The inequality sign defines not only the set of points on the contour,
but also all the points under this contour (product transformation space).

[4] The function will be derived and given an economic interpretation
later in the paper.

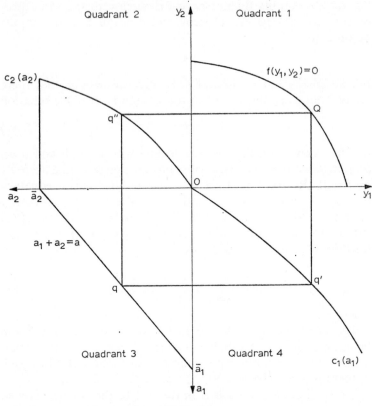

FIG. 5.1

indicates through its distance from the origin 0 the size of the total resource(s) of the economy. Any movement along the line shows the distribution of the total resource(s) between products y_1 and y_2. In the fourth quadrant we have

$$y_1 = y_1(a_1) \tag{3}$$

where a_i indicates that part of total resource(s) a devoted to production of y_i, $i = 1, 2$.

Alternatively, we can draw the total cost curves

$$c_1 = c_1(y_1) \quad \text{since} \quad y_1 = y_1(a_1) \tag{4}$$

i.e. for a given output y_1, certain costs measured in inputs **a** must be incurred. For the moment we assume the cost function

c_1 to be everywhere increasing. In the second quadrant the curve

$$y_2 = y_2(a_2) \tag{5}$$

or
$$c_2 = c_2(y_2) \tag{6}$$

is drawn in a similar way. From these curves the transformation curve $F[c_1(y_1), c_2(y_2)] = 0$ or $f(y_1, y_2) = 0$ can be deduced. It shows all combinations of y_1 and y_2 that a country, given the resource(s), is able to produce. Any point **Q** of the product transformation curve is obtained from the corresponding points **q**, **q'** and **q''**. Under the competitive assumption the ratio of the slopes at **q'** and **q''** (marginal costs) must be equal to the reciprocal of the ratio between Δy_1 and Δy_2 at **Q** (where Δ indicates increment).

A necessary condition for obtaining the minimum total cost of aggregate production is that the slope of $c_1(y_1)$ at **q'** be equal to the slope of $c_2(y_2)$ at **q''** for outputs at **Q**. So far, both cost curves are of the increasing marginal cost type and, accordingly, the transformation curve is concave with respect to the origin. Complications arise if one of the industries operates under increasing and the other under decreasing marginal costs. Then the curvature of the transformation curve depends on the exact form of the two cost curves.[5] Henceforth, we can relax the assumption of one single input or that inputs be used in the same fixed proportions in all industries in the following sense: the increase in the marginal product of variable inputs to outweigh the relative change of input prices (as a consequence of factor transfer between industries) is more likely to happen with factor substitution under type B increasing returns than

---

[5] From the cost functions in (4) and (6) we have

$$\frac{dy_2}{dy_1} = -\frac{c_1'}{c_2'}$$

where c_1' and c_2' are marginal costs, and

$$\frac{d^2y_2}{dy_1^2} = -\frac{1}{c_2'}\left[c_1'' + \frac{(c_1')^2 c_2''}{(c_2')^2}\right] \gtreqless 0 \tag{7}$$

Since c_1' and c_2' are always positive, we see that $\dfrac{d^2y_2}{dy_1^2}$ is a weighted sum of c_1'' and c_2''. The transformation curve can be either concave or convex with respect to the origin depending on whether (7) is less or greater than zero.

under type A. Starting with the general S-shaped long run total cost curves, we shall determine the regions which are characterized by strictly convex and strictly concave transformation curves as well as the areas in which such curvatures cannot be stated unambiguously.

(1) Beginning with very small *values* of a_1 and a_2 (indicating two collections of variable inputs), the corresponding values of c_1 and c_2 are on the concave (from below)

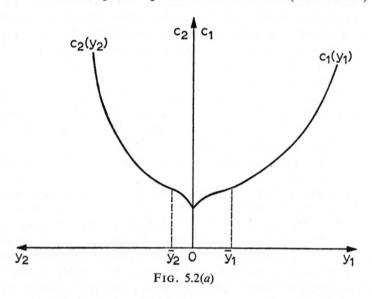

FIG. 5.2(*a*)

portions of the cost functions and accordingly the corresponding contours on the transformation curve are all convex from the origin.[6] This is illustrated in Figure 5.2(*a*). For outputs not exceeding the points of inflexion $\bar{y}_1$ and $\bar{y}_2$, the total cost curves are concave from below. The corresponding contours on the transformation curves are shown in quadrant III of Figure 5.2(*b*).

(2) In the range of outputs greater than $\bar{y}_1$ and $\bar{y}_2$ the total cost curves are strictly rising, and the corresponding contours of the transformation curve are concave from the origin as shown in quadrant I of Figure 5.2(*b*).

(3) For the range of outputs in which one good is producing

[6] Mathematically, the condition is (7) > 0.

at decreasing and the other at increasing marginal costs, the corresponding contours may be either concave or convex. If we let DD in regions II, IV be the locus of inflection points in Figure 5.2(*b*), then in the area above DD the contours are concave and in the area below DD convex.[7] In the range of output above DD all solutions will be interior solutions which are obtained mathematically by application of the marginal cost conditions

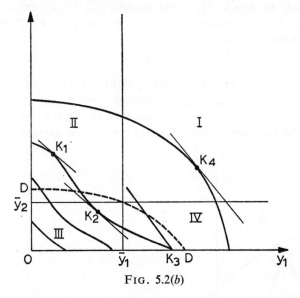

FIG. 5.2(*b*)

and all solutions below DD must necessarily be boundary solutions since there exist no interior solutions in these regions that will satisfy the second order conditions.

A typical interior solution for large enough resources is illustrated at point K_4 in Figure 5.2(*b*). The solution is obtained by application of the marginal cost conditions of the usual Lagrange multiplier. A typical boundary solution is illustrated by a transformation curve which has portions below as well as above DD. For example, points K_1 and K_2 satisfy the marginal conditions while K_3 satisfies the boundary conditions. By

[7] The line DD is determined by the condition of setting Equation (7) equal to zero, i.e. by joining all inflection points of a family of product transformation curves $f(y_1, y_2) = 0$.

application of the second order conditions we can eliminate K_2 and leave K_1 there. By application of the total conditions to K_1 and K_3 it is seen that K_3 gives a larger total revenue than K_1 and is therefore preferred to K_1.

These examples support a general procedure for locating a maximum maximorum as follows. Check the necessary marginal and boundary conditions. From the set, retain only those that satisfy the local second order conditions. Then reject subsets that fail to satisfy the total conditions. Whatever solutions remain (the optimum need not be unique) constitute the maximum maximorum.

3.

The expansion path of outputs y_1 and y_2 in the set of maximum maximorum solutions generated by our taking account of expansion of resources is illustrated by the heavy line in Figure 5.3. The transformation and DD curves are derived from the

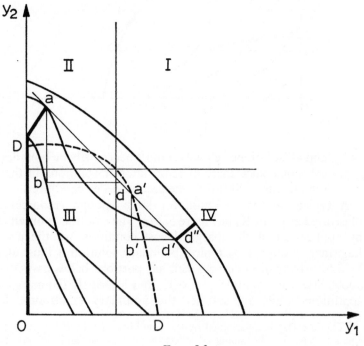

Fig. 5.3

cost curves as we did in Figure 2(*b*) except that the terms of trade (relative price) line is drawn somewhat steeper than in the earlier figure. The expansion path will always follow one of the two boundaries in region III in which the transformation curves are convex with respect to the origin. Note the abrupt discontinuity in the expansion path from ODa to d' d". Discontinuity results whenever one or more goods are produced under declining marginal costs over some range.

The impact on international trade is that goods previously exported will be imported and vice versa for goods imported previously. For example, in Figure 5.3 the country exported ab of y_2 in exchange for b d of y_1. It may, instead, export b' d' of y_1 in exchange for a'b' of y_2. Such a drastic shift may not take place quickly unless there is perfect information. The change is nevertheless inevitable, i.e. the trade expansion path will follow the direction of d' d" in Figure 5.3 when one realises that decreasing marginal cost, although it exists, may not last for long in all stages of economic growth. While such a phenomenon does exist, it deserves our analytic attention because it may well explain sudden change of trade patterns of developing nations.

References

[1] CAVES, R. E. *Trade and Economic Structure*, Cambridge, Mass.: Harvard University Press, 1960.

[2] KEMP, M. C. *The Pure Theory of International Trade*, Englewood Cliffs, N.J.: Prentice-Hall, 1964.

[3] DORFMAN, R., SAMUELSON, P. A. and SOLOW, R. M. *Linear Programming and Economic Analysis*, New York: McGraw-Hill, 1958.

[4] TINBERGEN, JAN. *International Economic Cooperation*, Amsterdam: Elsevier, 1945.

6 Adjustment Costs, Optimal Currency Areas, and International Reserves

MORDECHAI E. KREININ AND
H. ROBERT HELLER*

WHEN a country faces a disequilibrium in its Balance of Payments, it must make several choices. Paramount among them are (*a*) the choice (or the optimal balance) between adjustment to the disturbance and financing of the disequilibrium by the use of international monetary reserves, and (*b*) the choice of the optimal adjustment technique. Several factors relating to the internal as well as external position of the country have an important bearing on these decisions. This paper is concerned with the economic costs of adjustment on the assumption that the rational policy-maker would select the course of action that minimises these costs. With this in mind, the second choice listed above has implications for the optimum currency area problem, for it provides a criterion for the least cost policy to rectify external imbalances. The next two sections develop criteria for measuring the cost of adjustment and apply them to the determination of optimum currency areas. Some rough empirical estimates are also provided, with data pertaining to the 1960s. The final section is devoted to the choice between adjustment and financing, and its implications for optimal international reserves.

1. The Cost of Adjustment to External Imbalances

In this section we derive the costs of adjustment to an external imbalance associated with (*a*) an exchange rate change and (*b*)

* Michigan State University and the University of Hawaii.

an income change, both designed to achieve a one dollar improvement in the Balance of Payments. The country is treated as one whole entity, so that distributional effects are ignored. For simplicity's sake we assume that the Balance of Payments is initially balanced.

(a) *The costs of exchange rate changes*

The cost of exchange rate adjustment is twofold: first, the internal adjustment of the economy to a new exchange rate, involving shifts of resources between industries and perhaps geographical locations; and second, changes in the country's terms of trade. In this paper we concentrate solely on the second cost, recognising that the first may well be important, so that our cost estimates are strictly lower bound. The rationale for doing this is that the internal adjustment costs cannot readily be measured at the current state of our knowledge. Future work, utilising the framework developed here, could pay special attention to the possibility of measuring these costs.

A change in the exchange rate, in our example a devaluation, by one percentage point will affect the terms of trade[1] by

$$t = \frac{e_m}{e_m + \eta_m} - \frac{\eta_x}{e_x + \eta_x} \tag{1}$$

where e = supply elasticity

η = demand elasticity

and the subscripts

x = exports and

m = imports

At the same time, the one percent devaluation will improve the Balance of Payments by

$$b = \frac{e_x(\eta_x - 1)}{e_x + \eta_x} + \frac{\eta_m(e_m + 1)}{e_m + \eta_m} \tag{2}$$

[1] See: [8, Appendix to Chapters 8 and 9] or any other standard textbook for derivation of formulas (1) and (2) in the text.

Combining these two expressions we obtain the terms of trade cost of any given improvement in the Balance of Payments

$$c = \frac{t}{b} = \frac{\dfrac{e_m}{e_m + \eta_m} - \dfrac{\eta_x}{e_x + \eta_x}}{\dfrac{e_x(\eta_x - 1)}{e_x + \eta_x} + \dfrac{\eta_m(e_m + 1)}{e_m + \eta_m}} \tag{3}$$

or after manipulation

$$c = \frac{e_m e_x - \eta_m \eta_x}{e_m e_x \eta_m + e_m e_x \eta_x + e_m \eta_m \eta_x + e_x \eta_m \eta_x - e_m e_x + \eta_m \eta_x} \tag{4}$$

Since it is practically impossible to obtain estimates of export-supply elasticities, we assume – as a first approximation – that $e_x = e_m = \infty$. This assumption is justified if exports are small in relation to total domestic production. To derive c for this special case we divide (4) by $e_m e_x$ and obtain

$$c = \frac{1 - \dfrac{\eta_m \eta_x}{e_m e_x}}{\eta_m + \eta_x + \dfrac{\eta_m \eta_x}{e_x} + \dfrac{\eta_m \eta_x}{e_m} - 1 + \dfrac{\eta_m \eta_x}{e_m e_x}} \tag{5}$$

At $e_x = e_m = \infty$, this reduces to

$$c = \frac{1}{\eta_m + \eta_x - 1} \tag{6}$$

This expression for the terms of trade cost of devaluation is an expected result. For under infinite export-supply elasticities the terms of trade deteriorate by the degree of devaluation (1 per cent) and the balance of payments improves by $\eta_x + \eta_m - 1$. The difference that the assumption of infinite supply elasticity makes can be seen in Equation (5). Supply elasticities appear in the denominator of four terms; all these terms would be larger had the elasticities been finite. Since the four terms appear either in the denominator of the expression or in the numerator but with a negative sign, they all bias the result in the same direction: the infinity assumption makes the terms of trade cost of devaluation (c) larger than it would be under finite export supply elasticities. Consequently by using Equation

(6) to represent (5) we are actually presenting the upper bound of devaluation cost.

(b) *The costs of income changes*

We next turn to an analysis of the costs associated with income changes as a means of rectifying an external imbalance, assuming that no other adjustment takes place. Foreign repercussions are ignored throughout.

We define

Y = national income
C = consumption
I = investment
G = government expenditures
X = exports
M = imports
B = Balance of Payments, and
A = domestic absorption ($= C + I + G$)

Lower case letters denote marginal propensities and the subscript o indicates autonomous components. Our model consists of the following equations

$$Y = C + I + G + X - M \qquad (7)$$
$$C = C_o + cY \qquad (8)$$
$$I = I_o + iY \qquad (9)$$
$$G = G_o + gY \qquad (10)$$
$$M = M_o + mY \qquad (11)$$
$$X = X_o \qquad (12)$$

Furthermore

$$A = C + I + G \qquad (13)$$
$$B = X - M \qquad (14)$$
$$s = 1 - (c + i + g) = 1 - a \qquad (15)$$

Substituting into (7) above we obtain

$$Y = A_o + aY + X_o - M_o - mY \qquad (16)$$

and for changes

$$\Delta Y = \Delta A_o + a\,\Delta Y + \Delta X_o - \Delta M_o - m\,\Delta Y \qquad (17)$$

Rearranging and writing s for $(1 - a)$ we derive the traditional foreign trade multiplier equation showing the effect on national income of an autonomous disturbance

$$Y = \frac{1}{s + m}(\Delta A_o + \Delta X_o - \Delta M_o) \qquad (18)$$

In a similar fashion we calculate the effect of an autonomous change on the Balance of Payments

$$\Delta B = \Delta X - \Delta M \qquad (19)$$

or

$$\Delta B = \Delta X_o - \Delta M_o - m \Delta Y \qquad (20)$$

Substituting (18) into (20) we get

$$\Delta B = \Delta X_o - \Delta M_o - \frac{m}{s + m}(\Delta A_o + \Delta X_o - \Delta M_o) \qquad (21)$$

or

$$\Delta B = \frac{s}{s + m}(\Delta X_o - \Delta M_o) - \frac{m}{s + m}\Delta A_o \qquad (22)$$

This is to say that after an initial autonomous change in the external accounts (ΔX_o or ΔM_o) the country's national income will change automatically by $1/(s + m)$ times the initial disturbance (Equation 18) and the country's Balance of Payments will be in disequilibrium by $s/(s + m)$ times the initial disturbance (Equation 22). This Balance of Payments disequilibrium can be eliminated by *policy induced* changes in consumption, investment, or government expenditures. From Equation (22) we can calculate the change in A needed to eliminate any specified Balance of Payments disequilibrium

$$\Delta A = -\frac{s + m}{m}\Delta B \qquad (23)$$

Substituting from (22) we get[2]

$$\Delta A = -\frac{s + m}{m} \cdot \frac{s}{s + m}(\Delta X_o - \Delta M_o) \qquad (24)$$

$$\Delta A = -\frac{s}{m}(\Delta X_o - \Delta M_o) \qquad (25)$$

---

[2] Equation (24) can be viewed more directly as the change in A_0 that would compensate for a change in $(X_0 - M_0)$, leaving B unchanged ($\Delta B = 0$). In other words, it is obtainable from Equation (22) by setting

$$\frac{s}{s + m}(\Delta X_0 - \Delta M_0) = -\frac{m}{s + m}\Delta A_0$$

The effect of this policy change of A on national income is easily obtained from (18)

$$\Delta Y = \frac{s}{m(m + s)} (\Delta X_0 - \Delta M_0) \qquad (26)$$

Equation (26) shows the national income changes which result from *policy* measures adopted to restore Balance of Payments equilibrium after the initial disturbance. The *total costs* of adjusting to an external autonomous disequilibrium via *income changes* are made up of two components: (*a*) the *automatically* induced national income changes which result from the operation of the foreign trade multiplier, and (*b*) the *policy* induced income changes designed to restore external balance. The automatic income adjustments are given by Equation (18) and the policy induced changes by Equation (26). The total cost of rectifying an external imbalance is therefore given by

$$\Delta Y = \frac{1}{s + m} (\Delta X_0 - \Delta M_0) + \frac{s}{m(m + s)} (\Delta X_0 - \Delta M_0) \qquad (27)$$

which simplifies to

$$\Delta Y = \frac{1}{m} (\Delta X_0 - \Delta M_0) \qquad (28)$$

Thus, the cost of attaining \$1 external adjustment via income policies is the inverse of the marginal propensity to import $(1/m)$.

(c) *Relative costs of adjustment*

The rational policy-maker will select the least costly method of rectifying a given external imbalance. On the admittedly oversimplified model employed here, he would prefer income to switching policy if $\dfrac{1}{m} < \dfrac{1}{\eta_m + \eta_x - 1}$ and vice versa.[3]

---

[3] This restrictive criterion also assumes that the external balance is the government's overwhelming concern, rather than one of several policy targets. Additionally, we compare the costs of only two policy instruments whereas in effect a government may also resort to controls over trade or capital flows.

Can anything be said about these relative costs of adjustment on *a priori* grounds? Theoretically, we might expect the mpm to rise and the cost of income adjustment to decline, with the reduction in the size (increase in 'openness') of the economy. On the other hand the effect of country size on formula (6), and therefore on the cost of adjustment via switching policies, is unclear: η_x (the foreign demand elasticity for the country's exports) is likely to be negatively related to country size for it rises as the country becomes a less important supplier of its exports on world markets;[4] but η_m (the country's import-demand elasticity) is likely to be positively related to country size, since it rises as the share of imports in domestic production and consumption declines. Even these conflicting influences of size of country on demand elasticities (based on the country's share in the world's total trade, and on the share of imports in its domestic production and consumption) are partial equilibrium in nature, and refer to changes in individual products or industries. In actual fact all other things are not equal. The nature of the products traded (and their elasticities) varies from country to country; not all countries produce home substitutes for their imports; and finally, smaller countries tend to specialise in the exports of a few products, in which they may occupy an important share in world markets despite their size.

There is one important influence in determining the size of the relevant demand elasticities: time. The short-run demand curves for products tend to be quite inelastic, but the elasticity tends to increase with the passage of time. The main reason for this phenomenon is that information about price change must be disseminated, and buyers must be allowed time to adjust their consumption patterns. It follows that the longer the time span allowed for, the less costly is exchange rate adjustment relative to income adjustment in eliminating balance of payments disequilibria. However, for much of economic policy, we are interested in neither the very short run nor the very long run. What is relevant for many economic decisions is a three to five year time horizon. It would be important for policy purposes to shed some light on the relative costs of

---

[4] This could easily be offset if smaller nations were highly specialised in a few export products (as they are purported to be), of which they are important suppliers despite their size.

expenditure and switching policies for that time horizon. And this can be done only by empirical estimation.

There are numerous studies of price and income elasticities in international trade, the latest one being that by Houthakker and Magee [3]. For each of a score of countries, they estimate an import-demand function of the form:

$$\log M = a + b \log Y + c \log \left(\frac{PM}{WPI}\right) + u$$

where: M is the country's merchandise imports at constant prices

Y is the country's real G.N.P. (index)

PM is the country's import price index

WPI is the country's wholesale price index and

u is an error term

In such an equation (subject to the well known conceptual and statistical shortcomings) the parameters b and c are the income and relative price (η_m) elasticities respectively. Estimates of mpm are readily obtainable as a product of b and the apm. The fact that the estimates so obtained are not too different from those derived by other methods lends a measure of confidence to the elasticities.

Secondly, for each country they estimate the following 'demand for exports' function:

$$\log X = d + e \log (YW) + f \log \left(\frac{PX}{PXW}\right) + v$$

where X is the country's merchandise exports at constant dollars

YW is an index of G.N.P. for 26 major importing countries (representing the 'world')

PX is the country's export price index

PXW is the weighted average export prices of 26 other exporting (competing) countries, and

v is an error term

Here e and f are the income and relative price elasticities of demand. Strictly speaking, f represents an elasticity of substitution between the country and all its competitors combined, since export prices can differ from domestic prices by reason of export subsidies and other factors. But, following other scholars, we take it to represent η_x.

Apart from the generally recognised difficulties with this estimating procedure, it should be emphasised that where imports are subject to quantitative restrictions (i.e. import quotas and/or exchange control) which displace the market mechanism, the elasticity estimates based on market performance data are not meaningful. This rules out practically all of the

TABLE 6.1. *Costs of Adjustment to a $1 Deficit via Switching and Expenditure Policies*

Country	η_m (1)	η_x (2)	e_y (3)	apm (4)	Cost of adjustment to $1 deficit	
					Via switching policy $\dfrac{1}{\eta_m + \eta_x - 1}$ (5)	Via income policy $\dfrac{1}{m}$ (6)
Canada	−1·46	−0·59	1·2	0·16	0·95	5·21
Denmark	−1·66	−0·56	1·3	0·29	0·82	2·65
Germany	−0·24	−1·25	1·4	0·11	2·04	6·49
Italy	−0·13	−1·12	2·3	0·15	4·00	2·90
Japan	−0·72	−0·80	1·2	0·11	1·92	7·58
South Africa	−0·52	−2·41	0·9	0·17	0·52	6·54
Sweden	−0·79	−0·47	1·8	0·21	3·85	2·65
Switzerland	−0·84	−0·58	2·0	0·28	2·38	1·79
United Kingdom	−0·21	−1·24	2·0	0·16	2·22	3·13
United States	−1·03	−1·51	1·5	0·03	0·64	22·22

Sources: H. S. Houthakker and S. P. Magee, 'Income and Price Elasticities in World Trade', *Review of Ecomomics and Statistics*, LI (May 1969), 111-25.
Column (4) from International Monetary Fund, *International Financial Statistics*.

underdeveloped world. And in the O.E.C.D. countries, trade in agricultural products as well as in certain raw materials should ideally be excluded. But data limitations militate against such an exclusion. Also, the fact that annual rather than quarterly data were used in most cases reduces the reliability of the results.

Table 6.1 presents estimates of the relevant parameters, with the costs of adjustment to external imbalance shown in columns 5 and 6. They are based on formulae (6) and (28) respectively.

While the previous discussion indicates no theoretical reason for countries with high income adjustment costs to have low exchange rate adjustment costs, we do find such an empirical relationship. The rank correlation coefficient between the exchange rate adjustment costs calculated in column 5 and the income adjustment costs calculated in column 6 is equal to −0·58. There is a presumption for large countries to find exchange rate adjustment less expensive, and for smaller countries to find income adjustment less costly, but this seems a rough and unreliable rule of thumb. With particular reference to our sample of countries, Canada, Denmark, Germany, Japan, South Africa, the United Kingdom and the United States will find exchange rate adjustment less costly; Italy, Sweden and Switzerland will find income adjustment less costly.

2. Optimum Currency Areas

The results obtained above have a direct ramification for the theory of optimal currency areas. Such an area is defined to contain two or more currencies which are immutably pegged to each other, but which fluctuate jointly *vis-à-vis* the outside world. The idea, in one form or another, dates back quite some time now. In recent years it was advanced in a policy context by the Brookings Report on the United States Balance of Payments [7], which proposed the establishment of two blocs of currencies (E.E.C. bloc and a dollar-sterling bloc). The problem was then formulated along theoretical lines, with major contributions by Mundell [6], McKinnon [5] and Kenen [4]. Mundell defines an optimum currency area as one within which factors of production – primarily labour – are mobile (geographically), so that factor mobility can lubricate the adjustment mechanism. Other points of view, such as an intergovernmental agreement to co-ordinate fiscal and monetary policies, can easily be articulated as an alternative or supplemental criterion. Kenen relates the concept to degree of diversification, believing that fixed rates are most appropriate for well diversified national economies, where the internal cost of adjustment is less painful. McKinnon discusses the cost of adjustment under alternative systems and relates them to the degree of openness of the economy.

What the various criteria actually amount to is an attempt to identify the crucial variable(s) that determine whether the cost of external adjustment via devaluation exceeds or falls short of the cost of adjustment via domestic income policies. (Obviously, the more independent nations are willing to behave like regions of one country, the more suitable they are to form a currency area.) Indeed, a rational decision by an individual country on whether to adopt a fixed (i.e. join a currency area) or flexible exchange rate must be based on the relative costs of adjustment under the two regimes. And these are the costs identified in the previous section on the assumption that each country is one whole entity, and internal redistributional effects are ignored. In an optimal international financial system the costs of exchange rate changes and income changes must be equal at the margin. Hence, an optimal currency area may be defined as an area where exchange rate adjustments involve the same marginal costs as income adjustments. This condition may be obtained from Equations (6) and (28), which give the marginal costs associated with the respective adjustment types

$$\frac{1}{\eta_m + \eta_x - 1} = \frac{1}{m} \qquad (29)$$

Thus, if a country's marginal exchange rate adjustments are costlier than its marginal income adjustments, it should join with some other countries in a larger currency area, up to a point (size) in which the two types of costs are equal at the margin. If the reverse is true, then the country should keep its own currency flexible and without 'attachment'. Similarly, a currency area with higher marginal income than exchange rate adjustment costs might find it advantageous to separate into several smaller currency areas. Of course, this argument focuses narrowly on adjustment costs to external imbalances as the only determinant of optimal currency area, to the neglect of other considerations. But on this criterion only Italy, Sweden and Switzerland in our sample of ten countries should be interested in joining a currency area.

3. Optimal International Reserves

This section is concerned with the optimal international reserves which a country should maintain if it is to minimise the cost of (a) adjusting and (b) financing any external imbalance by the use of international reserves. The methodology used in determining optimal reserve levels was developed in a previous paper [2] and need not be repeated here. Only the modification in it will be spelled out. The optimal amount of international reserves equates the marginal costs of holding one dollar of additional reserves with the marginal costs of adjusting to the imbalance. Thus, ideally

$$MC_{\substack{\text{income} \\ \text{adjustment}}} = MC_{\substack{\text{exchange rate} \\ \text{adjustment}}} = MC_{\substack{\text{financing} \\ \text{by reserves}}}$$

From this equality we derive the formula for the optimal reserve level, R_{opt}, which will minimise the cost of correcting the external imbalance

$$R_{\text{opt}} = h \frac{\log (r/MC_{\text{adj}})}{\log 0\cdot5} \qquad (30)$$

where h shows the average yearly imbalance in the external accounts, r the opportunity cost of holding reserves (i.e. the yield foregone by holding part of the nation's assets in the form of reserves), and MC_{adj} the marginal cost of adjusting to the imbalance.

In two ways we improve upon previous calculations. (*a*) Instead of using an interest rate to estimate the opportunity cost of holding reserves, we use the contribution of capital to the country's aggregate growth rate. This has been estimated by Edward Denison [1] at $0\cdot109$ for the United States, $0\cdot102$ for France, $0\cdot104$ for Germany and $0\cdot086$ for the United Kingdom. In the absence of detailed estimates for all the countries in our sample, we assume that the opportunity cost of holding reserves, rather than investing the resources in imported physical capital, is approximately 10 per cent.[5] (*b*) We shall replace the costs of income adjustment by the lower of the two adjustment costs [formulae (6a) and (28)], i.e. for each country we use the devaluation *or* the income policy, whichever is lower.

Table 6.2 shows optimal reserve levels for both types of adjustment policies. A country which is always willing and able to choose the least costly adjustment technique would want to

---

[5] Note that this 10 per cent differs from the arbitrary five per cent figure used in the earlier calculations [2]. However, the estimates are not very sensitive to even a doubling of the interest rate due to the fact that the logarithm changes only by one.

TABLE 6.2. *Optimal Reserve Levels*

Country	h (millions of $) (1)	Cost of exchange rate adjustment per $1 deficit (2)	Cost of income adjustment per $1 deficit (3)	Optimal reserve level with exchange rate adjustment (millions of $) (4)	Optimal reserve level with income adjustment (millions of $) (5)
Canada	122·7	0·95	5·21	398·7	699·9
Denmark	40·4	0·82	2·65	119·1	191·0
Germany	527·0	2·04	6.49	2293·2	3172·8
Italy	275·2	4·00	2·90	1464·8	1337·0
Japan	235·8	1·92	7·58	1005·3	1472·6
South Africa	112·8	0·52	6·54	268·3	680·4
Sweden	58·4	3·85	2·65	307·6	276·1
Switzerland	100·1	2·38	1·79	457·8	416·7
United Kingdom	553·8	2·22	3·13	2447·1	2751·8
United States	862·0	0·64	22·22	2259·3	6720·7

Source: column (1): [2].
   column (2): Table 1, Col. 5.
   column (3): Table 1, Col. 6.
   column (4) and (5): Equation 30.

hold only the lower one of the reserve levels calculated in columns (4) and (5).

References

[1] DENISON, EDWARD. *Why Growth Rates Differ*, Washington, D.C.: The Brookings Institution, 1967.

[2] HELLER, H. ROBERT. 'Optimal International Reserves', *The Economic Journal*, LXXVI, (June 1966), 296–311.

[3] HOUTHAKKER, H. S. and MAGEE, S. P. 'Income and Price Elasticities in World Trade', *The Review of Economics and Statistics*, LI (May 1969), 111–25.

[4] KENEN, PETER B. 'The Theory of Optimum Currency Areas: An Eclectic View', in Mundell and Swoboda (eds.), *Monetary Problems of the International Economy*. Chicago: The University of Chicago Press, 1969, 41–60.

[5] MCKINNON, RONALD I. 'Optimum Currency Areas', *American Economic Review*, LIII (September 1963), 717–25.

[6] MUNDELL, ROBERT A. 'A Theory of Optimum Currency Areas', *American Economic Review*, LI (September 1961), 657–65.

[7] SALANT, WALTER et al. *The United States Balance of Payments in 1968*, Washington, D.C.: The Brookings Institution, 1963.

[8] YEAGER, LELAND B. *International Monetary Relations*, New York: Harper and Row, 1966.

7 The Role of Home Goods and Money in Exchange Rate Adjustments*

ANNE O. KRUEGER

EVER since Alexander's introduction of the 'absorption' approach, there has been a certain schizophrenia in balance-of-payments theory. On one hand, the macroeconomic identity that a payments deficit means that expenditures exceed income suggests that analyses of the balance of payments should proceed upon macroeconomic lines. On the other hand, analysis of exchange rate adjustment is, almost by definition, analysis of a relative price change.

There are many models focusing upon each of these aspects of the adjustment process separately. In most cases, an effort is made to relate the relative-price and macro aspects of the analysis. Nonetheless, the results of relative-price models sound rather different from those of absorption models. Relative-price models derive conclusions such as: devaluation is more likely to succeed the larger the price elasticities of demand and supply. Absorption models typically conclude that the success of devaluation is contingent upon the community's reduction of its real expenditures relative to its real income.

Good macrotheory should be derived from a consistent theory of microeconomic behaviour underlying it. Similarly, good microtheory should be consistent with its general equilibrium implications. In this sense, there should be an equivalence of relative price and macroeconomic analyses of balance of payments adjustment. That the relationship of the micro and macro aspects of balance of payments determination is not adequately understood may be seen by considering the

* The research underlying this paper was supported by the National Science Foundation's grant to this author, GS-1198. The paper was considerably improved by the helpful comments of James M. Henderson, Harry G. Johnson and Ronald Jones, to whom I am indebted.

following proposition:

> A 10 per cent decrease in domestic prices at a constant
> exchange rate will have the same effects as a 10 per cent
> increase in the price of foreign exchange with domestic
> prices constant.

This is superficially plausible, and seems to follow directly
from the homogeneity properties of excess demand functions.
Yet, upon closer inspection, it is not evident that the proposition holds in general. What, for example, is assumed about the
money supply in the above statement? If the money supply is
assumed the same in both cases, (*a*) domestic price determination must be explained and (*b*) the price level and, hence, money
income is unequivocally lower in the first case than in the second.
For that matter, *can* domestic prices rise by 10 per cent with a
fixed exchange rate, or remain unaltered with an increase in the
price of foreign exchange? What domestic prices are meant?
If all goods are internationally traded, then at any exchange rate
domestic prices cannot change unless foreign prices change also.
If domestic prices change at a fixed exchange rate, that surely
implies that some relative price within the system is changing, or
the role of *both* the domestic price level and the price of foreign
exchange is ambiguous. If it is assumed that the economy is
completely specialised in the production of export goods, then
the role of money is lost from the system; the price of export
goods is fixed relative to either domestic money or to the
exchange rate, and the system becomes a real system.

In this paper, a model is developed which incorporates both
the macro and micro aspects of trade balance determination.
Focus is upon the role of home goods (a class of goods and
services for which transport costs are assumed prohibitive) and
money in trade balance determination. As such, the model
represents a hybrid of the real analyses of Pearce [7] and
Komiya [5] in which home goods' relative prices have emerged
as an important variable and of monetary analyses of Hahn [1]
and Kemp [4] in which there exist only traded goods and a
domestic asset. The model is similar to that of Kemp [3], but
focuses upon the inter-relation of the real and monetary aspects
of exchange rate adjustment, and the reconciliation of the two
approaches.

Such an analysis enables the incorporation of a link between money, on the one hand, and aggregate expenditures on the other, via the link between the money supply, the price of home goods and money income. Relative prices (of home and traded goods) and macro phenomena (the relationship of the money supply, expenditure and the price level) are both important in exchange rate adjustment, and in generating payments imbalances.

Throughout, it is assumed that full employment is maintained, and that outputs of goods are functions of relative prices only. In addition, it is assumed that the country under discussion is small, and cannot affect the international prices at which it buys and sells goods. The former assumption has been widely used in models of trade balance determination, e.g. those of Pearce [7], Hahn [1] and Negishi [6]. The latter assumption is rather more limiting, since it ignores any effects on the terms of trade that might result from exchange rate changes. It is useful largely because it enables vast simplifications of the model, and highlights important aspects of the adjustment process that are obscured by the terms of trade question. In particular, traded goods may be treated as a composite commodity at any money exchange rate, since their relative prices will remain unchanged.

In Section 1, the properties of a model incorporating home goods and traded goods are established. In Section 2, it is shown that an increase (decrease) in the price of foreign exchange results in a decrease (increase) in the relative prices of home goods and an increase (reduction) in the desired money stock. Similarly, an increase in the money supply results in an increase in the relative prices of home goods and an increase in the desired stock of money. Finally, it is shown that devaluation will fail to improve the trade balance if and only if increasing the money supply and, hence, increasing real income, will improve the trade balance.

1. Monetary and Relative Price Models

It is useful to begin with two simple models. The first covers an economy with money in which all goods are internationally traded. It highlights the key macroeconomic relations and shows the symmetry between exchange rate and money supply adjustment mechanisms. The second simple model covers trade balance determination with home and traded goods. This model highlights the 'real' or 'relative price' aspects of payments adjustment. The monetary and real factors are then incorporated into a single model.

1.1 *Money and traded goods*
Let

D_i = the demand for the ith commodity ($i = 1, 2$)
X_i = the output of the ith commodity
E_i $\equiv D_i - X_i$, the excess demand for the ith commodity
M^* = the desired stock of money
M = the actual money stock
p_i = the domestic price of the ith commodity
q_i = the foreign price of the ith commodity
R = the price of a unit of foreign exchange, in domestic currency.

By assumption of constant foreign prices, it follows that

$$q_i = \bar{q}_i; \qquad p_i = R\bar{q}_i \tag{1.1}$$

for all exchange rates.

Domestic outputs of the two goods are functions of relative prices

$$X_i = X_i(p_1/p_2) \tag{1.2}$$

where $\qquad \dfrac{\partial X_1}{\partial(p_1/p_2)} > 0; \qquad \dfrac{\partial X_2}{\partial(p_1/p_2)} < 0$

The demand for money is assumed to be homogeneous of degree one in prices

$$M^* = M^*(p_1, p_2) \tag{1.3}$$

where $\quad \dfrac{\partial M^*}{\partial p_1} > 0 \quad$ and $\quad M^* = \dfrac{\partial M^*}{\partial p_1} p_1 + \dfrac{\partial M^*}{\partial p_2} p_2$

If consumers *always* hold their desired money stock,[1] the demand for goods will be derived from individual maximising

---

[1] If consumers adjust their actual money holdings to their desired holdings at some specified rate, so that, for example, $\bar{M} - M^* = b(M - M^*)$, where $0 < b < 1$ and $\bar{M}$ is the money they are willing to hold, then the budget constraint will be: (1.4') $M - \bar{M} - p_1 E_1 - p_2 E_2 = 0$.

behaviour subject to a budget constraint of the form

$$M - M^* - p_1E_1 - p_2E_2 = 0 \qquad (1.4)$$

Demand functions will then be zero degree homogeneous in p_1, p_2 and $(M^* - M)$

$$D_i = D_i[p_1, p_2; M^*(p_1, p_2) - M] \qquad (1.5)$$

Since supply functions are also zero degree homogeneous, excess demand functions

$$E_i \equiv D_i - X_i = E_i(p_1, p_2; M^*(p_1, p_2) - M) \qquad (1.6)$$

have the same homogeneity properties as demand functions. In particular,

$$\frac{\partial E_i}{\partial p_1} p_1 + \frac{\partial E_i}{\partial p_2} p_2 + \frac{\partial E_i}{\partial (M^* - M)} (M^* - M) = 0$$

Hence, if desired and actual money stocks are equal,

$$\frac{\partial E_i}{\partial p_1} p_1 + \frac{\partial E_2}{\partial p_2} p_2 = 0$$

If desired and actual money stocks are unequal,

$$\frac{\partial E_i}{\partial p_1} p_1 + \frac{\partial E_i}{\partial p_2} p_2 \lessgtr 0 \qquad \text{as} \qquad M \lessgtr M^*.$$

The equation system (1.1) through (1.6) consists of four equations in six unknowns (E_1, E_2, M, R, p_1, p_2). The demand for money, Equation (1.3), is not independent of the excess demand relations Equations (1.6), since if the latter are satisfied, the former must be also, via the budget constraint. The homogeneity properties of the system, however, are such that the choice of numeraire is arbitrary: regardless of how the system is closed, the values of the real variables E_1 and E_2 will be functions of M/R.

One way of closing the system would be to add the equilibrium condition

$$\sum_i p_i E_i = 0 \qquad i = 1, 2 \qquad (1.7)$$

Equation (1.7), combined with the budget constraint, Equation (1.4), implies that the demand for money equals the money supply. One can then solve uniquely for M/R.

Alternatively, one could treat either R or M as exogenous, with the other variable endogenous. Using Equation (1.7) as an equilibrium condition, the behaviour of the other variable with respect to changes in the exogenous variables can be investigated. The homogeneity properties of the system, however, are such that this is a trivial exercise. If the money supply is exogenous, the endogenous exchange rate will change in proportion to any change in the money supply. Conversely, if the exchange rate is exogenous, the money supply will adjust proportionately.[2] In a closed economy, of course, Equations (1.1) are dropped, and the summation Equation (1.7) is replaced by setting excess demand equal to zero in each market. Then, an increase in the money supply results in a proportionate increase in prices.

An alternative treatment of this model has been developed by Kemp [4]. Suppose that the money supply is endogenously determined by:

$$\dot{M} = B \tag{1.8}$$

where $B = -\sum_i q_i E_i$, $i = 1, 2$. That is, the time rate of change of the money supply is equal to the trade deficit per period of time. This is the classical price-specie-flow mechanism.

From an initial position of equilibrium ($B = 0$), investigate the effects on the system of an exogenous change in the exchange rate. In such a system, the equilibrium values of the variables are functions of time. Initially, ($t = 0$),

$$dB_o = -q_1 \left[\frac{\partial E_1}{\partial p_1} \frac{dp_1}{dR} + \frac{\partial E_1}{\partial p_2} \frac{dp_2}{dR} + \frac{\partial E_1}{\partial (M^* - M)} \frac{d(M^* - M)}{dR} \right]$$

$$\tag{1.9}$$

$$- q_2 \left[\frac{\partial E_2}{\partial p_1} \frac{dp_1}{dR} + \frac{\partial E_2}{\partial p_2} \frac{dp_2}{dR} + \frac{\partial E_2}{\partial (M^* - M)} \frac{d(M^* - M)}{dR} \right]$$

[2] The system is stable if neither money nor goods are strictly inferior. If changes in the terms of trade can occur, the stability condition becomes more stringent. In this model, if the exchange rate is endogenous, instability can occur only if an increase in the money supply results in an increase in the demand for money (prices constant) by more than the increase in the money supply. Similarly, if the money supply is endogenous, the system will be unstable only if an increase in the price of foreign exchange leads to increases in the quantities of goods demanded (at higher absolute prices and a constant money supply) and an absolute decrease in the desired money holdings. From the homogeneity properties of the system, the two conditions are equivalent.

Now,

$$\frac{d(M^* - M)}{dR} = \frac{\partial M^*}{\partial p_1}\frac{dp_1}{dR} + \frac{\partial M^*}{\partial p_2}\frac{dp_2}{dR} > 0$$

Equation (1.9) can be simplified by recalling that $\frac{dp_i}{dR} = q_i = \frac{p_i}{R}$,
and that, in the initial situation the desired and actual money
stocks are equal so that

$$\frac{\partial E_1}{\partial p_1} p_1 + \frac{\partial E_1}{\partial p_2} p_2 = 0$$

Hence,

$$dB_o = -\frac{1}{R}\left[q_1 \frac{\partial E_1}{\partial(M^* - M)} + q_2 \frac{\partial E_2}{\partial(M^* - M)}\right]\frac{d(M^* - M)}{dR} > 0 \tag{1.10}$$

The expression in brackets is negative, and $\dfrac{d(M^* - M)}{dR}$
positive. Therefore, the trade balance initially improves with an
increase in the price of foreign exchange. But, $\dot{M} = -B = (M^* - M)$. The domestically-held money supply therefore
increases, and the system returns to its initial state,[3] with a
higher price level and higher nominal money holdings.

If individuals adjust money holdings gradually to their
desired levels, the approach to a new zero trade balance
equilibrium will be asymptotic. Conversely, if the monetary
authority maintains the money supply in the face of trade
imbalances (as, for example, through continuous open market
operations or continuous printing of money at a rate equal but
opposite in sign to the trade imbalance), the initial imbalance
will be repeated continuously. In such cases, a distinction must
be made between the money supply (M) and privately held
money (M^*).

The system is of interest because it shows the conditions under
which money supply and exchange rate changes are equivalent,
and because it illustrates the impossibility of an 'autonomous
monetary policy' in a fully open economy with fixed exchange

---

[3] In Kemp's two-country model, the adjustment is asymptotic, rather
than immediate. The reason is that the price level is adjusting in both
countries.

rates.[4] Of course, one can question the need for autonomous monetary policy in a continuously fully employed economy.

1.2 *Home goods and traded goods*

Consider now a barter world in which there are any number of traded goods and a home good for which transport costs are infinite.[5] By the assumption of a perfectly elastic world supply of all traded commodities, the relative prices of traded goods cannot change, and hence the traded goods can be considered a composite commodity. Notation can remain the same as for the previous model, with $i = 1, 2$ where the first commodity represents the composite traded good. The system then becomes

$$p_1 = R\bar{q}_1 \tag{1.11}$$

$$E_i = E_i(p_1/p_2) \qquad (i = 1, 2) \tag{1.12}$$

$$E_2 = 0 \tag{1.13}$$

Equation (1.11) is equivalent to Equation (1.1) and fixes the absolute prices of traded goods. Excess demand relations are as before, except that excess money holdings are not an argument, and the relative price of home goods in terms of traded goods determines the excess demands for commodities. Equation (1.13) is the equilibrium condition for the system: the excess demand for home goods must be zero. If Equation (1.13) is satisfied, the excess demand for traded goods will also be zero, via Walras' Law. Hence, the full system will be in equilibrium.

The model is illustrated with Figure 7.1. Home goods are on the vertical axis and traded goods on the horizontal. The

[4] In fact, let the exchange rate be fixed. Then there will be one and only one money supply consistent with Equations (1.1), (1.6) and (1.7). Any autonomous change in the money supply would result in an inconsistent system. Therefore, rewrite Equation (1.7) as $\sum_i p_i E_i = B$. From an initial position of $B = 0$, differentiate the system totally with respect to a change in the money supply. $B = -dM$. That is, the trade balance deficit will eractly equal the money supply change. This follows immediately from Equation (1.4) since with R fixed, nominal and real balances will not change. If the rest of the world is perfectly willing to hold any amount of the home country's currency, welfare would be increased indefinitely, with continuous money creation at an infinite rate.

[5] In practice, transport costs need only be sufficient so that the good will not be traded within the relevant range of relative prices.

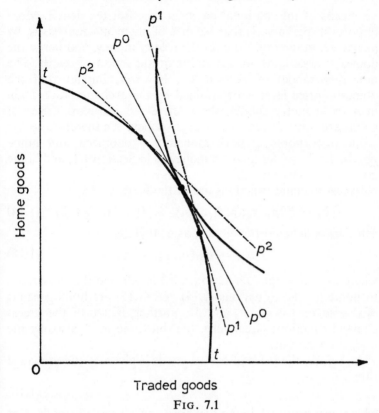

Traded goods

Fig. 7.1

community's production possibilities are represented by the transformation curve *tt*. As drawn, the price line p^0p^0 represents the equilibrium relative price of home goods in terms of traded goods. The price line p^1p^1 represents a higher relative price of traded goods; it is not an equilibrium since there would be a positive excess demand for home goods. Likewise, at prices p^2p^2, home goods prices are relatively higher than at p^0p^0 and there would be an excess supply of home goods.

1.3 *Home goods and traded goods*
Both the models presented above are artificial in important ways. In the home goods model, payments imbalances are possible only in a disequilibrium situation. Even then, there is

no means of international payment to offset the deficit. More important, perhaps, is that balance of payments analysis is, by its nature, monetary. To omit the role of money, and hence the domestic price level, misses an important aspect of reality. The monetary model of Section 1.1, however, implies that the domestic price level is determined by the exchange rate. Even in a two-country model, the relative (equilibrium) prices of goods are not affected by monetary policy. We therefore seek a model incorporating both monetary phenomena and home goods. To do so, let there be money as in Section 1.1, and home goods as in Section 1.2.

Excess demand functions are of the form

$$E_i = E_i[p_1, p_2; M^*(p_1, p_2) - M] \qquad (i = 1, 2) \quad (1.14)$$

The excess demand for money, as a stock, is

$$E_M = E_M(p_1, p_2, M) \qquad (1.15)$$

where the subscript $_1$ refers to traded goods and the subscript $_2$ to home goods. Equations (1.14) and (1.15) are homogeneous of degree zero in p_1, p_2 and M. Further, if two of the excess demand functions equal zero, the third one must also, by the budget constraint.

As before, the price of traded goods is given by the exchange rate

$$p_1 = R\bar{q}_1 \qquad (1.16)$$

where commodity 1 is the composite of all traded goods. For equilibrium, the home goods market must clear

$$E_2 = 0 \qquad (1.17)$$

As specified so far, the system contains five equations, of which four are independent and the six variables E_1, E_2, p_1, p_2, M and R.

As in the monetary model, the system can be closed by adding the equilibrium condition

$$E_1 = 0 \qquad (1.18)$$

and solved for a unique R/M. Alternatively, R can be taken as a parameter of the system, in which case there will be a unique M such that the system of equations is satisfied. The symmetry of the monetary model persists, so that M can be taken as given and the system solved for the corresponding R. So long as

Equation (1.18) holds as an equilibrium condition, it follows that E_M will equal zero via the budget constraint. Moreover, the equilibrium conditions of Equations (1.17) and (1.18) are sufficient to determine p_1/p_2, the relative price of traded goods in terms of home goods. With a fixed R, the absolute price of home goods will then be determined, and the money supply must be such as to satisfy the demand for money at that price level. Alternatively, given Equations (1.17) and (1.18), fixing the money supply determines a price level such that desired and actual money stocks are equal, and, given the equilibrium p_1/p_2, R is determined endogenously.

Setting an exchange rate, and allowing the money supply to adjust corresponds roughly to the price-specie-flow mechanism. Setting the money supply and allowing the exchange rate to adjust corresponds to a flexible exchange rate system. There is, however, a difference between the two systems, at equilibrium. Under a flexible exchange rate system, with instantaneous adjustments in the price of foreign exchange, there can be no trade imbalances. Under a price-specie-flow mechanism, trade imbalances will occur to equate desired and actual money holdings, even with instantaneous adjustments.

Under the Bretton Woods rules of the game, neither the exchange rate nor the money supply is determined endogenously. Most developed countries attempt to maintain a fixed exchange rate and to alter their domestic money supplies in response to their internal economic objectives. To represent this, the exchange rate and the money supply can be taken as parameters of the system. The two equations (1.14) combined with (1.16) and the equilibrium condition of Equation (1.17) then constitute a system of four equations in the four unknowns p_1, p_2, E_1 and E_2.

In this system, the trade balance will, in general, not be zero.[6] The first point to be noted is that a payments deficit or surplus can exist with the private community spending subject to its budget constraint: the excess of payments to foreigners over

[6] It may be objected that payments deficits combined with finance ministry operations to maintain the money supply do not leave the private sector's net asset position unchanged. This stock effect could tend to restore payments balance from any position of deficit or surplus, but is ignored in what follows.

receipts from them is exactly offset by the excess of the actual money stock over the desired. Moreover, if foreigners are willing to hold the country's currency, and the reduction in domestically-held money is offset through sterilisation of the payments imbalance, all consumers and producers can be maximising subject to their budget constraints: no individual will wish to alter his behaviour[7] and there will be no *unsatisfied* excess demands.

The second feature of the system is that altering the exchange rate and the money supply 'proportionately will leave the real variables of the system unaffected. We turn, therefore, to an examination of the comparative statics of the system when either the exchange rate or the money supply is altered, the other remaining constant.

2. The Effects of a Change in the Exchange Rate or the Money Supply

The system of Equations (1.14), (1.16) and (1.17) can be rewritten as

$$E_1 = \hat{E}_1(R, p_2, M)$$
$$E_2 = \hat{E}_2(R, p_2, M) \qquad (2.1)$$
$$E_2 = 0$$

[7] The situation is analogous to that which would result if an otherwise functionless government fixed the price of, e.g. corn, and paid for its operations by distributing the proceeds to its citizens or taxing them for its costs of operations. If the government set the price of corn below its equilibrium level (in the absence of interference), and had sufficiently large inventories, it could meet the excess demand from inventory, and distribute the proceeds among all citizens. Ignoring income distributional considerations, there is no reason why this behaviour could not continue as long as the inventory of corn held out. Similarly, if the price of corn were set above its no-interference equilibrium level, the Government could accumulate inventories indefinitely, taxing its citizens to pay for its purchases. In both cases, private citizens would be maximizing subject to their budget constraints, and there would be no tendency for the situation to alter until such time as the Government changed its policies. Note that, if the Government were not to tax or distribute its proceeds, the privately-held stock of money would alter over time, and all other prices could adjust relative to the fixed price until all excess demands were again zero.

where $\quad \dfrac{\partial \hat{E}_i}{\partial p_j} = \dfrac{\partial E_i}{\partial p_j} + \dfrac{\partial \hat{E}_i}{\partial M^*} \dfrac{\partial M^*}{\partial p_j}$, $i = 1, 2$ $\qquad$ and $\qquad \dfrac{\partial \hat{E}_i}{\partial M} > 0$

It is readily seen that both terms of $\dfrac{\partial \hat{E}_i}{\partial p_i}$ are negative. However, the sign of $\dfrac{\partial \hat{E}_i}{\partial p_j}$ is indeterminate without further assumptions, since its first term is positive and its second negative. It will be assumed, at this point, that both cross-partial derivatives are positive. Below, consideration will be given to the effects of relaxing this assumption.

2.1 *Effects on the trade balance and the money supply*
We wish to ascertain the effects on the trade balance and the price of home goods of a change in the exchange rate or the money supply. Totally differentiating Equation (2.1)

$$dB \equiv -dE_1 = - \frac{\partial \hat{E}_1}{\partial p_1} dR - \frac{\partial \hat{E}_1}{\partial p_2} dp_2 - \frac{\partial \hat{E}_1}{\partial M} dM \quad (2.2)$$

$$0 = \frac{\partial \hat{E}_2}{\partial p_1} dR + \frac{\partial \hat{E}_2}{\partial p_2} dp_2 + \frac{\partial \hat{E}_2}{\partial M} dM$$

Taking a change in the price of foreign exchange first, and setting $dM = 0$

$$dp_2 = \frac{\dfrac{\partial \hat{E}_2}{\partial p_1} dR}{-\dfrac{\partial \hat{E}_2}{\partial p_2}} \quad (2.3)$$

The price of home goods rises with an increase in the price of foreign exchange. From the homogeneity properties of the system

$$p_2 = \frac{\dfrac{\partial \hat{E}_2}{\partial p_1} R + \dfrac{\partial \hat{E}_2}{\partial M} M}{-\dfrac{\partial \hat{E}_2}{\partial p_2}} \quad (2.4)$$

Dividing Equation (2.3) by Equation (2.4) yields

$$\frac{dp_2}{p_2} = \frac{\dfrac{\partial \hat{E}_2}{\partial p_1} dR}{\dfrac{\partial \hat{E}_2}{\partial p_1} R + \dfrac{\partial \hat{E}_2}{\partial M} M} < \frac{dR}{R} \qquad (2.5)$$

Thus, the price of home goods rises, but proportionately less than the exchange rate. Hence, the price of home goods relative to that of traded goods declines with an increase in the price of foreign exchange if the money supply is kept constant. This result was obtained by Pearce [7]. It follows, therefore, that on any index, the price level will change in the same direction as any alteration in the exchange rate, but by proportionately less. The smaller the proportionate increase in home goods prices, the smaller will be the once-and-for-all increase in the price level accompanying devaluation.

The fact that devaluation will typically result in an increase in the domestic price level is usually taken as an argument against devaluation. In a sense, however, the increase in the absolute price of home goods can be interpreted as the nullification of repressed inflation of the past occurring under a fixed exchange rate system. This can be seen by solving Equations (2.2) for the change in home goods prices that will result from a change in the money supply under a fixed exchange rate. Setting $dR = 0$,

$$dp_2 = \frac{\dfrac{\partial \hat{E}_2}{\partial M} dM}{-\dfrac{\partial \hat{E}_2}{\partial p_2}}, \quad \frac{dp_2}{p_2} = \frac{\dfrac{\partial \hat{E}_2}{\partial M} dM}{\dfrac{\partial \hat{E}_2}{\partial p_1} R + \dfrac{\partial \hat{E}_1}{\partial M} M} < \frac{dM}{M} \qquad (2.6)$$

That is, at a fixed exchange rate, the price of home goods will increase with an increase in the money supply, but less than proportionately. Stated another way, increasing the money supply at a fixed exchange rate lowers the relative price of traded goods, and therefore, the price level will increase less than proportionately with changes in the money supply. The smaller the proportionate change in home goods prices resulting from a 1 per cent increase in the money supply, the larger will be the proportionate increase in home goods prices resulting from a 1 per cent increase in the price of foreign exchange, and conversely. The sum of the percentage changes in home goods prices in response to a 1 per cent change each in the money supply and in the exchange rate must sum to unity.[8]

The symmetry of money supply and exchange rate changes can now be seen. There is always a decrease in the money supply which will result in exactly the same relative price of home goods, and values of other real variables, as a given increase in the price of foreign exchange.

At the limit, in a perfectly open economy (no home goods) with fixed exchange rates, the domestic price level will be invariant with respect to money supply changes. At the other extreme, in a perfectly closed economy, the price level will move with the money supply. Between these limits, the price-level effects of a money supply change will be smaller, the more open the economy, whilst the change in the relative price of traded to home goods will be greater, the more closed the economy.

We now turn to the effects of changes in either parameter on the trade balance. With a composite traded good, the trade balance, B, measured in units of foreign currency, is $-q_1 E_1$. With foreign prices initialised at unity and constant, $dB = -dE_1$. Solving Equations (2.2) for dE_1 yields

$$dB = \frac{\left[\dfrac{\partial \hat{E}_2}{\partial p_2}\dfrac{\partial \hat{E}_1}{\partial p_1} - \dfrac{\partial \hat{E}_1}{\partial p_2}\dfrac{\partial \hat{E}_2}{\partial p_1}\right] dR + \left[\dfrac{\partial \hat{E}_2}{\partial p_2}\dfrac{\partial \hat{E}_1}{\partial M} - \dfrac{\partial \hat{E}_1}{\partial p_2}\dfrac{\partial \hat{E}_2}{\partial M}\right] dM}{-\dfrac{\partial \hat{E}_2}{\partial p_2}}$$

(2.7)

The denominator is unequivocally positive. Hence, for the trade balance to improve with an increase in the price of foreign exchange,

$$\frac{\partial \hat{E}_2}{\partial p_2}\frac{\partial \hat{E}_1}{\partial p_1} - \frac{\partial \hat{E}_1}{\partial p_2}\frac{\partial \hat{E}_2}{\partial p_1} > 0$$

But this is necessary for any equilibrium to exist in the first

[8] This suggests a possible way of estimating the change in home goods' prices that would result from devaluation. If one could estimate and correctly identify the response of home goods' prices to changes in the money supply, one could then predict the effect of a change in the exchange rate on home goods' prices.

place.[9] The trade balance unequivocally deteriorates with an increase in the money supply.

2.2 *Expenditures or relative prices?*
The relationship between the expenditure-absorption approach and the relative-price approach to analyses of devaluation and/or trade imbalances should now be obvious.

A payments deficit equilibrium can exist only when desired cash balances are less than the money supply; likewise, a deficit equilibrium can exist only when the relative price of home goods is too high. For, at the zero-deficit equilibrium price of home goods, there would (with an excess supply of money) exist an excess demand for home goods; and, at the trade-deficit equilibrium price of home goods, there would exist an excess supply of home goods in the absence of an excess supply of money.

Conversely, a trade deficit can be eliminated only by reducing the excess supply of money *and* lowering the relative price of home goods. For, if relative prices remain unaltered, but the excess supply of money is eliminated, there would be a disequilibrium (with an excess supply of home goods and an excess demand for traded goods). Likewise, if the relative price of home goods were lowered with the excess demand for money unaltered, there would remain an excess demand for traded goods *and* home goods.

[9] This can be seen by using the homogeneity property, that

$$\frac{\partial \hat{E}_1}{\partial p_1} R + \frac{\partial \hat{E}_1}{\partial p_2} p_2 + \frac{\partial \hat{E}_1}{\partial M} M = 0$$

$$\frac{\partial \hat{E}_2}{\partial p_1} R + \frac{\partial \hat{E}_2}{\partial p_2} p_2 + \frac{\partial \hat{E}_2}{\partial M} M = 0$$

Solving for R and p_2 in terms of M yields

$$\frac{R}{M} = \frac{-\dfrac{\partial \hat{E}_1}{\partial M}\dfrac{\partial \hat{E}_2}{\partial p_2} + \dfrac{\partial \hat{E}_2}{\partial M}\dfrac{\partial \hat{E}_1}{\partial p_2}}{\dfrac{\partial \hat{E}_1}{\partial p_1}\dfrac{\partial \hat{E}_2}{\partial p_2} - \dfrac{\partial \hat{E}_1}{\partial p_2}\dfrac{\partial \hat{E}_2}{\partial p_1}} \; ; \qquad p_2 = \frac{-\dfrac{\partial \hat{E}_1}{\partial p_1}\dfrac{\partial \hat{E}_2}{\partial M} + \dfrac{\partial \hat{E}_2}{\partial p_2}\dfrac{\partial \hat{E}_1}{\partial M}}{\dfrac{\partial \hat{E}_1}{\partial p_1}\dfrac{\partial \hat{E}_2}{\partial p_2} - \dfrac{\partial \hat{E}_1}{\partial p_2}\dfrac{\partial \hat{E}_2}{\partial p_1}}$$

The denominator must be positive for a solution to exist at positive prices, and hence

$$\frac{\partial \hat{E}_1}{\partial p_1}\frac{\partial \hat{E}_2}{\partial p_2} > \frac{\partial \hat{E}_1}{\partial p_2}\frac{\partial \hat{E}_2}{\partial p_1}$$

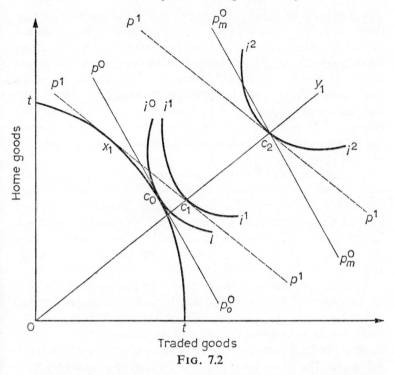

Traded goods

Fig. 7.2

Devaluation, proximately, raises the absolute price of traded goods. As such, it raises the price level, thereby increasing desired cash balances, and lowering the *relative* price of home goods. Hence, it is simultaneously, in Johnson's [2] terminology, an expenditure-reducing policy (via the increase in desired cash balances) *and* an expenditure-switching policy (via the decrease in the relative price of home goods).

Likewise, reducing the money supply (in a world of flexible prices) reduces expenditures, and lowers the absolute, and therefore also the relative price of home goods. Monetary policy, therefore, is also expenditure-switching *and* expenditure-reducing.

The underlying mechanism can perhaps be better understood with the help of Figure 7.2. The curve *tt* represents the transformation curve between home and traded goods. There will exist a community indifference curve, such as i^0i^0 at which producers will choose to produce the combination of outputs c^0 at prices p^0p^0, while consumers choose to consume c^0; trade, therefore, will be balanced. To construct a trade-deficit equilibrium, consider prices such as p^1p^1. Producers will choose the output combination x_1. At those relative prices, if consumers maximised subject to their budget constraints (with zero excess supply of money), they would select a consumption point such as c^1; hence, there would be an excess demand for traded goods and an excess supply of home goods: with no excess cash balances, the prices p^1 are not an equilibrium. But now draw the income-consumption line associated with prices p^1 (labelled oy^1 in Figure 7.2).

An excess supply of money shifts the budget constraint to the right. If the excess money supply is the horizontal distance between c^2 and x^1, prices p^1 can be an equilibrium in the sense defined above. The excess money supply is equal to the trade deficit (again, the horizontal distance between c^2 and x^1), and the quantity of home goods demanded equals the quantity supplied.

At prices p^0, but with excess money in the amount of c^2 less x^1, there would be a trade deficit, but also an excess demand for home goods. At prices p^1, without the excess money supply, there would be a trade deficit, and an excess supply of home goods. Hence, between equilibrium positions, *both* relative prices and the relation of desired to actual cash balances must change. With price flexibility and full employment, the difference between reducing the money supply and increasing the price of foreign exchange lies only in the determination of the absolute domestic price level; all real variables of the system will be the same under the two policies.

2.3 *Perverse behaviour*

The above results were derived on the basis of assumptions made about the signs of the partial derivatives in the excess demand functions (2.1). A wide range of literature exists as to cases where altering the exchange rate might lead to perverse effects on the trade balance. Much of this discussion has centred upon changes in the terms of trade between imports and exports consequent upon devaluation, a possibility ignored in the model presented here. An important empirical question, of course, is the relative magnitude of home goods-traded goods price changes contrasted with likely export-import price changes.

If a decline in real income and consequent reduction in expenditure is the primary effect of devaluation, terms-of-trade changes are likely to be of second-order importance.

It is therefore important to inquire whether perverse behaviour of the trade balance can occur in the money-home goods model. That it is possible can be seen by considering, for example, the outcome if home goods are inferior goods.

Several implications of such perversity can be derived, and are empirically observable. First, regardless of the signs of the various partial derivatives, the signs of the change in the trade balance with respect to exchange rate changes must be opposite to the sign with respect to changes in the money supply, since proportionate changes in both parameters will lead to a zero change in the trade balance. More generally, therefore, and without any assumptions about the signs of the partial derivatives,

(1) An increase in the price of foreign exchange will result in a deterioration in the trade balance if and only if an increase in the money supply will lead to an improvement in the trade balance.

This can be seen as follows. Substituting for p from Equation (2.4) in (2.8) yields:

$$\left(\frac{\partial \hat{E}_1}{\partial p_1} - \frac{\frac{\partial \hat{E}_1}{\partial p_2} \frac{\partial \hat{E}_2}{\partial p_1}}{\frac{\partial \hat{E}_2}{\partial p_2}} \right) R = -\left(\frac{\partial \hat{E}_1}{\partial M} - \frac{\frac{\partial \hat{E}_1}{\partial p_2} \frac{\partial \hat{E}_2}{\partial M}}{\frac{\partial \hat{E}_2}{\partial p_2}} \right) M \quad (2.8)$$

Algebraic manipulation of (2.7) gives

$$dB = \left(-\frac{\partial \hat{E}_1}{\partial p_1} + \frac{\frac{\partial \hat{E}_1}{\partial p_2} \frac{\partial \hat{E}_2}{\partial p_1}}{\frac{\partial \hat{E}_2}{\partial p_2}} \right) R \frac{dR}{R} - \left(\frac{\partial \hat{E}_1}{\partial M} - \frac{\frac{\partial \hat{E}_1}{\partial p_2} \frac{\partial \hat{E}_2}{\partial M}}{\frac{\partial \hat{E}_2}{\partial p_2}} \right) M \frac{dM}{M}$$

$$= R \left(-\frac{\partial \hat{E}_1}{\partial p_1} + \frac{\frac{\partial \hat{E}_1}{\partial p_2} \frac{\partial \hat{E}_2}{\partial p_1}}{\frac{\partial \hat{E}_2}{\partial p_2}} \right) \left(\frac{dR}{R} - \frac{dM}{M} \right)$$

$$= -M\left(\frac{\partial \hat{E}_1}{\partial M} - \frac{\dfrac{\partial \hat{E}_1}{\partial p_2}\dfrac{\partial \hat{E}_2}{\partial M}}{\dfrac{\partial \hat{E}_2}{\partial p_2}}\right)\left(\frac{dM}{M} - \frac{dR}{R}\right) \qquad (2.9)$$

Q.E.D.

Abandoning the assumptions made with regard to the signs of the relevant partial derivatives yields some other results. It was noted earlier that $\dfrac{\partial \hat{E}_2}{\partial p_1}$ might be negative, due presumably to a strong negative real balance effect of an increase in the price of traded goods. If this were the case, the question arises whether the price level could decline as a result of devaluation, in the absence of assumptions about the signs of the partial derivatives. While such a result cannot be directly ruled out, the following results are useful:

(2) The desired level of money holdings will increase with an increase in the price of foreign exchange if and only if the price level increases. This follows directly from the properties of the demand-for-money function.

(3) The trade balance will improve with an increase in the price of foreign exchange if and only if the desired level of money holdings increases. This follows directly from Walras' Law, and the nature of the budget constraint.

(4) If the price of home goods will decline with an increase in the price of foreign exchange, their price will increase more than proportionately with an increase in the money supply (from Equation 2.6).

Combining propositions (1), (2) and (3),

(5) The trade balance will fail to improve with an increase in the price of foreign exchange, the money supply held constant, if and only if the price level will decline with devaluation.

The assertion that devaluation would fail to improve the trade balance, therefore, implies that domestic inflation would improve it. These implications are empirically testable, and can limit controversy about the efficacy of exchange rate changes as instruments for righting trade imbalance. Needless to say, however, if devaluation is accompanied by a sufficiently large increase in the money supply, the trade balance will deteriorate.

2.4 Conclusions

A model incorporating home goods and money for analysis of determinants of the trade balance has been developed. It has been shown that, even under conditions of full employment, changes in the money supply or the exchange rate will affect the community's real expenditure and relative prices. Relative price changes and changes in the excess supply of money are both components of any comparative statics shifts.

Moreover, if the trade balance will not improve with devaluation, it must follow that increasing the money supply and domestic price level will do so. Whilst the direct proposition that home goods might be inferior seems plausible, the general equilibrium implications for the rest of the system do not.

References

[1] HAHN, FRANK. 'The Balance of Payments in a Monetary Economy', *Review of Economic Studies*, XXVI (February 1959) 110–25.

[2] JOHNSON, HARRY G. 'Towards a General Theory of the Balance of Payments', chap. VI of his *International Trade and Economic Growth*, Cambridge, Mass.: Harvard University Press, 1958.

[3] KEMP, MURRAY C. 'The Balance of Payments and the Terms of Trade in Relation to Financial Controls', *Review of Economic Studies*, XXXVII (January 1970) 25–31.

[4] KEMP, MURRAY C. 'The Rate of Exchange, the Terms of Trade and the Balance of Payments in Fully Employed Economies', *International Economic Review*, III (September 1962) 314–27.

[5] KOMIYA, RYUTARO, 'Non-Traded Goods and the Pure Theory of International Trade', *International Economic Review*, VIII (June 1967) 132–52.

[6] NEGISHI, TAKASHI. 'Approaches to the Analysis of Devaluation', *International Economic Review*, IX (June 1968) 218–27.

[7] PEARCE, I. F. 'The Problem of the Balance of Payments', *International Economic Review*, II (January 1961) 1–28.

8 A Two-Country Model of the Gold Standard

JAY H. LEVIN*

The objective of this paper is to construct and analyse a two-country short-run model of the gold standard. Wages and prices respond flexibly in both countries; gold flows in reaction to payments imbalance at the mint par exchange rate; and the authorities refrain completely from sterilising these gold movements. The model and two of its variants are similar to one introduced by Metzler in a recently published article, but the conclusions here differ from his in several respects. Moreover, this paper considers two important disturbances not discussed in the Metzler article and extends his coverage of other disturbances.

1. The Basic Model

The basic model consists of five equations that yield a solution to the domestic and foreign price levels and interest rates and the distribution of the world monetary gold stock. This system can be truncated into a three equation model that determines the two interest rates and the terms of trade. A monetary disturbance will have no effect on the equilibrium values of these latter variables because the remaining two equations describe equilibrium in the monetary sectors of the two countries. The following notation will be used:

S = domestic saving in constant domestic currency
I = real investment expenditures on domestic output
X = volume of domestic exports
M = volume of domestic imports
H = open market portfolio of home central bank
R = domestic monetary gold stock

* Associate Professor Wayne State University.

L = home demand for money in constant domestic currency
K = domestic currency value of net capital inflow into home country
$\hat{K}$ = net capital inflow into home country in constant domestic currency
W = world stock of monetary gold
B = domestic trade surplus in constant domestic currency
P = domestic price level
r = domestic interest rate
T = terms of trade, (P/P^*)
α = ratio of domestic bank reserves to domestic money supply

Asterisks designate corresponding variables in the foreign country. The symbols σ, ϕ and θ are shift parameters. The model is the following:

$$S = I(r, \sigma) + X(T) - (1/T)M(T, \phi) \tag{1}$$

$$H + R = \alpha PL(r) \tag{2}$$

$$S^* = I^*(r^*) + M(T, \phi) - TX(T) \tag{3}$$

$$H^* + W - R = \alpha^* P^* L^*(r^*) \tag{4}$$

$$PX(T) - P^*M(T, \phi) + P\hat{K}(r, r^*, \theta) = 0 \tag{5}$$

where $I_r, X_P, M_{P^*}, L_r, I_{r^*}^*, I_{r^*}^*, \hat{K}_P, \hat{K}_{r^*} < 0;$[1]

$X_{P^*}, M_P, \hat{K}_{P^*}, \hat{K}_r > 0;$

$X_{P^*} = -X_P; M_{P^*} = -M_P; \hat{K}_{r^*} = -\hat{K}_r; \hat{K}_{P^*} = -\hat{K}_P;$

and $M_\phi = \hat{K}_\theta = I_\sigma = 1.$

H, H^* and W are exogenous variables.

Equation (1) describes equilibrium in the home country's market for goods and services. Notice that the volume of imports must be deflated by the terms of trade because the variables are expressed in constant domestic currency. Any effect of the terms of trade on the volume of real saving has been ignored. In addition, it is assumed that only trade in consumption goods occurs with the result that investment expenditures

---

[1] X_Y refers to the partial derivative of X with respect to Y.

on domestic output are independent of the terms of trade.[2] Equation (3) is analogous to Equation (1). There the volume of home exports is multiplied by the terms of trade since the variables are expressed in constant foreign currency.

Equation (2) describes equilibrium in the home country's monetary sector. The demand for bank reserves is taken simply to be a constant fraction of the nominal demand for money. The stock of bank reserves equals the sum of the central bank's open market portfolio and its gold holdings. Equation (4) is analogous to Equation (2).

Equation (5) describes Balance of Payments equilibrium. It may be derived by first noticing that the nominal value of net capital imports, K, depends on the two price levels. A rise in the domestic price level increases the nominal value of domestic saving. This nominal increase in portfolio growth is distributed among domestic and foreign assets, and the latter is equivalent to a larger gross capital outflow. A rise in the foreign price level likewise increases the gross capital inflow. Thus, the net capital inflow in value terms may be written $P\hat{K}(r, r^*, \theta, 1/T)$ since it is homogeneous of degree one in P and P^*. However, the terms of trade effect on $\hat{K}$ is omitted in Equation (5) in accordance with Metzler's treatment but will be reintroduced in Section 4. Observe finally that only the pure flow formulation of capital movements is used in Equation (5). This is an oversimplification, and a more realistic approach will be attempted in Section 5.

2. Balance of Payments Adjustment

Equations (1), (3) and (5) are sufficient to determine equilibrium values of the two interest rates and the terms of trade. In order to deduce and understand the changes in these variables that occur when the Balance of Payments initially is in disequilibrium, it will be convenient to simplify the truncated model as

[2] In this respect the model differs from the absorption approach, which postulates import demand to depend on the level but not composition of expenditures. The real income effect of a change in the terms of trade is assumed to alter the demand for imports and domestic goods in the same proportion as does a change in domestic interest rates [1, chap. 15 and 2, 77–91; 152–53]. The most general approach, suggested in Section 6, would include an import content of investment expenditures different from the import content of consumption expenditures.

follows:

$$S = I(r, \sigma) + B(T, \phi) \qquad (1a)$$

$$S^* = I^*(r^*) - TB(T, \phi) \qquad (3a)$$

$$B(T, \phi) + \hat{K}(r, r^*, \theta) = 0 \qquad (5a)$$

where $B = X(T) - (1/T)M(T, \phi)$, the domestic trade surplus in constant domestic currency. In the rest of this paper the terms 'trade surplus' and 'net capital inflow' will refer to B and $\hat{K}$ respectively.

Consider an initial position of payments deficit for the home country. An increase in the trade surplus, produced by worsened terms of trade,[3] requires higher interest rates at home and lower interest rates abroad[4] to preserve goods market equilibrium in both countries, as seen from inspection of Equations (1a) and (3a). At the same time the widening of the interest differential, $r - r^*$, enlarges the net capital inflow. Clearly, the gold flow adjustment mechanism eliminates the deficit by improving both current and capital accounts through its effect on the terms of trade and the two interest rates. In particular by introducing F, defined as the domestic country's Balance of Payments surplus, into the right hand side of Equation (5a), differentiation of the above model yields

$$dr/dF = \frac{I_{r*}^* B_T}{\Delta} > 0;$$

$$dr^*/dF = \frac{-I_r(B_T + B)}{\Delta} < 0;$$

$$dT/dF = \frac{-I_r I_{r*}^*}{\Delta} < 0$$

where $\Delta = I_{r*}^* B_T(\hat{K}_r - I_r) + I_r \hat{K}_r(B_T + B) > 0$. These results suggest three important special cases. First, if home investment

---

[3] B_T is assumed negative. An equivalent condition under a pegged rate system is that a devaluation at fixed outputs and price levels improves the nominal trade balance valued in domestic currency.

[4] $(B_T + B)$ is assumed negative, where T is normalised at unity. An equivalent condition under a pegged rate system is that a devaluation at fixed outputs and price levels improves the nominal trade balance valued in foreign currency.

demand is completely interest inelastic, only one trade surplus is compatible with goods market equilibrium there. As a result the terms of trade must remain unaffected, and goods market equilibrium abroad requires a constant foreign interest rate as seen from inspection of Equation (3a). The gold flow mechanism eliminates the deficit by raising the home interest rate and improving only the capital account. In the same way completely interest inelastic foreign investment demand implies that the mechanism works solely through a lower foreign interest rate. To generalise, the ratio of the interest rate changes is inversely proportional to the ratio of interest sensitivities of investment demand. Moreover, the larger these sensitivities, the greater the adjustment in the current relative to the capital account because a given increase in the trade surplus requires a smaller interest rate change for goods market equilibrium and consequently a smaller improvement in the capital account. Finally, we may consider the case of perfect capital mobility $(\hat{K}_r = \infty)$ in which financial assets at home and abroad are regarded as such nearly perfect substitutes that gold flows cannot affect the interest differential between them. The slightest flow of gold, producing a negligible rise in r and fall in r^*, stimulates a capital flow sufficient to erase the deficit.[5] More generally the greater the degree of capital mobility, the greater the adjustment in the capital relative to the current account and the smaller the required change in the real variables, r, r^* and T.

Another important aspect of the adjustment mechanism is the direction and size of gold flows and price level changes necessary for removal of a payments imbalance. To determine how these variables are affected we differentiate the full model of Equations (1)–(5) with respect to F, the home country's payments surplus, introduced into the right hand side of Equation (5). First, we may expect that gold is redistributed to the surplus country, as verified by

$$dR/dF = \frac{\alpha\alpha^* L I_r [L_{r^*}^* (B_T + B) - L^* I_{r^*}^*] + \alpha\alpha^* L^* I_{r^*}^* L_r B_T}{\Delta'} < 0$$

---

[5] Actual gold flows may still play a role in the initial impact effect of disturbances discussed in the next section. Their function there is to preserve interest rate equality throughout the world.

where $\Delta' = (\alpha L + \alpha^* L^*) \Delta$.[6] The size of this gold movement declines with the degree of capital mobility because a given gold outflow with its impact on the two interest rates increases the net capital inflow more as K_r rises. On the other hand, the gold movement increases with increased interest sensitivity of the demand for money in either country. The reason is that a given gold flow, which changes bank reserves in the two countries by equal but opposite amounts, has a smaller effect on the interest differential and terms of trade the larger L_r or L_{r*}^* is. Finally, higher ratios of bank reserves to money supplies, α and α^*, increase the gold movement by diminishing the effect of a given gold flow on money supplies and hence on interest rates and the terms of trade.[7]

It may be surprising, perhaps, that elimination of the deficit need not involve lower prices at home accompanied by higher prices abroad,[8] as verified by

$$dP/dF = \frac{-\alpha I_{r*}^* L_r B_T + \alpha^* I_r L_{r*}^* (B_T + B) - \alpha^* L^* I_r I_{r*}^*}{\Delta'} \gtrless 0 ;$$

$$dP^*/dF = \frac{-\alpha I_{r*}^* L_r B_T + \alpha^* I_r L_{r*}^* (B_T + B) + \alpha L I_r I_{r*}^*}{\Delta'} \gtrless 0 .$$

[6] This gold redistribution implies a stable dynamic adjustment process, at least in the simplest case of instantaneous adjustment in the goods and money markets of the two countries. A decline in bank reserves in the deficit country and rise in the surplus country at the rate dR/dt ($= F$), produced by a gold outflow from the former, instantaneously reduces the imbalance by $F(dF/dR)$. Thus, the gold flow declines exponentially at the rate dF/dR, which depends among other things on the degree of capital mobility, the interest elasticities of the demand for money, and the ratios of bank reserves to money supplies, as described in the text. For a discussion of the possibility of instability in the single country case when the internal markets do not adjust instantaneously, see Mundell, [5, Note 8].

[7] This means that the adjustment process is slowed by higher ratios of bank reserves to money supplies as pointed out by Meade, [1, 185]. Conversely, if open market operations are used to reinforce the effect of gold flows on the money supply, the required gold movement declines, and the adjustment process accelerates.

[8] Although Metzler neglects this possibility, inspection of the formulas below still confirms his argument [3, pp. 483–84] that 'other things being equal, most of the price adjustment will fall upon the country which has the smaller elasticity of demand for real cash balances'. By the same token, as Meade argues [1, p. 185], *ceteris paribus*, the country with the lower ratio of bank reserves to the money supply will bear the larger burden of price adjustment. Finally, other things being equal, the country with the higher interest sensitivity of investment expenditures will undergo more of the price adjustment.

In fact, three cases are possible, as shown in Figure 8.1. In this diagram the Balance of Payments equilibrium ray is drawn for the terms of trade and implicit interest rates consistent with initial payments balance and goods market equilibrium in both countries. Its slope is normalised at unity. The Balance of Payments deficit ray is drawn for some particular higher terms of trade, corresponding to which r is lower and r^* higher for goods market equilibria. Along this ray the home country is experiencing an initial payments deficit measured in constant domestic currency units. It is also possible to derive a locus of

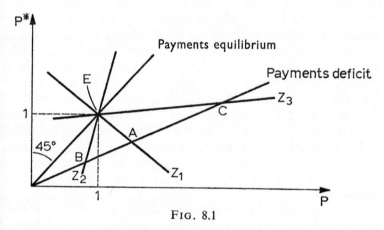

FIG. 8.1

combinations of the two price levels consistent with a given level of world bank reserves and equilibrium in the goods and monetary sectors of the two countries.[9] Its slope is the ratio of dP^*/dF to dP/dF because the redistribution of gold reserves that eliminates the payments imbalance does not alter the world total of bank reserves. In Figure 8.1 are drawn three such loci, Z_1, Z_2 and Z_3, intersecting the Balance of Payments deficit ray at points A, B and C respectively. The adjustment process can be viewed as a movement along these loci to point E, where the final price levels are normalised at unity.

If the demand for money is highly interest inelastic in both countries, the iso world bank reserve locus has a negative slope, such as Z_1. At point A the loss of gold by the home country raises its interest rate and creates deficient demand that reduces

[9] This locus is obtained from equations (1)–(4) by differentiating with respect to R to produce dP/dR and dP^*/dR, which yield dP in terms of dP^*.

the price level. The reverse occurs abroad. In fact, the ratio of the percentage price level changes equals the reciprocal of the ratio of the two countries' bank reserves, and the world price level rises or falls as the ratio of bank reserves to national income at home exceeds or falls short of the foreign ratio.[10] On the other hand, suppose that *ceteris paribus* the demand for money is highly interest elastic at home. Now the slope of the iso world bank reserve locus exceeds unity, as in the case of Z_2. In addition to the *direct price effects* of the bank reserve changes, a *cross price effect* operates in this case, for the rise in P^* increases the demand for the home country's exports and possibly demand for its own consumption goods. As long as the demand for money at home has some interest elasticity, these demand shifts tend to drive up domestic prices. In fact, the larger this interest elasticity, the greater is this cross price effect and the smaller is the direct price effect. In the case of Z_2 the former dominates, and prices rise at home as well as abroad. Similarly, a highly elastic demand for money abroad *ceteris paribus* corresponds to an iso world bank reserve locus with positive slope less than unity, as in the case of Z_3. The fall in domestic prices produces a cross price effect, and because of its dominance the gold flow entails lower prices in both countries.

To summarise, a higher interest elasticity of the demand for money at home tends to reduce the direct price effect at home and consequently the cross price effect on P^*. A higher interest elasticity of the demand for money abroad tends to reduce the direct price effect abroad and consequently the cross price effect on P. Thus, dP/dF and dP^*/dF are directly related to $|L_r|$ and inversely related to $|L_{r^*}^*|$. Similarly, because a given gold flow has a smaller impact on money supplies the higher the ratios of bank reserves to money supplies, dP/dF and dP^*/dF are directly related to α and inversely related to α^*.

Two final points concerning the price changes are worth making. First, high interest sensitivity of investment demand

---

[10] This is strictly true only for $L_r = L_{r^*}^* = 0$. With fixed outputs in each country, Y and Y^*, the world price level rises or falls with world national income. The criterion for a higher world price level is therefore $Y\,dP + Y^*\,dP^* > 0$ or $(dP^*/dP) < -Y/Y^*$. Since $dP^*/dP = -\alpha L/\alpha^* L^*$, the statement in the text follows. See also Mundell. [4, pp. 195–98].

at home makes a price drop there more likely by increasing the direct price effect, and for the same reason high interest sensitivity of foreign investment demand increases the probability of a price rise abroad. Secondly, the absolute price changes in both countries decline with the degree of capital mobility since, as shown above, the gold movement declines with increasing values of this parameter.

3. Disturbances to Equilibrium

Let us now consider a number of disturbances, denoted by changes in the shift parameters, σ, ϕ and θ or the exogenous variables H, H^* and W, and analyse their effects on the endogenous variables r, r^*, T, R, P and P^*. It will sometimes prove convenient to use the following two techniques. T_1: Assume that despite the disturbance the initial trade surplus is maintained along with goods market equilibrium in the two countries by means of changes in r, r^*, and/or T. Since removal of the ensuing *hypothetical* payments imbalance requires further movement in these variables as discussed in Section 2, it is possible to infer their actual net change caused by the disturbance. T_2: Assume that the goods and money markets of the two countries adjust instantaneously to the disturbance prior to any gold flows. This adjustment may be termed the *initial impact effect* (hereafter I.I. Effect).[11] By determining whether a payments surplus or deficit will arise, we can ascertain the direction of gold redistribution. This knowledge along with information about the overall interest rate changes from T_1 and the requirement of monetary sector equilibria enables us to determine the price level changes.

1. *Change in* θ

An increased capital inflow at the existing interest differential, caused perhaps by a change in asset preferences, produces an initial external surplus for the home country without affecting internal balance in either country. The adjustment in the

---

[11] The actual dynamics may be considerably more complicated than assumed here. Metzler's verbal discussion, for example, presupposes relatively slow speeds of adjustment in the two countries' goods markets.

endogenous variables has been discussed earlier in Section 2 for the case of an initial home deficit.

2. *Change in H, H*, or W*

A monetary disturbance in either country, such as an open market operation, a shift in the demand for money, or an increase in the world stock of gold, initially creates excess demand for or supply of world bank reserves. Since a monetary disturbance cannot alter the equilibrium interest rates and terms of trade, the excess demand or supply is relieved simply by equiproportional price changes at home and abroad. For example, under T_2 an open market purchase, dH, in the domestic country reduces interest rates temporarily and creates excess demand, causing domestic prices to rise. The cross price effect induces a proportionately smaller rise in foreign prices, which pulls up the foreign interest rate by way of an increased demand for money.[12] Consequently, the I.I. Effect is a reduction in the trade surplus and net capital inflow, stimulating a gold outflow. From the analysis of the adjustment mechanism it is clear that the gold flow produces a worsening of the terms of trade, higher r and lower r^* and, in fact, ceases only when these variables are restored to their initial levels. Bank reserves and prices in both countries will have risen in the same proportion as the increase in world bank reserves, $dH/(H + H^* + W)$. By similar reasoning it can be shown that an increase in the world gold stock is distributed in the two countries in the same proportion as their shares of world bank reserves and that prices in both rise in the same proportion as the increase in world bank reserves, $dW/(H + H^* + W)$.

3. *Change in σ*

Under T_1 a purely internal increase in demand for domestic output, such as a domestic investment boom, requires a higher r to maintain goods market equilibrium at home. As a result of a larger net capital inflow a payments surplus now arises, the removal of which by the adjustment mechanism involves a

---

[12] The I.I. Effect on the foreign price level must be less than on the domestic price level because equilibrium in the foreign goods market at a higher foreign interest rate can prevail only if the terms of trade improve.

higher foreign interest rate and improved terms of trade. From the change in the latter we may infer that the trade surplus has become smaller in the new equilibrium. Since external balance requires a larger net capital inflow, the overall rise in the domestic interest rate must exceed the rise in the foreign interest rate.[13]

Under T_2 the investment boom inflates domestic prices and induces the domestic interest rate to rise by increasing the demand for money. The cross price effect pushes up foreign prices and thereby induces a rise in the foreign interest rate. Although the terms of trade must show an improvement,[14] reducing the trade surplus, the interest differential may widen or narrow, depending among other things on the interest sensitivity of the demand for money in the two countries. In short the home country may experience either a deficit or surplus, causing an outflow or inflow of gold.[15] If gold flows abroad, equilibrium in the foreign monetary sector at a higher interest rate, deduced from T_1, requires a net rise in foreign prices. The improvement in the terms of trade, also deduced from T_1, implies higher domestic prices too. If gold flows to the home country, equilibrium in the domestic monetary sector at a higher interest rate requires a net rise in home prices. However, foreign prices may rise or fall.[16]

[13] In the special case of zero capital mobility payments remain balanced despite the initial rise in the home interest rate. The foreign interest rate and terms of trade are unaffected. The terms of trade also remain fixed if the foreign interest sensitivity of investment expenditures is zero, as discussion of the adjustment mechanism in Section 2 indicated.

[14] See Note 12.   [15] Differentiating the basic model yields

$$dR/d\sigma = \frac{\alpha\alpha^* L^* I_{r*}^* (L_r B_T - L\hat{K}_r) + \alpha\alpha^* \hat{K}_r (B_T + B)(LL_{r*}^* - L^* L_r)}{\Delta'} \lessgtr 0.$$

Meade [1, pp. 196–97 and 2, p. 79] seems to imply that the domestic country must lose gold.

[16] That domestic prices must rise may be verified from the basic model by

$$dP/d\sigma = \frac{\hat{K}_r[(B_T + B)(\alpha L_r + \alpha^* L_{r*}^*) - \alpha^* L^* I_{r*}^*] - \alpha B_T L_r I_{r*}^*}{\Delta'} > 0.$$

The ambiguity of the foreign price change is verified by

$$dP^*/d\sigma = \frac{\alpha I_{r*}^* (L\hat{K}_r - L_r B_T) + \hat{K}_r (B_T + B)(\alpha L_r + \alpha^* L_{r*}^*)}{\Delta'} \lessgtr 0.$$

In the special case of zero interest sensitivity of foreign investment expenditures, the failure of the terms of trade to change requires that foreign prices rise.

4. *Change in* ϕ

Under T_1 an increase in demand for imports by the home country at the expense of domestically produced consumption goods necessitates a deterioration in the terms of trade to preserve the initial trade balance. Thus, the foreign trade balance in constant foreign currency units, $-TB$, remains unchanged if trade is initially balanced, increases algebraically if the home trade balance is in surplus, and decreases algebraically if the home trade balance is in deficit. To preserve goods market equilibrium abroad at the initial home trade balance, r^* must remain constant in the first case, rise in the second and fall in the third. Consequently, the Balance of Payments remains in equilibrium in the first case, moves into deficit in the second, and moves into surplus in the third. In the second case the adjustment mechanism raises interest rates at home,[17] lowers them abroad and further worsens the terms of trade. Since the latter effect implies an expansion in the home trade surplus, external balance requires a smaller net capital inflow. In view of the rise in the home interest rate, the net increase in the foreign interest rate must be greater. In the third case the adjustment mechanism lowers interest rates at home,[18] raises them abroad and improves the terms of trade. Using an argument analogous to that employed in the case of initial home trade surplus, one can still infer a net drop in foreign interest rates. Moreover, goods market equilibrium abroad, in the face of a lower foreign interest rate and exogenous demand shift in favour of foreign exports, requires a net deterioration in the terms of trade. These conclusions are summarised in Table 8.1.[19]

In the case of initial trade balance under T_2 the import demand shift drives down domestic prices and lowers interest rates by reducing the demand for money. The opposite occurs

[17] In the special case of zero capital mobility the domestic interest rate does not rise because Balance of Payments equilibrium is maintained at the initial trade surplus.

[18] The domestic interest rate does not fall in the special case of zero capital mobility because Balance of Payments equilibrium prevails at the initial trade deficit.

[19] Metzler [3, pp. 477–78] argues that the two interest rates remain fixed, but he neglects the difference between the trade balance in constant domestic and constant foreign currency units that can only be ignored when trade is initially balanced.

TABLE 8.1. *Effect of a Rise in Home Import Demand on Equilibrium* r, r^*, *and* T

	$X = M$	$X > M$	$X < M$
r	No Effect	+	−
r^*	No Effect	+	−
T	−	−	−

abroad.[20] Since the lower interest rate at home must be offset by a trade deficit to preserve goods market equilibrium, and since the narrowing of the interest differential, $r - r^*$, induces a capital outflow, a payments deficit arises. Gold flows abroad until the original interest rates are restored, and the terms of trade deteriorate even further. With unchanged interest rates equilibrium in the two monetary sectors requires lower prices at home and higher prices abroad.

In the case of initial trade surplus the I.I. Effect again involves higher foreign prices and interest rates. Here, however, the cross price effects of the former may be sufficiently strong to reverse the opposite movement of prices and interest rates at home.[21] Should this occur, the trade surplus must increase to maintain goods market equilibrium at home. If the interest differential, $r - r^*$, widens at all or narrows only slightly, a payments surplus materialises. Thus, the direction of the gold movement is uncertain.[22] If gold flows abroad, equilibrium in the foreign monetary sector at a higher interest rate, deduced from T_1, requires higher foreign prices. However, domestic prices may rise or fall. If gold flows to the home country,

[20] The cross price effects cushion but do not reverse these price changes when trade is initially balanced. Movement to a trade deficit requires opposite changes in the two interest rates for goods market equilibrium in the two countries. The price level in each country must shift in the same direction as the interest rate to maintain monetary sector equilibrium.

[21] When the foreign interest rate rises, goods market equilibrium abroad requires the foreign trade deficit in constant foreign currency units, $TB(T, \phi)$ to contract. This is compatible with a larger trade surplus in constant domestic currency units, $B(T, \phi)$, provided the terms of trade deteriorate sufficiently. A larger B necessitates higher domestic interest rates for goods market equilibrium at home.

[22] Differentiating the basic model yields

$$dR/d\phi = \frac{\alpha\alpha^*(X - M)[LL_r^* I_r + \hat{K}_r(L^*L_r - LL_{r^*}^*)] - \alpha\alpha^* LL^*[I_r I_{r^*}^* - \hat{K}_r(I_r + I_*^*)]}{\Delta'} \lessgtr 0$$

when $X \neq M$.

domestic prices must rise for the analogous reason. The deterioration in the terms of trade implies an even greater proportionate price rise abroad.[23]

In the case of an initial trade deficit the I.I. Effect involves lower domestic prices and interest rates. In fact, the cross effect of the former may be strong enough to reverse the opposite movement of prices and interest rates abroad.[24] The trade deficit does increase to maintain goods market equilibrium at home, but if the interest differential widens sufficiently, a payments surplus emerges. Thus, gold may move in either direction. If gold flows abroad, equilibrium in the domestic monetary sector at a lower interest rate, deduced from T_1, requires lower prices at home, whereas foreign prices may rise or fall. If gold flows to the home country, foreign prices must fall for the analogous reason. The deterioration in the terms of trade implies a proportionately greater price fall at home.[25]

The above results are summarised in the following table.

TABLE 8.2. *Effect of a Rise in Home Import Demand on Equilibrium* P, P^*, *and* R

	$X = M$	$X > M$	$X < M$
P	−	− + +	− − −
P^*	+	+ + +	+ − −
R	−	− − +	− − +

[23] That foreign prices must rise regardless of the direction of gold flow is confirmed in the basic model by

$$dP^*/d\phi = \frac{(X - M)[\alpha^* L_{r^*}^*(I_r - \hat{K}_r) - \alpha L_r \hat{K}_r] + \alpha L[I_r I_{r^*}^* - \hat{K}_r(I_r + I_{r^*}^*)]}{\Delta'} > 0$$

if $X \geq M$.

[24] When the domestic interest rate falls, goods market equilibrium at home requires a larger trade deficit. This is compatible with a smaller foreign trade surplus in constant foreign currency units, $-TB(T, \phi)$, provided the terms of trade deteriorate sufficiently. In this event the foreign interest rate must fall to preserve goods market equilibrium abroad.

[25] That domestic prices must fall regardless of the direction of gold flows is verified in the basic model by

$$dP/d\phi = \frac{(X - M)[\alpha^* L_{r^*}^*(I_r - \hat{K}_r) - \alpha \hat{K}_r L_r] - \alpha^* L^*[I_r I_{r^*}^* - \hat{K}_r(I_r + I_{r^*}^*)]}{\Delta'} < 0$$

if $X \leq M$.

4. Terms of Trade Effect on Capital Flows

An improvement in the terms of trade reduces the net capital inflow, $\hat{K}$, by lowering the gross foreign capital inflow measured in constant domestic currency. In the removal of a deficit this effect supplements the widening of the interest differential in improving the capital account. As a result it cuts down the gold flow required to eliminate the deficit and thereby diminishes the absolute interest rate, price and terms of trade changes.

Only in the case of an import demand shift does this terms of trade effect modify the conclusions about disturbances to equilibrium. It remains true that an increase in demand for imports by the home country causes the terms of trade to deteriorate, for at the initial terms of trade r must fall and r^* rise to preserve goods market equilibrium in the two countries. Removal of the ensuing hypothetical deficit involves a worsening of the terms of trade. Now the actual capital inflow associated with the worsened terms of trade may be treated as an exogeneous shift in the $\hat{K}$ function in the basic model. By itself it would produce a payments surplus eliminated by a gold inflow. Thus, r is lower and r^* higher than previously indicated. Table 8.1 should be revised to show that r falls and r^* rises in the case of initial trade balance; r^* rises but r may rise or fall in the case of initial trade surplus; and r falls but r^* may rise or fall in the case of initial trade deficit. Table 8.2 should be expanded as follows. In the case of initial trade balance a sufficiently strong terms of trade effect on capital flows results in the I.I. Effect producing a payments surplus. Because of the gold inflow, the lower r, and higher r^*, prices may rise or fall in either country for equilibrium in the two monetary sectors. The same is true in the case of an initial trade surplus if the terms of trade effect fosters both a gold inflow and a lower domestic interest rate. It is also true in the case of an initial trade deficit if the terms of trade effect fosters both a gold inflow and a higher interest rate.

5. Capital Stock Adjustment Effect

Although a change in interest rates alters the level of sustained net capital inflows, given the volume of new saving at home and abroad, it also produces a transitional stock adjustment out of existing portfolios quickly followed by a permanent change in net interest payments. To isolate this effect the terms $r^*A(r, r^*, \theta) - rA^*(r, r^*)$ are introduced into the left hand side of Equation (5), where A is the stock of foreign short-term securities held by domestic residents and A^* is the stock of domestic short-term securities held by foreign residents. It is assumed that

$$A_{r^*}, A_r^* > 0; \qquad A_r, A_{r^*}^* < 0;$$

$$A_r = -A_{r^*}; \qquad \text{and} \qquad A_r^* = -A_{r^*}^*.$$

The interest payment flows are denoted by the terms r^*A and rA^*.

In this extended model interest payment flows are independent of the price levels because the same is assumed of existing portfolios. Suppose net interest payment outflows are \$Z at initial Balance of Payments equilibrium. A rise in all prices of p per cent results in a surplus of \$$pZ$, prompting gold inflows. In order to avoid this complicating effect of price levels on the Balance of Payments, net interest payment outflows are restricted to zero initially.

In the removal of a deficit the capital stock adjustment effect constitutes an obstacle to the adjustment mechanism. The higher domestic interest rate and lower foreign interest rate propel net interest payments in the direction opposite of the capital account.[26] If the net effect is perverse, stability of the adjustment mechanism requires the response of the trade surplus to the terms of trade to dominate it.[27] In any event the

---

[26] Let J represent the fraction of domestic portfolios, V, held as foreign assets and the fraction of new saving, S, devoted to the acquisition of additional foreign assets. Then the net capital inflow less net interest payment outflow is $J^*(r, r^*)S^* - J(r, r^*, \theta)S + r^*J(r, r^*, \theta)V - rJ^*(r, r^*)V^*$. The response of this sum to say a change in the domestic interest rate is $J_r^*(S^* - rV^*) - J_r(S - r^*V) - J^*V^* \gtrless 0$, where $J_r^* > 0$ and $J_r < 0$.

[27] The Jacobian of the new system is

$$\Delta^* = (\alpha L + \alpha^* L^*)[I_{r^*}^* B_T(\hat{K}_r + r^*A_r - rA_r^* - A^* - I_r)$$
$$+ I_r(B_T + B)(\hat{K}_r + r^*A_r - rA_r^* - A)] > 0$$

for stability. The term $-I_r I_{r^*}^* B_T$, which reflects the response of the trade surplus, must be sufficiently positive if the remaining quantity inside the brackets is negative.

interest payment reflows increase the amount of gold redistribution and therefore the absolute interest rate, price and terms of trade changes. Increased capital mobility may even intensify these effects.[28]

Let us finally reconsider the effects of the disturbances discussed in Section 3. When interest rates have a greater impact on net capital inflows than net interest payment outflows, the previous conclusions remain unaffected. The discussion below is restricted to the case in which both interest rates have the reverse effect, but the adjustment mechanism remains stable. A third case, in which one interest rate has the usual effect and the other the perverse effect, seems too restrictive to justify separate analysis.[29]

A reduced preference by domestic residents for foreign assets may give rise to either a surplus or deficit depending on whether the reduction in gross capital outflow exceeds the reduction in gross interest receipts due to the liquidation of existing foreign assets. An equivalent criterion is whether the growth rate of domestic portfolios exceeds the foreign interest rate.[30] The previous conclusions are reversed if this condition is not fulfilled.

The overall effects of a monetary disturbance are the same as before. In the case of an investment boom the higher domestic interest rate that preserves goods market equilibrium under T_1 creates a payments deficit. As the adjustment mechanism proceeds, the foreign interest falls, the terms of trade worsen, and the home interest rate rises even further. It can be shown that gold must flow abroad and that prices may rise or fall in either country for equilibrium in the two monetary sectors. The previous conclusions that the terms of trade improve, that the

[28] In Note 26, if $S^* < rV^*$, an increase in J_r^* raises the net interest payment response more than the net capital inflow response. The same is true for an increase in $|J_r|$ if $S < r^*V$.

[29] This case is attributable to differences in the initial stocks A and A^*, leading to asymmetric interest payment responses to the two interest rates. It is ruled out in any event by the assumption $r^*A = rA^*$ initially, provided the elasticities of K, A and A^* with respect to r are identical to those with respect to r^*.

[30] From Note 26 the response of the net capitalin flow less net interest payment outflow to a reduced preference by domestic residents for foreign assets is $J_\theta(r^*V - S)$, where $J_\theta < 0$. The term is positive when $r^* < S/V$.

foreign interest rate rises, and that domestic prices must rise are invalidated here.

In the case of an import demand shift, the conclusions remain unaltered when trade is initially balanced. When trade is initially in surplus, the terms of trade deteriorate to maintain the initial trade surplus, and the foreign interest rate rises to preserve goods market equilibrium under T_1. Removal of the ensuing payments surplus by the adjustment mechanism calls for lower home interest rates, a further rise in foreign interest rates, and an improvement of the terms of trade. However, the net effect on the terms of trade is normally a deterioration.[31] It can also be shown that gold may flow in either direction and that prices may rise or fall in either country for equilibrium in the two monetary sectors. The previous conclusions shown in Tables 8.1 and 8.2, that home interest rates rise and that foreign prices must rise, are contradicted here. When trade is initially in deficit, the drop in the foreign interest rate that maintains goods market equilibrium abroad under T_1 produces a payments deficit. The adjustment mechanism raises interest rates at home, lowers them abroad even further and causes a further worsening in the terms of trade. It can be demonstrated that gold must flow abroad and that prices may rise or fall in either country for equilibrium in the two monetary sectors. The previous findings displayed in Tables 8.1 and 8.2, that the domestic interest rate falls and that domestic prices must fall, are refuted here.

6. Conclusions

The gold flow adjustment mechanism removes a deficit by worsening the terms of trade, which increases the trade surplus

[31] At the initial terms of trade r must fall and r^* rise for goods market equilibrium in the two countries. The trade surplus and net capital inflow decline, but the interest payment outflow may be sufficiently reduced to produce a payments surplus. Removal of the hypothetical surplus involves an improvement in the terms of trade. This possibility is confirmed by

$$dT/d\phi =$$
$$\frac{(\alpha L + \alpha^* L^*)[I^*_{r_*}(\hat{K}_r + r^* A_r - r A^*_r - A^* - I_r) + I_r(\hat{K}_r + r^* A_r - r A^*_r - A)]}{\Delta^*} \gtreqless 0.$$

However, the numerator can be positive only in the case of initial trade surplus. If we postulate stability of the adjustment mechanism regardless of the initial condition of the trade balance, the numerator must be negative to ensure that Δ^* is positive.

and capital inflows, and by raising (lowering) domestic (foreign) interest rates, which enlarges capital inflows but also interest payment outflows. The interest payment effect, which is caused by a transitional stock adjustment out of existing portfolios at home and abroad, impedes the adjustment mechanism and imposes larger changes on interest rates, prices and the terms of trade. The amount of adjustment in these variables and the quantity of gold redistribution is inversely related to the degree of capital mobility, provided interest rates have a greater impact on capital inflows than interest payment outflows, and to the terms of trade sensitivity of capital flows. The distribution of adjustment between the current and capital accounts depends directly on the interest sensitivity of investment expenditures at home and abroad, inversely on the terms of trade sensitivity of capital flows, and inversely on the degree of capital mobility, provided interest rates have a greater effect on capital inflows than interest payment outflows.

The frequent assertion that the adjustment mechanism necessarily involves opposite price movements in the two countries is incorrect. The bank reserve changes produced by the gold flow do tend to impose direct opposite price changes by initially lowering interest rates in the surplus country and raising them in the deficit country. However, the price rise in the former tends to switch demand on to the products of the latter, and the price fall in the latter tends to switch demand away from the products of the former. These cross price effects may be sufficient to produce jointly rising or falling price levels if the difference in the interest elasticities of the demand for money in the two countries is significant.

A reduced preference by domestic residents for foreign assets directly generates an external surplus or deficit depending on whether the growth rate of domestic portfolios exceeds the foreign interest rate. The gold flow mechanism then erases the ensuing imbalance as described above.

A monetary disturbance in either country creates excess demand for or supply of world bank reserves, which is relieved simply by equiproportional price changes at home and abroad. Although interest rates and the terms of trade are affected initially, the gold flow restores them to their original levels.

An investment boom raises domestic interest rates, but

foreign interest rates may rise or fall and the terms of trade improve or deteriorate depending on whether interest rates have a greater impact on capital inflows than interest payment outflows. Moreover, if this condition is not fulfilled, the boom may lower domestic prices.

The effects of an increase in demand for home country imports at the expense of domestically produced consumption goods depend on the initial state of the trade balance, although under all circumstances the terms of trade deteriorate. In the case of initial trade balance the terms of trade effect on capital flows is responsible for a drop in domestic interest rates and rise in foreign interest rates. Normally gold flows abroad, prices fall at home and rise in the foreign country, but a sufficiently strong terms of trade effect produces a gold inflow and renders the price changes ambiguous. In the case of initial trade surplus both interest rates normally rise, but a strong enough terms of trade effect on capital flows or capital stock adjustment effect leads to a fall in domestic interest rates. In general, gold may flow in either direction, and prices may rise or fall in either country. Finally, in the case of an initial trade deficit both interest rates normally fall. However, if the terms of trade effect on capital flows is strong enough, foreign interest rates rise, and if the capital stock adjustment effect is strong enough, domestic interest rates rise. Again, the direction of gold flow and price changes is uncertain.

These conclusions rely on a model that allows for trade only in consumption goods in the spirit of Metzler's analysis. Admitting trade in investment goods invites new possibilities. To show an example, the truncated model used in this paper may be extended as follows:

$$S = I(r, T, \sigma) + X_C(T) + X_I(T, r^*) - (1/T)M_C(T, \phi) \quad (1b)$$
$$S^* = I^*(r^*, T) + M_C(T, \phi) + M_I(T, r, \sigma) - TX_C(T) \quad (3b)$$
$$X_C(T) + X_I(T, r^*) - (1/T)M_C(T, \phi) - (1/T)M_I(T, r, \sigma)$$
$$+ \hat{K}(r, r^*, \theta) = 0 \quad (5b)$$

where the subscripts C and I refer to consumption and investment goods respectively. Introduce F, the payments surplus, into the right-hand side of (5b), constrain the terms of trade effect on total investment expenditures at home and abroad to zero, and differentiate with respect to F to obtain

$$dT/dF = \frac{-I_r I_{r*}^* + M_{Ir} X_{Ir*}}{B_T[I_{r*}^*(\hat{K}_r - I_r - M_{Ir}) + \hat{K}_r M_{Ir}]} \gtrless 0.$$
$$+ (B_T + B)[K_r I_r \hat{+} X_{Ir*}(K_r - I_r - M_{Ir})]$$

Removal of a deficit involves a deterioration of the terms of trade only if $-I_r I_{r*}^* + M_{Ir} X_{Ir*} < 0$ or equivalently

$$\left(\frac{M_{Ir}}{I_r + M_{Ir}}\right) + \left(\frac{X_{Ir*}}{I_{r*}^* + X_{Ir*}}\right) < 1$$

That is, the sum of the import content of investment expenditure responses must be less than unity. This condition differs from the absorption approach criterion, which constrains the import contents of investment and consumption expenditures to be identical. The relevance only of the former stems from the process of adjustment, which raises domestic interest rates and lowers foreign interest rates. In the home country domestic investment demand falls but exports of investment goods rise. The reverse occurs abroad. Whether deficient demand at home and excess demand abroad, requiring a deterioration of the terms of trade for goods market equilibrium, prevail depends only on the import contents of investment expenditures. Further analysis and extensions of this model should prove helpful in illuminating the workings of the gold standard.

References

[1] MEADE, J. E., *The Balance of Payments*, London: Oxford University Press, 1951.

[2] MEADE, J. E., *The Balance of Payments: Mathematical Supplement*, London: Oxford University Press, 1951.

[3] METZLER, L. A., 'The Process of International Adjustment under Conditions of Full Employment: A Keynesian View'. in R. E. Caves and H. G. Johnson, eds., *Readings in International Economics*, Homewood, Illinois: R. D. Irwin, 1968.

[4] MUNDELL, R. A., *International Economics*, New York: Macmillan, 1968.

[5] MUNDELL, R. A., 'The International Disequilibrium System', *Kyklos*, XIV, (fasc. 2, 1961) 154–72.

9 Private Short-Term Capital Flows and the Eurodollar Market

RAYMOND F. MIKESELL*

Introduction

THE operations of the Eurodollar market have had a sub-stantial influence on both the volume and the nature of private short-term capital flows in the U.S. international accounts on the one hand, and on the character of international dollar liquidity held by foreigners on the other. Most of the liquid dollar assets held by foreign commercial banks (excluding foreign branches of U.S. banks) and by foreign individuals and non-bank concerns is in the form of dollar deposits in com-mercial banks outside the U.S.[1] One consequence of the Eurodollar market has been the growth of the multinational

---

* The author is W. E. Miner, Professor of Economics, University of Oregon. This article was written in early 1971. For an analysis of sub-sequent developments in the Eurodollar market and the U.S. balance of payments, see Raymond F. Mikesell and J. Herbert Furth, *Foreign Dollar Balances and the International Role of the Dollar*, National Bureau of Economic Research, New York, 1973 (forthcoming).

[1] The total volume of foreign-held Eurodollar deposits is difficult to estimate but the following data provide some idea of the magnitude. At the end of 1969 foreign commercial banks held $17·7 billion in dollar deposits with foreign branches of U.S. banks. In addition, foreign indi-viduals and non-bank firms held $13·8 billion in Eurodollar deposits with Canadian commercial banks and with the commercial banks of the eight European countries reporting to the B.I.S. (These figures exclude foreign non-bank deposits with other foreign commercial banks as well as the large volume of inter-bank deposits between foreign banks other than foreign branches of U.S. banks.) The total of these two figures, $31·5 billion, may be compared with $14·6 billion in short-term dollar assets held in the U.S. by foreign commercial banks (excluding foreign branches of U.S. banks) and foreign individuals and non-bank concerns. (Data derived from [1, p. 158], [2], [5].)

banking structure. Of the $21 billion in U.S. short-term dollar liabilities to foreign commercial banks and other non-official entities as of the end of 1970, about $14 billion represented *intra-bank* accounting entries, i.e. liabilities of U.S. commercial banks to their foreign branches ($7.7 billion) plus liabilities of agencies and branches of foreign banking corporations in the U.S. to their head offices and branches abroad ($6.5 billion est.).[2] Intra-bank transactions have tended to dominate U.S. short-term capital movements arising from changes in foreign short-term assets held in the U.S. For example, not only did U.S. resident bank borrowings from their foreign branches account for 63 per cent of the net increase in foreign private liquid dollar holdings between 31 December, 1964 and 31 December, 1969, but quarterly changes in U.S. bank liabilities to their foreign branches over this period explained through their linear influence about 84 per cent of the quarterly variance in U.S. liquid liabilities to non-official foreigners.[3] In the opinion of the author, these short-term capital movements are not satisfactorily explained by models of short-term capital flows currently found in the literature on international finance.[4] Any realistic analysis of short-term capital movements must take account of the operations of the Eurodollar market and of the intra-bank transactions of multinational banks.

The purpose of this paper is to analyse the foreign private or non-official demand for dollar liquidity in the form of both

[2] Data on U.S. bank liabilities to their foreign branches are found in [5, p. A86]. Data on liabilities of agencies and branches of foreign banking corporations are estimated from the annual reports of the State of New York Banking Department and the State of California Superintendent of Banks.

[3] I have analysed the relationship between U.S. bank borrowings from the Eurodollar market and changes in U.S. liquid liabilities to foreigners in [11].

[4] The results obtained from empirical tests of the various models with respect to interest rate sensitivity of U.S. short-term capital movements, or the effects of trade flows and other independent variables on short-term capital flows have been generally conflicting and inconsistent. Moreover, regression estimates obtained for some periods in the past may have little validity for later periods; this is especially true for empirical studies made prior to the rapid growth of the Eurodollar market beginning in 1964. For a critical review of models of international capital movements, see [9].

liquid dollar assets held in the U.S. (American dollars) and dollar deposits in banks outside the U.S. (Euro-dollars) and to show how changes in the volume and composition of the foreign private demand for liquid dollar assets affects private short-term capital flows in the U.S. international accounts. No attempt will be made in this essay to formulate a complete model of short-term capital flows or to provide an empirical test of a model of the foreign private demand for dollar assets. Sufficient data on the composition of foreign liquid asset holdings as among American dollars, Eurodollars and non-liquid dollar assets together with the relevant interest rates, risk and other explanatory variables are presently not available to provide a satisfactory explanation of changes in the composition of liquid asset holdings by foreigners. Nevertheless, it seems desirable to discuss the type of model that might prove most useful for explaining such changes and to relate this model to the analysis of short-term capital movements.

1. The Analytical Framework

As a framework for my analysis I shall employ a portfolio adjustment model designed to explain changes in foreign holdings of liquid dollar assets by various categories of trans-actors, each of which has a unique preference function in terms of rates of return, risk and other preference variables, and a relevant net wealth variable.[5] Changes in the net wealth of a transactor will result in changes in the composition of the holdings of individual liquid assets without changes in relative interest rates or other preference variables, but such changes need not be in the same proportion as the initial composition of the assets. Thus, in any dynamic analysis of changes in the composition of liquid asset holdings of a particular category of transactor, we cannot properly abstract changes in liquid asset holdings from changes in net wealth. Nevertheless, for purposes of my analysis, I shall assume that total liquid asset holdings for each category of transactor is fixed, thereby concentrating solely on changes in liquid asset composition. I shall employ the following categories of foreign liquid dollar asset holders: (*a*) foreign commercial banks, excluding foreign

[5] Examples of the employment of portfolio-adjustment models include [6] and [3].

branches of U.S. banks; (*b*) foreign private non-banks and (*c*) foreign official agencies. I shall regard foreign branches of U.S. banks as a part of the U.S. banking system except that their deposit liabilities to foreigners will be regarded as Eurodollars but their claims on their head offices in the United States will not be regarded as foreign dollar holdings (except for Balance of Payments accounting in conformity with U.S. official statistics). I shall include as a part of foreign liquid dollar asset holdings dollar deposits in foreign branches of U.S. banks held by foreign commercial banks but I shall exclude from liquid dollar asset holdings all other foreign inter-bank deposits.[6] It would be simpler to regard foreign deposits in foreign branches of U.S. banks as American dollars but in U.S. official Balance of Payments statistics only foreign-owned obligations of U.S. residents enter into the Balance of Payments and foreign branches of U.S. banks are regarded as non-residents.

In my analysis I shall employ the following symbols:

L_n = American liquid dollar holdings of foreign private non-banks

L_{br} = U.S. bank liabilities to their foreign branches

L_{fb} = American liquid dollar holdings of foreign commercial banks excluding foreign branches of U.S. banks

$L_b = L_{br} + L_{bf}$ = U.S. liquid liabilities to foreign commercial banks including foreign branches of U.S. banks

L_o = American liquid dollar holdings of foreign official agencies

E_n = Eurodollar deposit holdings of foreign private non-banks

E_{fb} = Eurodollar deposit holdings of foreign commercial banks with foreign branches of U.S. banks

E_o = Eurodollar deposits of foreign official agencies

E_u = Eurodollar deposit holdings of U.S. residents

At any particular time, t, total foreign private liquid dollar holdings, will be given by $T_p^t = L_n^t + L_{fb}^t + E_{fb}^t + E_n^t$.

Total private non-bank liquid dollar holdings will be given by

$$T_n^t = L_n^t + E_n^t$$

[6] In its estimate of the size of the Eurodollar market the B.I.S. excludes all inter-bank deposits among banks in the eight European countries reporting to the B.I.S. ('inside area' banks), including foreign branches of U.S. banks [1, pp. 155ff].

Total foreign commercial bank liquid dollar holdings will be given by

$$T_{fb}^t = L_{fb}^t + E_{fb}^t$$

and total foreign liquid dollar holdings are given by

$$T_t^t = L_n^t + L_{fb}^t + L_o^t + E_{fb}^t + E_n^t + E_o^t$$

Let us express the total foreign private demand for liquid dollar assets as a general asset demand function relating the stock of foreign private liquid dollar assets, T_p, to a scale variable, W_p, constituting the total foreign private holdings of liquid assets, and a set of preference variables, τ, which determine the allocation of the total liquid asset portfolio, W_p, among competing assets. Thus, we may write

$$\frac{T_p^t}{W_p^t} = F(\tau^t) \qquad \text{or} \qquad T_p^t = F(\tau^t, W_p^t)$$

as the relation determining the equilibrium foreign private holdings of liquid dollar assets. We may also express the fraction of total foreign private non-bank assets, W_n, held in the form of liquid dollar assets as

$$T_n^t = F(\delta^t, W_n^t)$$

and the fraction of total foreign commercial bank liquid assets (excluding foreign branches of U.S. banks), W_{fb}, held in the form of liquid dollar assets as

$$T_{fb}^t = F(\beta^t, W_{fb}^t)$$

where δ and β constitute asset preference variables determining the allocation of total liquid assets between liquid dollar assets and non-dollar liquid assets for foreign private non-banks and foreign commercial banks respectively. We may express the fraction of total foreign private non-bank liquid dollar assets, T_n, held in the form of Eurodollars as

$$E_n^t = F(\phi^t, T_n^t)$$

where ϕ constitutes a set of preference variables determining the allocation of total foreign private non-bank liquid dollar assets between E_n and L_n. Finally, we may express the fraction of total commercial bank (excluding foreign branches of U.S. banks) liquid dollar assets, T_{fb}^t, held in the form of Eurodollars, as

$$E_{fb}^t = F(\lambda^t, T_{fb}^t)$$

where λ constitutes a set of preference variables determining the allocation of foreign commercial bank liquid dollar assets between E_{fb} and L_{fb}.

In employing the above relationships in the analysis of the effects of changes in the foreign demand for liquid assets on short-term capital movements, it is important to note that private short-term capital flows arising from a change in U.S. liquid liabilities to foreign commercial banks and private non-banks is equal to[7]

$$(\Delta L_n + \Delta L_{br} + \Delta L_{fb}) \quad \text{or} \quad (\Delta L_n + \Delta L_b)$$

The preference function of foreign official agencies with respect to the composition of their international reserves raises special problems for my analysis. Given the limited capacity of the U.S. Government to convert dollars presented by foreign central banks into gold and the reluctance of foreign governments to appreciate their currencies *vis-à-vis* the dollar, foreign official agencies must be regarded as residual holders of American dollars. They may choose between holding American dollars and Eurodollars on the basis of the interest rate differential, the desire to conceal their holdings of American dollars, or for other reasons. However, this option is also constrained for foreign official agencies as a group since unless the foreign official dollars deposited with Eurodollar banks are absorbed in increased holdings by foreign non-official entities or are loaned to U.S. residents, the Eurodollar deposits of foreign official agencies will be recycled back to the foreign central banks. Hence, foreign official agencies as a group cannot have an independent preference function relating to liquid dollar assets.

The purpose of setting down the above functional relationships is two-fold. First, I want to emphasise the necessity of disaggregation in any analysis for the foreign demand for liquid dollar assets. Second, an analytical framework is useful in analysing the interrelationships arising from the liquid asset demand patterns among the various categories of foreign liquid asset holders. For example, an increase in the foreign private

---

[7] Foreign branches of U.S. banks may hold small amounts of liquid dollar claims on U.S. residents other than claims on parents, but these will be ignored in this analysis.

non-bank demand for Eurodollars at the expense of either American dollars or non-dollar liquid assets immediately shifts the asset composition of foreign commercial banks. Given the U.S. and foreign demand for Eurodollar loans, the resulting adjustment in the portfolios of foreign commercial banks will affect both the dollar holdings of foreign central banks and private short-term capital flows in the U.S. Balance of Payments.

It will be noted that I have suggested using total liquid asset holdings (domestic and foreign) as the relevant wealth constraint for any particular category of liquid asset holders. Moreover, in any analysis of the foreign demand for liquid dollar assets I believe that it is necessary to include only those categories of foreign liquid asset holders that are also significant holders of international liquid assets. Large business firms concerned almost entirely with domestic business or even large banks that have few international transactions will tend to hold virtually all of their liquid assets in their own currencies so that they are oblivious to what happens to interest rates abroad or to the range of exchange rate expectations. Here we are confronted with serious data deficiencies. Data on foreign holdings of short-term assets are not published by many countries and, where published, they are frequently not broken down by commercial banks and private non-banks. Incomplete data on foreign exchange holdings of foreign commercial banks by country are provided by the International Monetary Fund but, except for certain countries, the data are not available on such holdings by currencies.[8] Even where estimates of private non-bank short-term capital flows are published they tend to be greatly underestimated since a large portion of the private capital flows tend to be reflected in the errors and omissions item. Thus a good deal of work needs to be done in the estimation of the total volume of international liquidity held by non-banks.[9] Although we know much more about foreign private liquid dollar holdings than we do about total liquid asset

[8] See table on 'Deposit Money Banks Foreign Exchange', in [8, p. 25].
[9] A review of the Balance of Payments of countries which have been large recipients of foreign private short-term capital, including Switzerland, Germany and the Netherlands, reveals large credit entries in the errors and omissions items [7]. For a discussion of the problems relating to the estimation of short-term capital movements, see [4].

holdings relevant for any particular category of portfolio holders, data on Eurodollar holdings disaggregated by bank and non-bank are quite limited except for a few countries. Finally, we lack data on domestic liquid asset holdings for the relevant categories of international liquid asset holders.

Because of the data limitations indicated above, I am presently unable to formulate and test portfolio preference functions for any specific category of foreign liquid asset holders. The following discussion must, therefore, be limited to the application of what little we do know about the behaviour of foreign commercial banks and private non-banks for the analysis of the foreign demand for liquid dollar assets and its effects on short-term capital movements in the U.S. Balance of Payments.

2. Foreign liquid asset preferences and short-term capital flows

The remainder of this article will be concerned with the following questions:

(1) What are the preference variables that determine the allocation of total liquid asset portfolios of private non-banks as between L_n, E_n and non-dollar liquid assets?

(2) What is the effect of a shift of assets by foreign private non-banks between American dollars and Eurodollars on T_n and on private short-term capital movements in the U.S. Balance of Payments?

(3) What is the nature of the preference function of foreign banks in allocating their liquid asset holdings among L_{fb}, E_{fb} and non-dollar liquid assets?

(4) What is the effect of shifts by foreign commercial banks between L_{fb} and E_{fb} on T_p and on private short-term capital movements?

(5) What are the effects of changes on U.S. resident and foreign official deposits in the Eurodollar market on T_p and on private short-term capital imports?

(6) What are the effects of changes in the interest rate structure involving Eurodollar rates, U.S. money market rates and foreign non-dollar interest rates on the volume and composition of foreign private liquid dollar asset holdings and on private short-term capital movements?

The allocation of foreign private non-bank liquid assets

The allocation of foreign private non-bank liquid assets among American dollars, Eurodollars and non-dollar liquid assets will be determined by a complex set of variables, including the pattern of interest rates, exchange rate expectations and the cost of hedging, and the relative risks relating to both the currencies themselves and where they are held.[10]

A generalised liquid asset preference function for all foreign private non-banks is wholly unrealistic. It is more meaningful to identify categories of foreign liquid asset holders operating in international financial markets and to investigate the preference function and wealth constraint relevant to each category. For example, it might be convenient initially to divide foreign liquid asset holders into two major groups: (*a*) those having a strong preference for holding liquid dollar assets; and (*b*) those having a strong preference for holding one or more non-dollar currencies, e.g. sterling or Swiss francs. In the first group we might include foreign affiliates of U.S. firms and residents of countries with strong economic and financial ties with the United States that normally hold any non-domestic currency assets in dollars. For this group of portfolio holders the demand for Eurodollars is likely to be more sensitive to the U.S. money market-Eurodollar deposit rate differential than to the Eurodollar deposit-non-dollar rate differential.

The second group of foreign portfolio holders, which might include residents of members of the sterling area and of continental European countries, may be more sensitive to changes in the differential between the Eurodollar deposit rates and the yields on non-dollar money market assets. There is doubtless a third group of portfolio holders for which no strong preference exists, say, as between U.S. liquid dollar assets and assets denominated in non-dollar currencies, but within this group there may exist strong preferences as to the country composition of their liquid asset holdings however denominated by currency. Within each group differentiated on the basis of

[10] Liquid assets denominated in dollars, sterling, Deutschmarks and other convertible currencies may be held in a number of countries other than the country whose currency is involved. Thus, the Eurocurrency market not only provides options as to the currency in which liquid assets may be denominated, but also as to the country in which any currency may be held.

preferences as between holding dollars and non-dollars, we need to distinguish functional groups such as non-financial corporations, non-banking financial institutions, wealthy individuals, etc. Each functional group will tend to have its own behavioural pattern and relevant wealth constraint. Thus, corporations engaged in producing commodities or services will tend to have an asset preference function which is quite different from that of a financial institution whose main concern is to maximise its returns from an international portfolio of deposits and securities.

Assuming we could identify a group of foreign liquid asset holders with a strong preference for holding liquid dollar assets, what factors other than interest rate differentials would determine their preference as between American dollars and Eurodollars? Although no element of exchange risk is involved, there are political and economic risks as between holding dollar assets in the United States and in foreign countries and among different foreign countries. These include the risk of the imposition of exchange controls by the foreign country in which the dollars are held and the risk of insolvency of the bank where the dollar deposits are held. There is also the matter of convenience; it is usually more convenient to hold deposits with a bank in your own country, but this might not be significant for multi-national firms.[11]

Since Eurodollars are not ordinarily used for making current payments, firms conducting an international business will need working balances in U.S. banks. However, demand deposit holdings in U.S. banks need not be large except where required as compensatory balances for borrowers from U.S. banks. Despite the large increase in international transactions financed with dollars, holdings of demand deposits in U.S. banks by foreign non-banking concerns and individuals have fluctuated by less than $300 million since 1964; they were $1737 million at the end of December 1970 as compared with $1531 million at the end of December 1964. Time deposits that can be shifted into demand deposits in U.S. banks on short notice may serve as a substitute for a portion of the demand deposit balances required for transactions purposes. Moreover, it would appear

[11] The fact that Eurodollar deposits are normally accepted only in units of 100,000 dollars not only keeps most investors out of the market but is also a factor of inconvenience even for relatively wealthy asset holders.

that very short-term and call deposits with, say, Chase Manhattan, London are virtually as liquid and readily available as time deposits with Chase Manhattan, New York. Thus, any additional liquid dollar asset holdings by foreign private non-banks required to satisfy the transactions function over the past several years may well have been met by the acquisition of short-term Eurodollar deposits, rather than by increased holdings of demand deposits in U.S. banks.

Short-term interest-earning assets in the United States held by foreign private non-banks totalled $2307 million at the end of 1970 as against $2231 million at the end of 1966 and reached an end-of-year high of $2647 million in December 1968. Moreover, month-to-month changes in the volume of these holdings do not appear to be correlated with relative movements of interest rates between the United States and abroad.[12] On the other hand, foreign non-bank holdings of Eurodollars rose by at least $9 billion between the end of 1966 and the end of 1969. We may conclude, therefore, that the foreign private non-bank demand for American liquid dollar assets has been both stable and rather insensitive to relative levels of interest rates over the period between the end of 1966 and the end of 1970. Hence, changes in liquid dollar asset holdings of this group appear to have taken the form mainly of changes in their holdings of Eurodollar deposits rather than changes in their holdings of American liquid dollar assets, at least over the period between December 1966 and the end of 1970.

For most foreign private non-bank liquid asset holders who are residents of convertible currency countries, the principal option in allocating their assets is likely to be between liquid dollar assets and their own currency rather than between liquid dollar assets and third currencies. Major exceptions would be a speculative demand for a currency which is expected to appreciate, e.g. the Deutschmark in early 1969, or a desire by residents of a relatively weak currency country to hold foreign

---

[12] Foreign private non-bank holdings of long-term deposits in U.S. banks have fluctuated within a narrow range above and below $50 million over the same period. Foreign private non-bank holdings of long-term government securities have also been relatively stable between the end of 1966 and the end of 1970. Data on foreign holdings of dollar assets derived from the *Federal Reserve Bulletin*, (various issues).

exchange for speculative reasons, in which case their principal options might be between liquid dollar assets and, say, Swiss francs.[13] During the period 1967–1969 at least, Eurodollar rates, both covered and uncovered, tended to be higher than rates paid on assets of similar maturity in the United States and in domestic European money markets. Hence, except for those foreign private liquid asset holders that have a strong preference for liquid dollar assets, e.g. Latin Americans in countries with unstable currencies, allocation has probably been governed mainly by factors affecting preferences between Eurodollars and the domestic currency of the asset holder rather than between the domestic currency and American liquid dollar assets or between the domestic currency and liquid assets dominated in a third currency. This hypothesis could be tested if there were sufficient time series data available on both the Eurodollar and third currency holdings of residents of foreign countries. Nevertheless, it illustrates the kind of disaggregated analysis that may prove fruitful in investigating the demand for Eurodollars.

Effects of a shift of assets by foreign private non-banks from American dollars to Eurodollars

A shift of American dollars by foreign private non-banks into Eurodollars does not reflect any increase in the aggregate foreign demand for liquid dollar assets, while a shift from non-dollar liquid assets into liquid dollar assets does reflect such an increase. However, a shift from American liquid dollar assets into Eurodollars may increase the total supply of foreign private dollar liquidity and, if there is no corresponding increase in aggregate private demand for liquid dollar assets, dollars will flow into the central banks. In order to determine the effects of a shift from American dollars into Eurodollars by foreign private non-bank holders, let us assume that between time t and $t + 1$ there is no increase in either U.S. resident deposits or in foreign official deposits in the Eurodollar market. The effects of a shift of American dollars to Eurodollar banks on foreign private non-bank holdings of dollar liquidity will depend in considerable measure on what the Eurodollar banks

[13] Most of the speculative movements out of Italian lire tend to go into Swiss francs.

do with the American dollars deposited with them. If all the dollars deposited with the Eurodollar banks by foreign private non-banks are lent to U.S. resident banks, there would be no change in the supply of private non-bank dollar liquidity, T_n, and foreign private holdings of American liquid dollar assets would not be affected.[14] This situation may be expressed as follows:

$$[(E_n^{t+1} - E_n^t) - (L_n^{t+1} - L_n^t)] = 0$$

and

$$[(L_n^{t+1} - L_n^t) - (L_b^{t+1} - L_b^t)] = 0$$

However, if all or part of the American dollars deposited with Eurodollar banks were loaned to non-residents of the United States, T_n would increase (momentarily) since

$$[(E_n^{t+1} - E_n^t) - (L_n^{t+1} - L_n^t)] > 0$$

Unless there is an increase in the aggregate foreign private demand for dollar liquidity, a portion of the privately held American dollars would flow into the foreign central banks with a consequent outflow of foreign private capital from the United States.

Now let us suppose that foreign private non-banks shift a portion of their non-dollar liquid assets into the Eurodollar market, thereby increasing the foreign demand for American dollars in the exchange market. If the entire amount of the dollars acquired by the Eurodollar banks were lent to U.S. resident banks, there would be a net increase in foreign private non-bank liquid dollar holdings, T_n, and a flow of private short-term capital to the United States equal to the amount of the shift from non-dollar liquid assets into Eurodollars. On the other hand, if the dollars deposited with the Eurodollar banks were loaned to non-residents of the United States, and there were no net increase in the foreign non-official demand for American dollars, the dollars acquired from the foreign exchange market (or from the central banks) to finance the shift from non-dollar liquid assets to Eurodollars would simply be channelled (or recycled back) to the foreign central banks

[14] This would hold true regardless of whether the dollars were deposited with foreign branches of U.S. banks or with other foreign commercial banks.

and there would be no net private short-term capital flow to the United States. This might occur, for example, if the dollars borrowed from the Eurodollar banks were used to finance non-dollar expenditures.

The preference function of foreign commercial banks for American liquid dollars, Eurodollars and non-dollar liquid assets

The vast bulk of the liquid dollar holdings of foreign commercial banks (excluding foreign branches of U.S. banks) are held in the form of Eurodollar deposits with foreign branches of U.S. banks or with agencies and branches of foreign banks located in the United States. (As noted above, we have excluded from liquid dollar holdings of foreign commercial banks inter-bank deposits between foreign commercial banks excluding foreign branches of U.S. banks.) Foreign commercial bank holdings of short-term dollar assets in the United States (excluding U.S. bank liabilities to foreign branches) totalled $10·6 billion at the end of 1969 and $9·2 billion at the end of 1970. However, of these assets an estimated $5·8 billion and $6·5 billion consisted of claims on agencies and branches of foreign banking corporations located in the United States at the end of 1969 and 1970 respectively.[15] (About half of these amounts constituted U.S. dollar claims of Canadian banks on Canadian bank agencies and branches in the United States.) The U.S. agencies and branches of foreign banks in turn invest these funds in dollar loans to U.S. and non-U.S. resident firms, in balances with U.S. banks, and in other short-term dollar assets including acceptances. Foreign bank claims on their agencies and branches in New York State appear to have had a rather steady growth, quarter-by-quarter, from about $2·5 billion at the end of 1960 to $6·3 billion at the end of 1970.[16] The growth of these claims appears not to have been influenced significantly by changes in the relative level of interest rates in the United States and abroad. Demand deposit holdings of foreign commercial banks (excluding U.S. bank liabilities to their foreign branches) in large U.S. banks have also risen fairly steadily; they were $1·6

[15] Estimated from *Annual Reports* of the State of New York Banking Department and the Superintendent of Banks, State of California.
[16] See *Annual Reports*, Banking Department, State of New York. 1970 figure adjusted for overstatement of $700 million for the end of 1970.

billion at the end of 1966, $1·8 billion at the end of 1967, $2·1 billion at the end of 1968 and $2·5 billion at the end of 1969, declining to $2·4 billion at the end of 1970.[17] The growth of these demand deposit holdings of foreign commercial banks partially reflects the increase in the transactions demand for dollars but it may also reflect compensating balances of foreign banks borrowing in the United States.

Other foreign bank short-term assets in the United States can be estimated only by indirection. They were about $1·0 billion at the end of 1967; $1·5 billion at the end of 1968; over $2 billion at the end of 1969, declining to less than $0·5 billion at the end of 1970.[18] It is difficult to explain these changes in terms of changes in relative levels of interest rates in the United States and abroad. Long-term C.D.s held by foreign banks with U.S. resident banks were only $55 million at the end of 1969, rising to $160 million at the end of 1970. Holdings of long-term U.S. Government marketable securities were also small.

On the other hand, Eurodollar holdings of foreign commercial banks with foreign branches of U.S. banks have grown rapidly in recent years to sizeable levels. They were $17·7 billion at the end of 1969; $7·6 billion at the end of 1968; $4·4 billion at the end of 1967 and $3·4 billion at the end of 1966.[19] At the time of writing, data were not available on Eurodollar deposits of foreign commercial banks with foreign branches of U.S. banks for 1970, but such holdings were probably about the same level or higher than they were at the end of 1969 since total Eurodollar deposit liabilities of foreign branches of U.S. banks were higher at the end of 1970 than they were at the end of 1969.

[17] See Table entitled 'Assets and Liabilities of Large Commercial Banks', *Federal Reserve Bulletin*, (various issues).

[18] Treasury data on U.S. short-term liabilities to foreign commercial banks include both U.S. bank liabilities to their foreign branches and liabilities of branches and agencies of foreign banks to their head offices and branches abroad. However, these intra-bank liabilities are reported as demand or time deposits in accordance with internal accounting procedures of the reporting banks. In deriving the above estimates, I have sought to include only those short-term interest-earning assets of foreign commercial banks that do not represent intra-bank liabilities.

[19] See: [13, p. 130] for years 1966–1968; December 1969 figure from Federal Reserve Board.

The preference function of foreign commercial banks can be summarised by saying that the increase in their liquid dollar holdings in recent years has taken the form very largely of Eurodollar deposits in foreign branches of U.S. banks (which generally have yielded a higher rate of return than assets of similar maturity and risk in the United States) and of investments in their U.S. agencies and branches. The latter have been dominated by Canadian and, to a lesser extent, by Japanese agencies and branches. Foreign commercial banks hold relatively modest amounts of demand deposits in U.S. resident banks and, although the amount of these deposits have risen in recent years, this rise does not appear to be proportional to the increase in international transactions denominated in dollars.[20] Their holdings of short-term interest-earning American dollar assets also appear to have been rather modest. The growth of Eurodollar deposits of foreign commercial banks with foreign branches of U.S. banks probably reflects the rise in foreign commercial bank Eurodollar deposit liabilities to their own residents and to other foreign commercial banks, foreign official agencies and foreign private non-banks throughout the world. During 1970 there was a substantial growth in Eurocurrency deposits denominated in non-dollar currencies, particularly German marks, Swiss francs and, to a lesser extent, Dutch guilders. Thus the share of the non-dollar component of the Eurocurrency market had grown to nearly 20 per cent by September 1970 as against about 10 per cent at the end of 1969. At the same time, the relative share of the foreign currency deposits of foreign branches of U.S. banks declined during 1970.[21] How much of this was due to a change in relative levels of interest rates and how much to changes in other variables which determine the preference for liquid dollar assets as against assets denominated in European currencies, cannot be determined without more information on the relevant preference variables.

[20] Foreign commercial bank demand deposits in large U.S. banks rose from about $1·5 billion in December 1965 to $2·4 billion in December 1970, or by about the same percentage as the percentage increase in world trade. However, Eurodollar transactions have increased several-fold as indicated by the more than three-fold increase in the size of the Eurodollar market between December 1965 and December 1969.

[21] See: [12].

Effects of shifts by foreign commercial banks between L_{fb} and E_{fb} on T_p and U.S. short-term capital movements

Foreign commercial banks receive American dollars from a variety of sources including dollar deposits, dollar exchange from trade finance and purchases from or swaps with a central bank. Dollars in excess of the amounts needed for loans to customers are likely to be deposited by foreign commercial banks with other Eurodollar banks which in turn will either loan the dollars to customers outside the United States or transfer the dollars to U.S. residents, mainly U.S. banks. Foreign branches of U.S. banks were, at least until 1970, large residual holders of Eurodollar deposits of foreign commercial banks. At the end of 1969 $17·7 billion out of a total $29·9 billion in dollar liabilities of foreign branches of U.S. banks were to foreign commercial banks, while $13·8 billion out of a total of $22·9 billion in total dollar assets constituted claims on parents.

When American dollars held by foreign commercial banks are transferred to U.S. residents either directly or via Eurodollar deposits with foreign branches of U.S. banks, neither the total volume of liquid dollar assets held by foreign commercial banks, T_b, nor the total volume of private foreign liquid dollar assets, T_p, will change. If foreign commercial banks deposit dollars with foreign branches of U.S. banks, they simply exchange American dollars, L_{fb}, for Eurodollars, E_{fb}. Moreover, there is no effect on U.S. private short-term capital movements since the U.S. liquid liabilities are simply shifted from a foreign commercial bank to the foreign branch of the U.S. bank. However, if the dollars held by foreign commercial banks are lent to foreign private non-banks, T_{fb} will decline and T_p will also decline unless there is an increase in the aggregate foreign private demand for liquid dollar assets. Moreover, since the excess supply over the demand for American dollars will flow into the central banks, private short-term capital will flow out of the United States. Since foreign private non-bank American liquid dollar holdings have been quite stable in recent years, it seems evident that Eurodollar loans to foreign private non-banks have not been accompanied by an increase in the demand for American liquid dollars on the part of foreign private non-banks. Thus the sharp decline in U.S. bank borrowings from their foreign branches during 1970 and the evident shift of Eurodollar loans to foreign private non-banks contributed to the sharp rise in foreign official holdings of American dollars and to the outflow of foreign private short-term capital from the United States.

In the above analysis it was not indicated how the foreign commercial banks acquired the dollars. Let us assume that the dollars are deposited by foreign private non-banks who thereby exchange American liquid dollars, L_n, for Eurodollars, E_n. Let us also assume that the foreign commercial banks redeposit the dollars with a foreign branch of a U.S. bank which in turn shifts the dollars to its U.S. parent. As a consequence of these transactions, T_n remains the same but T_{fb} will have risen since the foreign commercial banks have acquired Eurodollar deposits with a foreign branch of a U.S. bank, E_{fb}. However, U.S. liquid liabilities to foreigners (including foreign branches of U.S. banks) remain the same so that there is no net short-term capital movement in the U.S. Balance of Payments. Now let us suppose that the foreign commercial bank receiving the dollar deposits from the foreign non-banks lend the dollars to other foreign non-banks and that there does not occur an increase in the aggregate foreign non-official demand for American liquid dollar assets. In this case there would again be an excess supply of American dollars over the foreign private demand for them and the dollars would flow into the central banks. T_n would not change but E_n would rise and L_n would decline by an equivalent amount. T_p would also remain at the same level but American liquid dollar asset holdings of foreign private non-banks would decline with a consequent net short-term private capital outflow from the United States.

Finally, let us assume that the American dollars were initially acquired by the foreign commercial banks from the foreign exchange market or from the central banks thereby constituting an increase in the foreign non-official demand for liquid dollar assets. If the foreign commercial banks redeposited the dollars with a foreign branch of a U.S. bank, E_{fb} would rise and if the foreign branch of the U.S. bank shifted the dollars to its U.S. parent, there would be a private short-term capital flow to the United States. On the other hand, if the dollars were lent by the foreign commercial banks to non-bank customers and there was no net increase in the aggregate foreign non-bank demand for American dollars, the dollars would be again recycled back to the foreign central banks and there would be no net U.S. private short-term capital movement and also no net increase in T_p. During 1969 excess American dollars accruing to private foreigners were channelled into the Euro-dollar market and these dollars were in large measure borrowed by U.S. banks with a consequent increase in both T_n and T_{fb} and a large movement of private short-term funds into the United States.

Effects of changes in U.S. resident and foreign official deposits in the Eurodollar market on T_p and on private short-term capital imports

If there is an increase in Eurodollar deposits from outside the foreign private sector, say as a consequence of increased de-posits by foreign official agencies, ΔE_o, or by U.S. residents, ΔE_u, the impact on foreign private liquidity and on private short-term capital flow to the United States will depend upon whether the dollars are initially deposited with foreign branches of U.S. banks or with other foreign commercial banks, and upon what the Eurodollar banks do with the dollars. Let us assume initially that foreign central banks increase their dollar deposits with foreign commercial banks, ΔE_o, and that the dollars are redeposited in foreign branches of U.S. banks which in turn shift the dollars to their U.S. parents. In this case

$$\Delta E_o = \Delta E_{fb} = \Delta T_p$$

and private short-term capital flow to the United States will also be equal to ΔE_o. However, if the foreign central banks deposit dollars directly with the foreign branches of U.S. banks, there will be no increase in E_{fb} or T_p, but the effects on U.S. private short-term capital flow will be the same as in the previous case.

Now let us assume that the dollars deposited by foreign central banks in foreign commercial banks are lent to foreign non-banks and that there is no increase in the foreign non-bank demand for American dollars. In this case the American dollars will simply be recycled back to the foreign central banks and there will be no increase in T_p or in private short-term capital flow to the United States. If, however, the dollars deposited by the foreign central banks are redeposited with foreign branches of U.S. banks which in turn lend the dollars to foreign non-banks, E_{fb} and hence T_p will rise, but again there will be no private short-term capital flow to the United States.

An increase in Eurodollar deposits by U.S. residents, ΔE_u, will be accompanied initially by a U.S. short-term capital outflow balanced by an inflow of foreign private short-term capital in the U.S. Balance of Payments. If the U.S. resident deposits are with a foreign branch of a U.S. bank and the branch in turn shifts the dollars to its U.S. parent, foreign private liquid dollar holdings in the United States will increase but there will be no *net* short-term capital movements. However, if the foreign branch lends the dollars to foreign non-banks and there is no aggregate increase in foreign non-bank demand for American dollars, the excess dollars will flow to the foreign central banks and there will be a *net* private short-term capital outflow. If the U.S. resident deposit is made with a foreign commercial bank, the same analysis applies so far as the effects on U.S. short-term capital flow is concerned. However, if the foreign commercial bank redeposits the dollars with a foreign branch of a U.S. bank, there will be an increase in E_{fb} and hence in T_p.

Effects of changes in the international interest rate structure
The effects of relative changes in interest rate levels as among U.S. money market rates, Eurodollar rates, and rates in non-dollar markets on foreign liquid asset holdings are exceedingly complex and there exist neither adequate models nor sufficient data for analysing their effects on short-term capital imports in the U.S. Balance of Payments. Nevertheless, in the following paragraphs I shall set forth certain tentative hypotheses for which empirical tests might be designed.

(*a*) Between the end of 1965 and mid–1970 the principal influence on interest rates in the Eurodollar market was the U.S. commercial bank demand for Eurodollars. The U.S. bank demand is to a considerable degree a function of the spread between the Eurodollar rate and the cost to U.S. banks of obtaining funds from alternative sources including in the cost determination such variables as differential reserve requirements. Changes in Federal Reserve Board regulations relating to reserve requirements on funds borrowed by U.S. banks from the Eurodollar market and to interest rates that may be paid on foreign and domestic deposits have had a substantial impact on the level of U.S. bank borrowings from their foreign branches. Thus, U.S. credit conditions together with Federal Reserve Board regulations have been major determinants of both Eurodollar rates and U.S. bank borrowings from their foreign branches.[22]

(b) Eurodollar interest rates are also affected by the foreign demand for loans from the Eurodollar market. At the end of 1965, U.S. resident borrowing from the Eurodollar market was only 17 per cent of total borrowing from the Eurodollar market, but by June 1969 total U.S. borrowing had risen to 50 per cent of total market uses.[23] However, with the sharp decline in U.S. borrowing from the market in 1970, U.S. borrowing probably accounted for no more than a quarter of total uses at the end of 1970, and the market became more responsive to the foreign demand for Eurodollars. In the absence of U.S. capital export controls on both U.S. bank lending and direct foreign investment, foreign firms, including foreign affiliates of U.S. corporations, would have the option of borrowing either in the Eurodollar market or of obtaining loans or other types of financing from the United States. However, U.S. capital export restrictions reduced the availability of U.S. financing and increased the spread between U.S. and Eurodollar loan rates. Foreign

[22] E. G. Massaro related by means of regression analysis monthly changes in gross Eurodollar liabilities of U.S. banks to their foreign branches (dependent variable) to the Federal Funds rate minus the Eurodollar call rate (adjusted for Eurodollar float), and changes in the amount of C.D.s outstanding. He found that the C.D.s and the interest rate differential accounted for about 45 per cent of the monthly changes in Eurodollar gross liabilities over the period January 1966 to May 1970. Variations in C.D.s were employed in the regression analysis since they constitute a substitute source of funds for U.S. banks [10].

[23] According to the B.I.S., U.S. resident borrowing from the Eurodollar market amounted to $2·0 billion out of total market uses of $11·5 billion at the end of December 1965. By the end of June 1969, U.S. resident borrowing had risen to $16·7 billion out of total market uses of $33·5 billion, but U.S. resident borrowing declined to $16·5 billion in December 1969 out of total market uses of $37·5 billion. [1, p. 158].

borrowers may also have the option of borrowing in non-dollar money markets, but these markets are often restricted, particularly when they involve the export of capital from the lending country.

When U.S. resident borrowing from the Eurodollar market declines, Eurodollar rates tend to decline and both the foreign demand for, and the availability of, Eurodollar funds tend to rise. However, a shift from U.S. resident borrowing to foreign borrowing from the Eurodollar market tends to induce a foreign private short-term capital outflow from the United States. This is true because most foreigners (including foreign affiliates of U.S. firms) borrow for financing foreign currency expenditures or imports from the United States rather than for increasing their dollar working balances.

(*c*) An increase in the Eurodollar deposit rate relative to U.S. money market rates tends to encourage foreigners to shift out of American dollars into Eurodollars entailing at least a momentary expansion in the total volume of foreign non-official dollar liquidity. Unless there is a compensating increase in the U.S. resident demand for Eurodollars (including that arising from U.S. bank borrowing from their foreign branches) some of the non-official holdings of American dollars will be transferred to the foreign central banks.

(*d*) An increase in Eurodollar deposit rates relative to U.S. money market rates will increase the flow of U.S. resident dollars to the Eurodollar market, thereby increasing U.S. dollar outflow. Unless this U.S. short-term capital outflow is accompanied by an increase in U.S. resident borrowing from the Eurodollar market, the American dollars will flow into foreign central banks.

(*e*) An increase in Eurodollar rates relative to U.S. money market rates is likely to induce a shift of foreign official (American) dollar holdings to the Eurodollar market. This will increase the supply of Eurodollar funds available for loans to both U.S. residents and foreign residents. Again, the effect on private short-term capital flow in the U.S. Balance of Payments will depend upon whether the dollars flow mainly to U.S. residents or to foreign borrowers. However, central banks are motivated by factors other than the desire to maximise returns on their dollar reserve assets.

(f) An increase in the Eurodollar deposit rate relative to interest rates in foreign currency money markets will tend to induce foreigners to exchange their foreign currency liquid asset holdings for Eurodollars (or to deposit current dollar receipts with Eurodollar banks rather than convert such receipts into another currency). While an increase in the foreign private demand for Eurodollars, whether by foreign non-banks or foreign commercial banks, would increase T_p, the effects on foreign non-official holdings of American dollars, and hence on short-term capital imports in the U.S. Balance of Payments will depend upon whether the dollars are lent by the Eurodollar banks to U.S residents or to foreign non-banks. Only in the former case would there occur a short-term private capital inflow. It should be noted, however, that if the rise in Eurodollar rates relative to foreign currency money market rates were accompanied by a rise in Eurodollar rates relative to U.S. money market rates, private short-term capital would tend to flow out of the United States, thereby tending to offset any short-term capital inflow induced by the rise in Eurodollar rates relative to foreign currency money market rates. Thus, in relating changes in relative interest rate levels to short-term capital movements it is necessary to consider the relationships among the constellation of relevant interest rates, together with the pattern of Eurodollar lending as between loans to U.S. residents and to foreigners.

3. Summary and Conclusions

In analysing the factors determining the foreign private demand for liquid dollar assets and short-term capital movements in the U.S. Balance of Payments, this paper has admittedly raised many more problems than it has solved. Nevertheless, fuller recognition of the complexities examined is essential for the formulation of more realistic models explaining short-term capital movements. My conclusions may be summarised as follows:

(1) The analysis of private short-term capital movements in the U.S. Balance of Payments must take into account not simply the foreign private demand for American liquid

dollar assets but the foreign demand for and supply of both American liquid dollar assets and Eurodollars. The foreign demand for and supply of liquid dollar assets is governed by a complex set of interest rate differentials, asset preferences, locational preferences for holding liquid dollar assets, exchange rate expectations and the special behavioural patterns of multinational banks in serving multinational corporations and other customers throughout the world. Moreover, the total supply of foreign private liquid dollar assets is not independent of the pattern of private demand as between American liquid dollar assets and Eurodollars. Thus, the Eurodollar market in its role as an international financial intermediary has substantially expanded the volume of foreign private dollar liquidity.

(2) Trade variables are probably not very important in the explanation of short-run changes in the foreign private demand for American liquid dollar assets. Foreign non-bank holdings of demand deposits in U.S. banks changed very little between December 1964 and December 1970 and to a lesser extent this was true of other American short-term dollar asset holdings of foreign non-banks. Eurodollars are a good substitute for American dollars with the exception of small dollar working balances that must be held in the form of U.S. demand deposits, and there is strong evidence that foreigners are able to conduct an increasingly large volume of dollar transactions with little or no increase in U.S. demand deposit holdings.

(3) At the end of 1970, over 80 per cent of the recorded U.S. short-term liabilities to foreign banks constituted intra-bank accounting entries, i.e. U.S. bank liabilities to their foreign branches plus the liabilities of U.S. agencies and branches of foreign banking corporations to their head offices or branches abroad. Changes in U.S. bank liabilities to their foreign branches reflect changes in credit conditions in the United States and the relative advantage of borrowing in the Eurodollar market as against other sources of funds, as determined both by interest rate differentials and Federal Reserve Board

regulations.[24] U.S. resident banks have also shifted portions of their foreign loans to their overseas branches from time to time, thereby reducing their liabilities to their foreign branches. Foreign banks have tended to increase their investments in the United States through their foreign branches at a fairly steady pace throughout the period 1960–1970. These developments in intra-bank transactions which are reflected mainly in U.S. private short-term capital movements cannot be adequately explained in terms of relative interest rate levels and trade variables; they are a consequence of the behavioural patterns of multinational banking corporations whose operations are closely tied to those of multinational corporations and influenced in various ways by governmental policies. Thus, for example, in serving the financial requirements of multinational firms both U.S. and foreign multinational banks borrow funds in a variety of markets and make loans in a number of currencies to the head offices or affiliates of multinational firms throughout the world.

(4) The problem of handling all of the variables described in this paper in a testable model of foreign private short-term capital flows in the U.S. Balance of Payments staggers the imagination. It seems likely that future progress in analysing both the operations of the Euro-dollar market and short-term capital movements will be made by formulating partial models for testing particular relationships rather than by formulating a comprehensive equilibrium model aggregating all classes of transactors and types of short-term capital movements. The importance of varying asset preferences among categories of transactors suggests the desirability of using

[24] In November 1970 the Federal Reserve Board took action to moderate the repayment of Eurodollar borrowings by U.S. banks by raising from 10 per cent to 20 per cent the reserves required to be held against Eurodollar borrowings in excess of the reserve-free base level and, at the same time, amended the regulations regarding the computation of the base. The effect of these changes was to discourage banks from further reducing their Eurodollar borrowings in order to maintain their reserve-free base level so as to enable the banks to maintain the option of having recourse to the Eurodollar market in the future, should the need arise.

portfolio models which reflect different preference functions. Such an analysis would require considerable knowledge of the behaviour patterns of various categories of foreign transactors. For example, it may be determined that wealthy individuals in certain Latin American countries tend to hold the vast bulk of their foreign currency liquid assets in dollars while those in other countries are more disposed to hold sterling or Swiss francs. However, we need to know far more than we do about the asset preferences of liquid asset holders both geographically and functionally. The selection of appropriate interest rate variables in preference functions also presents a serious problem. Are we to assume that foreign portfolio managers are sensitive to relative movements in the entire constellation of rates in the principal money markets around the world, or are their preferences limited mainly to American dollars, Eurodollars and their domestic currency? It is likely that every foreign portfolio manager has a unique preference function with respect to currencies, exchange rate expectations and risk (other than exchange risk) evaluation. Perhaps most difficult of all is the analysis of intra-bank transactions which account for a substantial portion of the recorded movements in foreign non-official liquid dollar holdings. One simplifying approach might be to regard all dollar obligations of foreign branches of U.S. banks as U.S. dollar obligations to foreigners and all transactions between U.S. banks and their foreign branches as domestic transactions.[25] A similar treatment might be applied to U.S. branches and agencies of foreign banking corporations. While this approach might simplify the analysis somewhat, there are difficulties arising from the paucity of published data on the assets and liabilities of the branches and agencies with which to test hypotheses relating to their behaviour.

[25] This approach would involve a change in U.S. Balance of Payments accounting which has been suggested in an unpublished memorandum by a former chief of the U.S. Balance of Payments Division, Department of Commerce.

References

[1] Bank for International Settlements, *Fortieth Annual Report*, June 1970.
[2] Bank of Canada, *Statistical Summary*, May 1970.
[3] BRYANT, RALPH C. and HENDERSHOTT, P. H., *Financial Capital Flows and the Balance of Payments of the United States: An Exploratory Empirical Study*. Princeton Essays in International Finance, No. 25, Princeton University, June 1970.
[4] DIAMOND, MARCUS, 'Trends in the Flow of International Private Capital, 1957–65', I.M.F. Staff Papers, (March 1967) 1–40.
[5] *Federal Reserve Bulletin*, February, 1971.
[6] GRUBEL, H. G., 'Internationally Diversified Portfolios', *American Economic Review*, L, (December 1968) 1299–1314.
[7] International Monetary Fund, *Balance of Payments Yearbook*, Vol. 21, 1964–68.
[8] International Monetary Fund, *International Financial Statistics*, April 1971.
[9] LEAMER, EDWARD E. and STERN, ROBERT M., 'Problems in the Theory and Empirical Estimation of International Capital Movements', *International Mobility and Movement of Capital*, Fritz Machlup, Walter S. Salant and Lorie Tarshis, eds, National Bureau of Economic Research, New York, 1972, 171–206.
[10] MASSARO, E. G., 'Eurodollars and U.S. Banks', *The Conference Board Record*, National Industrial Conference Board, October 1970, 15–22.
[11] MIKESELL, RAYMOND F., 'The Eurodollar Market and the Foreign Demand for Liquid Dollar Assets', *Journal of Money, Credit and Banking*, August 1972, 643–83.
[12] Morgan Guaranty Trust Company of New York, 'Recent Eurocurrency Market Developments', *World Financial Markets*, January 1971, 6–8.
[13] *The Treasury Bulletin*, November 1970.

10   Equalisation of Factor Prices by Sufficiently Diversified Production Under Conditions of Balanced Demand

PAUL A. SAMUELSON*†

1.

If we have two factors ('labour and land') and one good, the slightest geographical difference in factor endowments will make factor prices unequal. If a second good is added that differs not at all in factor intensities from the first, the same conclusion holds.

If there are two goods that differ in their factor intensities and factor endowments are identical, factor prices will be equal. A slight perturbation in relative endowments will not suffice to upset this factor-price equalisation. But sufficiently large differentiation of geographical endowments must, even under strong differences in factor intensities of the two goods, ultimately destroy factor-price equalisation by leading to complete specialisation.

What happens as we increase indefinitely the number of goods[1] of 'intrinsically-differing factor intensities'? If demand is kept 'balanced', the present paper shows that such an increase in numbers must result eventually in factor-price equalisation

* Massachusetts Institute of Technology.

† I owe thanks to the National Science Foundation for financial aid and to Mrs Jillian Pappas for editorial assistance.

[1] J. Vanek and T. J. Bertrand have considered related problems in the Kindleberger *Festschrift*, Chapter 3, i.e. in J. Bhagwati *et al.*, *Trade, Balance of Payments and Growth*, (Amsterdam: North Holland Publishing Company, 1971). They provide references to earlier articles by Tinbergen (1949), Meade (1950), Samuelson (1953), Land (1959), Johnson (1967, 1969), Vanek (1968), Bertrand (1969) and others.

no matter how large is the original discrepancy of the relative positive land/labour endowments geographically. And the same can be said to hold when there are three or more factors of production. The reader is warned that the rabbit of necessary factor-price equalisation is plucked out of the hat only because some strong assumptions are put into the hat.

2.

Definitions: Demand among n goods is said to be 'balanced' when equal amounts are always spent on every good. (This strong assumption could be somewhat relaxed, but not in this paper.) Two goods are, by definition, 'of intrinsically-differing labour/land intensities' if the shares of the factors in their production are constant and systematically different between goods; a set of $n = 2m + 1$ goods, by definition, are 'of intrinsically-differing factor intensities' if their labour/land shares (b_i) satisfy the lattice equalities

$$(b_m, b_{m-1}, \ldots, b_1, b_0, b_{-1}, \ldots, b_{-m})$$
$$= (a^m, a^{m-1}, \ldots, a, 1, a^{-1}, \ldots, a^{-m}) \qquad a > 1 \quad (1)$$

For m large, this assures that all relative factor intensities are 'well represented', particularly the two extremes. (Example: for $a = 2$, $m = 1$, we have $n = 3$ Cobb–Douglas production functions proportional to

$$(V_1^{1/2} V_2^{1/2}, \; V_1^{1/3} V_2^{2/3}, \; V_1^{2/3} V_2^{1/3})$$

Theorem (two-factor case): As the number of goods of 'intrinsically differing factor-intensities' increases toward infinity, factor-price equalisation occurs between any two regions no matter how far apart are their geographical endowment ratios. More precisely, equalisation occurs for all endowments satisfying

$$1 > A^*(a, m) < \frac{(\text{Labour/Land})_{\text{Region 1}}}{(\text{Labour/Land})_{\text{Region 2}}} < A^{**}(a, m) > 1 \quad (2)$$

where
$$\lim_{m \to \infty} \begin{cases} A^*(a, m) = 0 \\ A^{**}(a, m)^{-1} = 0 \end{cases}$$

Hence for m large enough factor-price equalisation is assured.

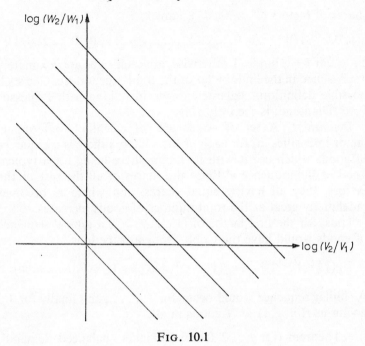

FIG. 10.1

Figure 10.1 can help explain the logic of what might otherwise seem like arbitrary assumptions. It portrays the well-known chart of factor/price ratio against factor proportions, but now on double-log scale so that the spread of the intensities can be identified with the statement that the parallel lines are distributed uniformly both on the right and the left of any intensity, *ad infinitum* in the limit.

3.

To generalise the result to any number of factors, retain the assumption of balanced demand. Now generalise the definition of a set of goods of 'essentially-differing factor intensities', in any one of a number of alternative ways, so as to ensure that the extreme poles – where each of r factors, taken by itself, suffices to produce a good – are increasingly well approximated as the number of goods is increased, i.e. the extreme points of relative shares of factors $(V_1, \ldots, V_1)$, namely

$$(1, 0, \ldots, 0) \cdots (0, 0, \ldots, \delta_{ij}, \ldots, 0), \ldots, (0, 0, \ldots, 0, 1),$$

$\delta_{ij} = 0$ if $i = j$ but $= 1$ otherwise, are each to be approximately approached in the limit by $1/r$ of the total expenditure. One such possible definition, suggested to me in talking with Professor Peter Diamond, is the following.

Definition: A set of goods are 'of essentially-differing r-factor intensities' if, for each of the r factors there is a sequence of goods which use it with its factor share being for a typical good of the sequence a^i times the shares of all the rest of the factors, they all having equal shares, and where a^i becomes indefinitely great as the total number of goods increases.

Thus, for the first factor of $(V_1, \ldots, V_r)$, a typical sequence of goods would have the Cobb–Douglas functions

$$V_1^{c_i}(\prod_2^r V_k)^{(1-c_i)/(r-1)}, \quad c_i/(1 - c_i) = a^i \quad (i = 0, 1, \ldots, m)$$

A similar sequence would occur for $V_2, \ldots,$ and finally for V_r, giving us $r(m + 1) = N$ goods in all.

> Theorem (for $r \geq 2$ factors): Under 'balanced demand', and for any number of factors, if there are enough goods N that are 'of effectively-differing factor intensities' equalisation of *all* factor prices is assured no matter how differentiated are geographical endowments of regions (provided only each region has positive amounts of all r factors.)

Specifically, factor prices are equalised between any two regions satisfying

$$1 > A^*(a, r, m) < \frac{[V_j \text{ endowment}/V_1 \text{ endowment}]_{\text{Region 1}}}{[V_j \text{ endowment}/V_1 \text{ endowment}]_{\text{Region 2}}} \quad (3)$$

$$< A^{**}(a, r, m) > 1 \quad (j = 2, \ldots, m)$$

with $\quad \lim_{m \to \infty} \begin{cases} A^*(a, r, m) = 0 \\ A^{**}(a, r, m)^{-1} \end{cases}$ for $a > 1, r > 2$

Only a sketch of a proof will be given. Note that if an economy has two Cobb-Douglas functions, the factor share of any V_j would be the mean of the k_j coefficients of the two industries' production function, calculated by using as industry weights the industry's share of total demand. If there were n industries, the same weighted mean of the nk_j shares would give aggregate share of the jth factor. Now the definition of intrinsically-differing factor intensities is so contrived that, as $m \to \infty$ and the number of goods becomes larger and larger, the weight of expenditure becomes spent almost completely among the r polar cases where each of the r factors is in effect the *only* factor and is earning 100 per cent share in its industry's product. Thus, we end up indefinitely close to the case of a world characterised by r industries each using only one of the r factors peculiar to it. Obviously, a world with the production functions

$$Q_1 = V_1, Q_2 = V_2, \ldots, Q_r = V_r$$

will have the same real factor prices everywhere regardless of geographical partition of total factor endowments, provided only that all endowments are positive. With each factor working alone, regional specialisation is quite impossible. If any doubt about the proof remains, the reader can think of the above limiting case as being generated by the following kind of limit

$$Q_1 = V_1^{1-\varepsilon}\left(\prod_2^r V_j\right)^{\varepsilon/(r-1)}, \ldots, Q_r = (V_1 \cdots V_{r-1})^{\varepsilon/(r-1)} V_r^{1-\varepsilon} \quad (4)$$

with $\varepsilon \to 0$ as $m \to \infty$. Clearly, for any geographical dispersion of endowments, so long as every region has something of each factor, by making ε small enough we can ensure factor-price equalisation. The concept of 'diagonal dominance', first introduced by McKenzie, is used here with a vengeance.

Figure 10.2 illustrates, for $r = 3$ factors, the logic of the argument. Any industry point in Figure 2 represents, by its distance from the respective sides of the equilateral triangle, the relative shares of three factors in the indicated industry. As we move toward corner 1, say, the industry is more and more 'purely-labour (or V_1) intensive'. The definition of 'effectively-differing factor intensities' ensures that most industry points end up clustering indefinitely near one of each of the three corners being shown here, on the altitude lines,

$$\left[\tfrac{1}{2}, \tfrac{4}{5}, \ldots, 2^i/(1 + 2^i), \ldots\right]$$

8

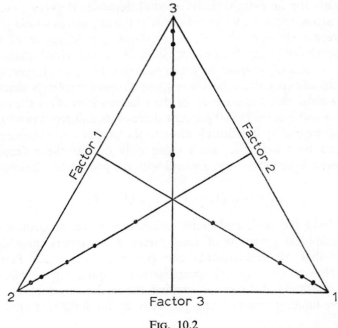

Fig. 10.2

fractions of the way toward the respective corners. That all the industry points fall on the angle-bisectors is a result of adopting the particular Diamond suggestion and is not an essential feature of a more general definition of 'differing factor intensities'.

4.

One singular, and surely objectionable, consequence of these strong assumptions of balanced demand and effectively-differentiated factor intensities is the fact that all r factors end up in the present model with equal shares. This is not at all an essential feature of the model: it would be easy to modify the assumption of balanced demand – as e.g. to assume that five times as much gets spent on land-intensive goods as on labour-intensive, with labour's final share of income being only one-sixth; but it is important for the present sufficiency conditions, that no significant expenditure must end up going for goods of mixed factor intensities, since otherwise one could not rule out completely specialised trade between diverse geographical regions.

It is of interest to note that the recent work of Professor Tinbergen has been with real-world models in which each nation should specialise in only a limited range of goods, which is in marked contrast with the non-specialisation results of the present artificial model. Empirical fact must decide among the competing theoretical models.

11 A Ten-Region Model of World Trade

ERIK THORBECKE AND
ALFRED J. FIELD, JR.*

Introduction

OVER the last two decades a number of important contributions have been made to the quantitative analysis of the pattern of world trade. It is possible to break down these contributions into three broad categories: (a) comprehensive studies of the changes in the pattern of world trade using non-econometric techniques such as the pathbreaking work of the League of Nations [1] which analysed the network of world trade between 1928 and 1938; the work of Thorbecke which extended the previous analysis to 1956 [12] and Maizels [3]; (b) econometric attempts at explaining trade flows between individual countries and regions by way of essentially single equation models such as the contributions of Tinbergen [10], Pöyhönen [6] and Linneman [2]; and, (c) transmission models which attempted to estimate quantitatively the main relationships between the level of domestic economic activities in the various countries and the international transactions. Perhaps most representative of this class of models are those of Neisser and Modigliani [4], Polak [5], Rhomberg [7] and Rhomberg and Boissonneault [8].

It is therefore somewhat surprising that the most disaggregated world trade model available at this time is that of Rhomberg which is limited to only three regions. It appears clear that a multiregional model embodying all the trade information contained in a comprehensive world trade matrix could provide significant insight into the nature and structure

* Professor of Economics, Iowa State University (Ames); Assistant Professor of Economics, University of North Carolina (Chapel Hill).

of the network of world trade. Taplin, in a recent review of world trade models [9], recommended that a multiregional, multicommodity model be built in terms of ten to twelve regions and six categories of goods.

The present attempt is a move in that direction – at least in terms of building a world trade model broken down into ten regions and capable of explaining the multi-regional trade flows resulting from short-run changes in income and prices.[1]

Section 1 is devoted to the structural specification of the model. Section 2 provides the quantitative estimation of the complete model and a discussion of some of the quantitative results obtained. The third section attempts to test the quality of the model particularly in terms of its predictive ability over the sample period. The final part of the paper ends with some conclusions.

1. The Structure of the Model

The present model is essentially demand-oriented and of a short-run nature. The world is divided into eleven regions as indicated in Table 11.1. The trade pattern of the Sino-Soviet

TABLE 11.1. *Description of Regions*

Region 1	United States
Region 2	Canada
Region 3	European Economic Community
Region 4	Non-E.E.C. Western Europe (residual group comprised of all non-E.E.C. countries in Western Europe)
Region 5	Japan
Region 6	Latin America
Region 7	Middle East (Aden, Bahrein, Cyprus, Ethiopia, Iran Iraq, Israel, Jordan, Kuwait, Lebanon, Libya, Qatar, Somalia, Sudan, Syrian, Arab Republic, U.A.R.)
Region 8	Australia, New Zealand, South Africa
Region 9	African countries not included in Regions 7 and 8 plus miscellaneous islands and territories
Region 10	South-East Asia, exclusive of Sino-Soviet bloc countries in Asia
Region 11	Sino-Soviet countries in Europe and Asia

[1] At a further stage a commodity-breakdown could be superimposed upon the regional breakdown included in this model.

bloc (region 11) is considered to be determined exogenously because of the difficulty of identifying the determinants of that region's trade and the general bilateral nature of its trading pattern. The major requirement imposed on the proposed model is that it explains the interregional commodity flows within the ten-region matrix consisting of five developed and five developing regions.

The theoretical structure of the model can be viewed as a sequel to the work of Rhomberg, although it is broader in scope and regionally much more disaggregated – using a ten-region breakdown compared to only three in Rhomberg's case. Since all of the trade matrix figures are expressed in f.o.b. terms, exports from region j to region i are equivalent to region i's imports from region j, avoiding thereby the problem of statistical discrepancies arising from mixed use of f.o.b. and c.i.f. data.

The structural form of the model is essentially that of a demand-oriented Keynesian system for the world economy. Income is determined by both the supply and demand for goods and services. Domestic and foreign effective demand, in turn, are assumed to be determined by the level of real income at home and abroad. This circularity gives rise to the multiplier effect so typical of the Keynesian system. Since the multiplier effects are concerned with real income changes, it is necessary to specify all relationships in real terms rather than money terms to separate the real income changes from price changes.

Table 11.2 presents the trade model in structural form which is followed by the list of variables. Equation (1) represents the national income account identity for the five developed regions. G.N.P. of each developed region is expressed as the sum of its components, i.e. consumption plus investment plus government expenditures (these last two variables taken as exogenous) plus total exports minus total imports plus two balancing exogenous variables.[2] Since exports of region i to region j are equal to the imports into region j from region i, it follows that $\sum_{j=1}^{10} M_{ji}$

[2] These variables represent, respectively, net exports of each region with the Sino-Soviet bloc and total exports to Region 8 and an adjustment for invisible trade terms and c.i.f.–f.o.b. valuation differences.

TABLE 11.2. *A Ten-Region Model of World Trade in Structural Form*

Number of Equations	
5	$Y_i = C_i + \bar{I}_i + \bar{G}_i + \sum_{j=1}^{10} M_{ji} - \sum_{j=1}^{10} M_{ij} + \bar{B}_i^{8,11} + \bar{B}_i^r$ (1)

$i = 1, \ldots, 5;\ j = 1, \ldots, 10$ (except in $\sum_{j=1}^{10} M_{ji}$ where $j \neq 8$); and $i \neq j$

1	$Y_1^P = Y_1 - U_1$ (2)
1	$T_1 = \gamma_0 + \gamma_1 Y_1^P$ (3)
1	$Y_1^{PD} = Y_1^P - T_1$ (4)
1	$C_1 = \beta_0 + \beta_1 Y_1^{PD} + \beta_2 \bar{T}_r$ (5)
4	$C_i = \beta_{i0} + \beta_{i1} Y_i + \beta_{i2} T_r$

$i = 2, \ldots, 5$

45	$M_{ij} = \delta_{ij0} + \delta_{ij1}[Y_i - \overline{\Delta BI_i}] + \delta_{ij2} \dfrac{\bar{P}_i}{\bar{r}_i \bar{p}_j^x} + \delta_{ij3} \bar{T}_r +$

$\qquad \delta_{ij4} \overline{DV}_K \qquad i = 1, \ldots, 5;\ j = 1, \ldots, 10$ for $i \neq j$

20	$M_{ij} = \alpha_{ij0} + \alpha_{ij1}\left[\underset{-1}{\bar{R}_i} + \sum_{j=1}^{5} M_{ji} + \bar{M}_{ri} \right] + \alpha_{ij2} \underset{-1}{\bar{M}_{ij}} +$

$\qquad \alpha_{ij3} \dfrac{\bar{P}_w^x}{\bar{P}_j^x} \qquad i = 6, 7, 9, 10;\ j = 1, \ldots, 5$ (7)

r = rest of world (the world exclusive of the developed regions $1, \ldots, 5$)

5	$r_1 P_i^x = z_{i0} + z_{i1} \bar{P}_i + z_{i2} \sum_{j=1}^{5} M_{ji} + z_{i3} \bar{T}_r \qquad i = 1, \ldots 5;$

$\qquad i \neq j$ (8)

___
83

EXPLANATION OF VARIABLES*

Y_i	G.N.P. in region i: $i = 1, \ldots, 5$.
C_i	Total consumption expenditures in region i: $1 = 1, \ldots, 5$.
G_i	Government expenditures in region i: $i = 1, \ldots 5$.
M_{ij}	Merchandise imports into region i from region j, expressed in f.o.b. terms: $i = 1, \ldots, 7, 9, 10$. $j = 1, \ldots, 10$, for $i \neq j$ (i.e. regional intratrade is not specified in the model).
Y_1^P	Personal income in region 1.
Y_1^{PD}	Personal disposable income in region 1.
T_1	Personal taxes in region 1 (i.e. disposable personal income + personal taxes = personal income).

U_i $Y_1 - Y_1^P$

$\bar{B}_i^{8,11}$ Net exports of region i with region 11 (the Sino-Soviet bloc) plus region i's total exports to region 8 (Australia, New Zealand, South Africa): $i = 1, \ldots, 5$.

B_i^r A balancing item which adjusts for (a) invisible trade items and (b) the c.i.f.-f.o.b. valuation difference in the G.N.P. income identity equation of region i. This adjustment is necessary since the import functions deal only with merchandise trade and are all stated in f.o.b. terms. $i = 1, \ldots, 5$.

$\overline{\Delta BI}_i$ Change in business inventories of region i: $i = 1, \ldots, 5$.

$\bar{T}_r$ Time trend $(1, 2, \ldots, n)$.

$\bar{P}_i$ Implicit (G.N.P.) price deflator for region i (1958 = 100): $i = 1, \ldots, 5$).

$\bar{P}_i^x$ Export price index of region i (1958 = 100): $i = 1, \ldots, 10$.

$\bar{P}_w^x$ Export (dollar) price index of total world exports (1958 = 100).

$\bar{P}_w^{xP}$ Export (dollar) price index of world exports of primary products (1958 = 100).

$\bar{r}_i$ Implicit exchange rate of region i *vis-à-vis* region 1 (the United States dollar; 1958 = 1·00); i.e. region i's G.N.P. in current United States dollars and 1958 exchange rates divided by region i's G.N.P. in current United States dollars and current exchange rates. $i = 2, \ldots, 5$.

$\bar{R}_i$ $_{-1}$ Foreign exchange reserves of region i at the end of the previous period $(t - 1)$, inclusive of gold holdings, reserve positions in the Fund, and foreign exchange: $i = 6, 7, 9, 10$.

$\hat{M}_{ri}$ Net balance on current account of the developing regions (i.e. 6, 7, 9, 10) *vis-à-vis* one another plus the net invisible balance *vis-à-vis* the developed regions (i.e. 1, …, 5): $i = 6, 7, 9, 10$.

$\bar{M}_{ij}$ $_{-1}$ Merchandise imports into a period region i from region j, expressed in f.o.b. terms and lagged one period $(t - 1)$: $i = 6, 7, 9, 10$; $j = 1, \ldots, 5$.

$\overline{DV}_K$ Dummy shift (0, 1) variable included to reflect unusual events. The variable takes the value of 1 for the years indicated by the subscript K and in all other years it is set equal to zero.

* All indexes use 1958 as the base year (i.e. 1958 = 100). All non-index variables are expressed in billions of United States dollars at 1958 prices and 1958 exchange rates. Exogenous variables are identified with a bar above the symbol.

represents exports of region i to all other regions.[3] Equations (2), (3) and (4), respectively, define for region 1 (United States) personal income, personal taxes and personal disposable income. Equation (5) gives the set of consumption functions applying to the five developed regions. There is a slight difference between the specification of the consumption function for the U.S. and that for the other four developed regions. U.S. consumption is expressed as a function of personal disposable income and a trend factor whereas consumption of the other four developed regions is expressed as a function of G.N.P. and a trend factor.

The demand for merchandise imports into the developed regions is given in relation (6). Imports into each developed region i from all regions j are assumed to depend upon the level of business activity, as indicated by G.N.P. corrected for changes in business inventory, the ratio of prices in the importing region $(\bar{P}_i)$ to the export index of the exporting region[4] and a time trend factor $(\bar{T}_r)$. Occasional dummy variables are included in several equations to act as proxy variables denoting shifts believed to result from various non-quantifiable autonomous factors. It should be recalled that the net value of the service entries in the current account of the Balance of Payments is given exogenously (i.e. $\bar{B}_i^r$ in the national income identities). With the help of these forty-five import equations (consisting of nine regional import functions into each of five developed regions), the effect of income and price changes are used to explain the level of imports on a regionally disaggregated basis. The model is demand-oriented in the sense that variations in the ten regions' exports to the developed regions are simultaneously explained by the above import functions. Nevertheless, supply and capacity limitations in the exporting regions would presumably be reflected by the export price variable which appears in the import functions. Finally, no attempt is made to

[3] Imports into Region 8 (Australia, New Zealand and South Africa) are taken as exogenously determined.

[4] Since all variables in the model (except for the price indices) are expressed in U.S. dollars at 1958 prices and 1958 exchange rates the G.N.P. price deflator of the importing region has to be corrected for exchange rate changes $(\bar{r}_i)$. In some cases the numerator of the price variable is replaced by the export (dollar) price index of total world exports $(\bar{P}_w^x)$ or by the export (dollar) price index of world exports of primary products $(\bar{P}_w^{xp})$.

explain intra-trade within Region 3 (E.E.C.) or Region 4 (Non-E.E.C. Western Europe).

Imports into the developing regions from the developed regions, are considered to be determined by the capacity to import of the former, the lagged value of imports and a relative price variable (see Equation (7)). The capacity to import, in turn, is assumed to depend on the level of lagged foreign exchange reserves, the current level of exports to the developed world and the net balance on current account of the developing regions, *vis-à-vis* one another ($\bar{M}_{ri}$). There are twenty such equations explaining imports into four developing regions (Latin America, Middle East, Africa and Southeast Asia) from the five developed regions [5].[5]

It is clear that the time pattern of adjustment of a developing region's imports to the availability of foreign exchange is a complex process. The simplest approach would be to assume that imports into these regions are exactly equal to their respective capacities to import in any given year. Indeed, the tendency for the less developed countries to resort to defensive measures in the form of quantitative controls would lend credence to such an assumption. At the same time, however, it is obvious that a decision-making lag exists even if the afore-mentioned assumption is reflective of the decision rules em-ployed. Consequently, the estimated coefficients (the α's in relation (7)) can be considered to reflect the adjustment process.

Finally, the last set of relations (8) in Table 11.2 is meant to express the determinants of the dollar export price indices for the five developed regions as a function of respectively each region's G.N.P. price deflator, total exports to the developed world, and a time trend. It should be noted that the correspond-ing five export price equations are not an integral part of the model in the sense that the model itself is run by assuming all price variables determined exogenously, i.e. in deriving the reduced form of the estimated model no use was made of the export price equations in relation (8). Thus the export price relations can be considered as an adjunct part of the model. The only reason for specifying and estimating the five export price equations was to indicate that the regions' export prices seem

[5] The intra- and interregional trade flows within and among the de-veloping regions are not specified endogenously in the model.

to be relatively highly correlated with the above independent variables.

In summary, the model consists of seventy-eight equations in seventy-eight endogenous variables and eighty-eight exogenous variables. The simultaneous solution of the model can perhaps most clearly be viewed by means of reaction functions. The reaction function is generated for a region by specifying its national income as a function of its own domestic endogenous and exogenous income components (i.e. consumption, imports, investment and government expenditures) and as a function of its exports which are, in turn, linked to the national incomes of the other developed regions. Since the model contains as many endogenous variables as linearly independent equations the equilibrium levels of G.N.P. for the five developed regions are solved simultaneously after the reduced form has been derived. In the reduced form, all the seventy-eight endogenous variables (including thus the five developed regions' G.N.P.) are expressed exclusively as a function of the exogenous variables (which include a number of lagged endogenous variables).

2. The Model in Estimated Form

The model was estimated on the basis of annual observations covering the period 1953–67. All variables except for the price and dummy variables are expressed in constant 1958 U.S. dollars at 1958 exchange rates. All price indices used 1958 as the base year (i.e. 1958 = 100). The model was estimated using two different estimation procedures. It was first estimated on the basis of one stage least squares (O.L.S.). Since a time trend variable $(\bar{T}_r)$ appears in a large number of the equations and since time is obviously correlated with a number of the other independent variables appearing in these same equations, these other independent variables were regressed on $\bar{T}_r$ and the deviations from the regression trend were plugged in the behavioural equations of the model rather than the absolute values of these same variables.

A number of the equations estimated on the basis of O.L.S. revealed serial correlation as reflected by the Durbin-Watson (dW) statistic. The model was consequently re-estimated using a first order Cochrane-Orcutt iterative technique for estimating relationships containing serial correlation. The estimates obtained on the basis of this method were close to those obtained on the basis of the O.L.S. technique. Consequently, it was decided to present the model in its O.L.S. form.

The estimated model is given in Table 11.3. The coefficient of determination adjusted for degrees of freedom ($\bar{R}^2$), the F value, and the Durbin-Watson (dW) statistic are given for each estimated equation. Likewise the t ratio of each estimated coefficient is indicated in parentheses below it.

As can be seen from Table 11.3 the model consists of seventy-eight equations in seventy-eight endogenous variables and eighty-eight exogenous variables (including seventeen dummy variables). An examination of the estimated model reveals, in general, high coefficients of determination – 43 per cent of the estimated equations having an $\bar{R}^2$ above 0·95, 33 per cent between 0·85 and 0·95, and only two equations displaying an $\bar{R}^2$ between 0·40 and 0·50. Looking at the statistical significance of the various coefficients by region, it can be seen that the t value corresponding to the coefficients of the income variable for Region 1 (the United States) are all above 3·1 with one exception.[6] In contrast, the price coefficients reveal lower t ratios with, however, seven of the nine coefficients of the price variable in the import equations of Region 1 having t ratios of above 1·5.

In Region 2 (Canada) the same general pattern is noticeable, i.e. highly significant income coefficients and only relatively significant price coefficients. In this respect it is worth noting that the import functions into Canada from the developing regions yield less significant income and price coefficients than the import functions into Canada from the developed regions. With respect to the E.E.C. (Region 3) it can again be seen that most of the income coefficients are highly significant. However, it should be noted that the price variable is not significant in either the E.E.C. import function from the U.S. or from

[6] For a regression equation estimated on the basis of fifteen observations (1953–1967) with four independent variables, corresponding thus to eleven degrees of freedom, a t ratio of 3·1 would be statistically significant at the 1 per cent level, a t ratio of 2·2 would be statistically significant at the 5 per cent level and one of 1·9 at the 10 per cent level.

TABLE 11.3. *A Ten-Region Model of World Trade in Estimated Form*
(*variables are defined in Table 11.2*)

(1) $Y_1 = C_1 + \bar{I}_1 + \bar{G}_1 + M_{21} + M_{31} + M_{41} + M_{51}$
$+ M_{61} + M_{71} + M_{91} + M_{101} - M_{12}$
$- M_{13} - M_{14} - M_{15} - M_{16} - M_{17} - M_{18}$
$- M_{19} - M_{110} + \bar{B}_1^{8,11} + \bar{B}_1^r$

(2) $Y_1^P = Y_1 - \bar{U}_1$

(3) $Y_1^{PD} = Y_1^P - T_1$

(4) $T_1 = -1 \cdot 280 + 0 \cdot 128 \, Y_1^P$ $\qquad \bar{R}^2 = 0 \cdot 890$
$\quad \ (-0 \cdot 26) \quad (10 \cdot 72)$ $\qquad\qquad\quad F = 99 \cdot 4$
$\qquad\qquad\qquad\qquad\qquad\qquad\qquad\qquad dW = 1 \cdot 38$

(5) $C_1 = 28 \cdot 049 + 0 \cdot 775 \, Y^{PD} + 2 \cdot 919 \bar{T}_r$ $\qquad \bar{R}^2 = 0 \cdot 999$
$\quad \ \ (3 \cdot 30) \qquad (23 \cdot 43) \qquad\ (6 \cdot 85)$ $\qquad F = 7386 \cdot 2$
$\qquad\qquad\qquad\qquad\qquad\qquad\qquad\qquad dW = 2 \cdot 20$

(6) $M_{12} = 8 \cdot 735 + 0 \cdot 020[Y_1 - \overline{\Delta BI_1}] + 3 \cdot 871 \, \dfrac{\bar{P}_1}{\bar{P}_2^x}$ $\quad \bar{R}^2 = 0 \cdot 984$
$\qquad \ (-3 \cdot 50) \ (6 \cdot 33) \qquad\qquad\qquad\quad (1 \cdot 53)$ $\qquad F = 222 \cdot 1$
$\qquad - 0 \cdot 199 \bar{T}_r$ $\qquad\qquad\qquad\qquad\qquad\qquad dW = 2 \cdot 55$
$\qquad \ \ (-2 \cdot 90)$
$\qquad + 0 \cdot 90 \overline{DV}_{66-67}$
$\qquad \ \ (3 \cdot 54)$

[7] $M_{13} = -15 \cdot 356 + 0 \cdot 017[Y_1 - \overline{\Delta BI_1}] + 11 \cdot 088 \, \dfrac{\bar{P}_1}{\bar{P}_3^x}$ $\quad \bar{R}^2 = 0 \cdot 988$
$\qquad \ \ (-8 \cdot 20) \qquad (8 \cdot 90) \qquad\qquad\qquad (7 \cdot 10)$ $\qquad F = 368 \cdot 7$
$\qquad -0 \cdot 268 \bar{T}_r$ $\qquad\qquad\qquad\qquad\qquad\qquad\quad dW = 1 \cdot 58$
$\qquad \ \ (4 \cdot 91)$

[8] $M_{14} = -11 \cdot 208 + 0 \cdot 015[Y_1 - \overline{\Delta BI_1}] + 7 \cdot 221 \, \dfrac{\bar{P}_1}{\bar{P}_4^x}$ $\quad \bar{R}^2 = 0 \cdot 969$
$\qquad \ \ (-1 \cdot 93) \qquad (3 \cdot 78) \qquad\qquad\qquad (1 \cdot 47)$ $\qquad F = 110 \cdot 0$
$\qquad + 0 \cdot 346 \overline{DV}_{59} - 0 \cdot 199 \bar{T}_r$ $\qquad\qquad\qquad\qquad dW = 2 \cdot 18$
$\qquad \ \ (2 \cdot 40) \qquad\qquad (1 \cdot 70)$

[9] $M_{15} = -8 \cdot 219 + 0 \cdot 015[Y_1 - \overline{\Delta BI_1}] + 2 \cdot 981 \, \dfrac{\bar{P}_1}{\bar{P}_5^x}$ $\quad \bar{R}^2 = 0 \cdot 988$
$\qquad \ \ (-6 \cdot 32) \qquad (9 \cdot 94) \qquad\qquad\qquad (2 \cdot 41)$ $\qquad F = 289 \cdot 7$
$\qquad + 0 \cdot 174 \overline{DV}_{59} - 0 \cdot 165 T_r$ $\qquad\qquad\qquad\qquad\ dW = 2 \cdot 03$
$\qquad \ \ (1 \cdot 56) \qquad\qquad (-2 \cdot 96)$

TABLE 11.3 (*contd.*)

[10] $M_{16} = -2.456 + 0.007[Y_1 - \overline{\Delta BI}_1] + 3.84 \, \frac{\bar{P}_1}{\bar{P}_6^x}$ $\bar{R}^2 = 0.861$
      $\quad\quad (-1.31) \quad\quad (2.19) \quad\quad\quad\quad\quad\quad (3.36)$ $F = 22.7$
      $\quad\quad + 0.279 \overline{DV}_{56-57} - 0.167 \bar{T}_r$ $dW = 1.40$
      $\quad\quad\quad (2.50) \quad\quad\quad\quad (-1.92)$

[11] $M_{17} = 0.001[Y_1 - \overline{\Delta BI}_1] + 0.027 \frac{\bar{P}_w^x P}{\bar{P}_7^x}$ $\bar{R}^2 = 0.760$
      $\quad\quad\quad (3.45) \quad\quad\quad\quad (0.33)$ $F = 15.1$
      $\quad\quad + 0.036 DV_{59-67}$ $dW = 1.80$
      $\quad\quad\quad (1.09)$

[12] $M_{18} = -0.834 + 0.002[Y_1 - \overline{\Delta BI}_1] + 0.391 \, \frac{\bar{P}_1}{\bar{P}_8^x}$ $\bar{R}^2 = 0.881$
      $\quad\quad (-5.97) \quad\quad (4.97) \quad\quad\quad\quad\quad (1.67)$ $F = 50.8$
      $dW = 1.20$

[13] $M_{19} = -1.184 + 0.002[Y_1 - \overline{\Delta BI}_1] + 1.124 \, \frac{\bar{P}_w^x P}{\bar{P}_9^x}$ $\bar{R}^2 = 0.981$
      $\quad\quad (-2.16) \quad\quad (3.05) \quad\quad\quad\quad\quad (2.20)$ $F = 243.5$
      $\quad\quad + 0.027 \bar{T}_r$ $dW = 2.28$
      $\quad\quad\quad (2.75)$

[14] $M_{110} = -3.211 + 0.008[Y_1 - \overline{\Delta BI}_1] + 1.365 \, \frac{\bar{P}_1}{\bar{P}_{10}^x}$ $\bar{R}^2 = 0.984$
      $\quad\quad (-5.79) \quad\quad (12.25) \quad\quad\quad\quad\quad (0.33)$ $F = 290.2$
      $\quad\quad -0.108 \bar{T}_r$ $dW = 1.96$
      $\quad\quad (-5.48)$

[15] $Y_2 = C_2 + \bar{I}_2 + \bar{G}_2 + M_{12} + M_{32} + M_{42} + M_{52}$
      $\quad\quad + M_{62} + M_{72} + M_{92} + M_{102} - M_{21} - M_{23}$
      $\quad\quad - M_{24} - M_{25} - M_{26} - M_{27} - M_{28} - M_{29}$
      $\quad\quad - M_{210} + \bar{B}_2^{8,11} + \bar{B}_2^r$

[16] $C_2 = 5.461 + 0.414 Y_2 + 0.409 \bar{T}_r$ $\bar{R}^2 = 0.999$
      $\quad\quad (7.32) \quad\quad (14.05) \quad\quad (8.30)$ $F = 5060.9$
      $dW = 1.55$

[17] $M_{21} = -8.073 + 0.349[Y_2 - \overline{\Delta BI}_2] + 2.237 \, \frac{\bar{P}_2}{\bar{r}_2 \bar{P}_1^x}$ $\bar{R}^2 = 0.921$
      $\quad\quad (-3.91) \quad\quad (6.69) \quad\quad\quad\quad\quad (1.14)$ $F = 55.62$
      $\quad\quad -0.373 \bar{T}_r$ $dW = 1.50$
      $\quad\quad (4.29)$

TABLE 11.3 (*contd.*)

[18] $\quad M_{23} = 0\cdot730 + 0\cdot011[Y_2 - \overline{\Delta BI_2}] + 0\cdot563 \, \dfrac{\bar{P}_2}{\bar{r}_2 \bar{P}_3} \qquad \bar{R}^2 = 0\cdot973$

$\qquad (-5\cdot04) \ (3\cdot07) \qquad\qquad\qquad (4\cdot33) \qquad\qquad F = 170\cdot4$

$\qquad + 0\cdot007 \bar{T}_r \qquad\qquad\qquad\qquad\qquad\qquad\qquad dW = 1\cdot83$

$\qquad (1\cdot09)$

[19] $\quad M_{24} = -0\cdot775 + 0\cdot012[Y_2 - \overline{\Delta BI_2}] + 0\cdot998 \, \dfrac{\bar{P}_2}{\bar{r}_2 \bar{P}_4^x} \quad \bar{R}^2 = 0\cdot740$

$\qquad (-0\cdot80) \quad (6\cdot34) \qquad\qquad\qquad (2\cdot37) \qquad\quad F = 20\cdot5$

$\qquad\qquad\qquad\qquad\qquad\qquad\qquad\qquad\qquad\qquad\qquad dW = 0\cdot96$

[20] $\quad M_{25} = -0\cdot297 + 0\cdot009[Y_2 - \overline{\Delta BI_2}] + 0\cdot183 \, \dfrac{\bar{P}_2}{\bar{r}_2 \bar{P}_5^x} \quad \bar{R}^2 = 0\cdot974$

$\qquad (-6\cdot79) \quad (7\cdot49) \qquad\qquad\qquad (1\cdot83) \qquad\quad F = 262\cdot3$

$\qquad\qquad\qquad\qquad\qquad\qquad\qquad\qquad\qquad\qquad\qquad dW = 1\cdot58$

[21] $\quad M_{26} = -0\cdot395 + 0\cdot0001[Y_2 - \overline{\Delta BI_2}] + 0\cdot729 \, \dfrac{\bar{P}_w^{xp}}{\bar{P}_6^x} \quad \bar{R}^2 = 0\cdot660$

$\qquad (1\cdot99) \qquad (0\cdot07) \qquad\qquad\qquad (2\cdot91) \qquad\quad F = 14\cdot75$

$\qquad\qquad\qquad\qquad\qquad\qquad\qquad\qquad\qquad\qquad\qquad dW = 1\cdot76$

[22] $\quad M_{27} = -0\cdot142 + 0\cdot003[Y_3 - \overline{\Delta BI_2}] + 0\cdot118 \, \dfrac{\bar{P}_2}{\bar{r}_2 \bar{P}_7^x} \quad \bar{R}^2 = 0\cdot480$

$\qquad (1\cdot00) \qquad (1\cdot68) \qquad\qquad\qquad (0\cdot68) \qquad\quad F = 7\cdot4$

$\qquad\qquad\qquad\qquad\qquad\qquad\qquad\qquad\qquad\qquad\qquad dW = 0\cdot40$

[23] $\quad M_{28} = 0\cdot001[Y_2 - \overline{\Delta BI_2}] - 0\cdot009 \, \dfrac{\bar{P}_2}{\bar{r}_2 \bar{P}_8^x} + 0\cdot003 \bar{T}_r \quad \bar{R}^2 = 0\cdot920$

$\qquad (2\cdot23) \qquad\qquad\qquad (0\cdot47) \qquad\quad (3\cdot67) \qquad F = 54\cdot8$

$\qquad\qquad\qquad\qquad\qquad\qquad\qquad\qquad\qquad\qquad\qquad dW = 1\cdot69$

[24] $\quad M_{29} = 0\cdot040 + 0\cdot001[Y_2 - \overline{\Delta BI_2}] + 0\cdot036 \, \dfrac{\bar{P}_w^{xp}}{\bar{P}_9^x} \quad \bar{R}^2 = 0\cdot890$

$\qquad (0\cdot17) \quad (0\cdot17) \qquad\qquad\qquad (0\cdot17) \qquad\quad F = 38\cdot5$

$\qquad + 0\cdot009 \bar{T}_r \qquad\qquad\qquad\qquad\qquad\qquad\qquad dW = 2\cdot10$

$\qquad (1\cdot80)$

[25] $\quad M_{210} = -0\cdot066 + 0\cdot005[Y_2 - \overline{\Delta BI_2}] \qquad\qquad \bar{R}^2 = 0\cdot920$

$\qquad (1\cdot25) \qquad (3\cdot5) \qquad\qquad\qquad\qquad\qquad\quad F = 55\cdot3$

$\qquad -0\cdot002 \, \dfrac{\bar{P}_2}{\bar{r}_2 \bar{P}_{10}^x} - 0\cdot002 \bar{T}_r \qquad\qquad\qquad dW = 2\cdot23$

$\qquad (-0\cdot04) \qquad\quad (-0\cdot88)$

TABLE 11.3 (*contd.*)

[26] $Y_3 = C_3 + I_3 + \bar{G}_3 + M_{13} + M_{23} + M_{43} + M_{53}$
$\qquad + M_{63} + M_{73} + M_{93} + M_{103} - M_{31} - M_{32}$
$\qquad - M_{34} - M_{36} - M_{37} - M_{38} - M_{39}$
$\qquad - M_{310} + \bar{B}_3^{8,11} + \bar{B}_3^r$

[27] $C_3 = -20.788 + 0.826\,Y_3 - 2.004\,\bar{T}_r$
$\qquad\quad (-1.88) \qquad (8.46) \qquad\; (-2.17)$
$\qquad\qquad\qquad\qquad\qquad\qquad\qquad \bar{R}^2 = 0.998$
$\qquad\qquad\qquad\qquad\qquad\qquad\qquad F = 3981.6$
$\qquad\qquad\qquad\qquad\qquad\qquad\qquad dW = 1.57$

[28] $M_{31} = -11.185 + 0.054[Y_3 - \overline{\Delta BI}_3] + 6.031\dfrac{\bar{P}_w^x}{\bar{P}_1^x}$
$\qquad\quad\;\; (-1.42) \qquad (2.22) \qquad\qquad\qquad (0.72)$
$\qquad\qquad + 0.401\overline{DV}_{56-57} - 0.209\bar{T}_r$
$\qquad\qquad\quad (2.15) \qquad\qquad\quad (0.79)$
$\qquad\qquad\qquad\qquad\qquad\qquad\qquad \bar{R}^2 = 0.948$
$\qquad\qquad\qquad\qquad\qquad\qquad\qquad F = 64.7$
$\qquad\qquad\qquad\qquad\qquad\qquad\qquad dW = 1.78$

[29] $M_{32} = 0.027 + 0.003[Y_3 - \overline{\Delta BI}_3] - 0.075\dfrac{\bar{P}_w^x}{\bar{P}_2^x}$
$\qquad\quad (0.06) \quad (9.71) \qquad\qquad\qquad (-0.17)$
$\qquad\qquad\qquad\qquad\qquad\qquad\qquad \bar{R}^2 = 0.869$
$\qquad\qquad\qquad\qquad\qquad\qquad\qquad F = 47.4$
$\qquad\qquad\qquad\qquad\qquad\qquad\qquad dW = 2.14$

[30] $M_{34} = -6.941 + 0.084[Y_3 - \overline{\Delta BI}_3]$
$\qquad\quad\;\; (-6.17) \quad (8.17)$
$\qquad\qquad - 6.872\dfrac{\bar{P}_3}{\bar{r}_3\bar{P}_4^x} - 0.712\overline{DV}_{67}$
$\qquad\qquad\;\; (4.15) \qquad\qquad (2.59)$
$\qquad\qquad\qquad\qquad\qquad\qquad\qquad \bar{R}^2 = 0.993$
$\qquad\qquad\qquad\qquad\qquad\qquad\qquad F = 674.6$
$\qquad\qquad\qquad\qquad\qquad\qquad\qquad dW = 1.73$

[31] $M_{35} = -1.621 + 0.012[Y_3 - \overline{\Delta BI}_3]$
$\qquad\quad\;\; (-3.58) \quad (1.77)$
$\qquad\qquad + 0.349\dfrac{\bar{P}_3}{\bar{r}_3\bar{P}_5^x} - 0.085\bar{T}_r$
$\qquad\qquad\;\; (0.73) \qquad\qquad (-1.84)$
$\qquad\qquad\qquad\qquad\qquad\qquad\qquad \bar{R}^2 = 0.963$
$\qquad\qquad\qquad\qquad\qquad\qquad\qquad F = 122.5$
$\qquad\qquad\qquad\qquad\qquad\qquad\qquad dW = 1.54$

[32] $M_{36} = -0.872 + 0.012[Y_3 - \overline{\Delta BI}_3] + 0.527\dfrac{\bar{P}_3}{\bar{r}_3\bar{P}_6^x}$
$\qquad\quad\;\; (-0.81) \quad (1.63) \qquad\qquad\qquad (0.67)$
$\qquad\qquad - 0.018\bar{T}_r + 0.012\overline{DV}_{56-57}$
$\qquad\qquad\;\; (-0.22) \qquad\quad (0.19)$
$\qquad\qquad\qquad\qquad\qquad\qquad\qquad \bar{R}^2 = 0.973$
$\qquad\qquad\qquad\qquad\qquad\qquad\qquad F = 127.6$
$\qquad\qquad\qquad\qquad\qquad\qquad\qquad dW = 1.77$

[33] $M_{37} = -5.434 + 0.0179[Y_3 - \overline{\Delta BI}_3]$
$\qquad\quad\;\; (-3.63) \quad (12.65)$
$\qquad\qquad + 3.639\dfrac{\bar{P}_w^{xp}}{\bar{P}_7^x}$
$\qquad\qquad\;\; (2.64)$
$\qquad\qquad\qquad\qquad\qquad\qquad\qquad \bar{R}^2 = 0.926$
$\qquad\qquad\qquad\qquad\qquad\qquad\qquad F = 88.7$
$\qquad\qquad\qquad\qquad\qquad\qquad\qquad dW = 0.60$

TABLE 11.3 (*contd.*)

[34] $M_{38} = 0.006[Y_3 - \overline{\Delta BI_3}] - 0.131 \dfrac{\bar{P}_3}{\bar{r}_3 \bar{P}_8^x} - 0.026 \bar{T}_r$ $\bar{R}^2 = 0.85$
     (7.03) (-1.09) (-5.10) $F = 21.0$

     $+ 0.053 \overline{DV}_{56-57}$ $dW = 2.42$
       (2.04)

[35] $M_{39} = 0.007[Y_3 - \overline{\Delta BI_3}] + 0.972 \dfrac{\bar{P}_3}{\bar{r}_3 \bar{P}_9^x}$ $\bar{R}^2 = 0.962$
     (2.41) (2.17) $F = 120.1$

     $+ 0.289 \overline{DV}_{50-67}$ $dW = 1.21$
       (3.05)

[36] $M_{310} = -2.687 + 0.016[Y_3 - \overline{\Delta BI_3}]$ $\bar{R}^2 = 0.800$
       (2.79) (3.47) $F = 20.0$

         $+ 1.529 \dfrac{\bar{P}_w^{xp}}{\bar{P}_{10}^x} - 0.126 \bar{T}_r$ $dW = 1.77$
         (1.92) (-2.82)

[37] $Y_4 = C_4 + I_4 + \bar{G}_4 + M_{14} + M_{24} + M_{34} + M_{54}$
      $+ M_{64} + M_{74} + M_{94} + M_{104} + \bar{B}_4^{8,11} \bar{B}_4^r$

[38] $C_4 = -10.208 + 0.825 Y_4 - 1.739 \bar{T}_r$ $\bar{R}^2 = 0.990$
      (-0.93) (6.63) (-2.09) $F = 679.0$
                                 $dW = 1.26$

[39] $M_{41} = -7.518 + 0.020[Y_4 - \overline{\Delta BI_4}] + 6.575 \dfrac{\bar{P}_w^x}{\bar{P}_1^x}$ $\bar{R}^2 = 0.925$
      (-1.12) (1.13) (1.03) $F = 44.2$

     $+ 0.313 \overline{DV}_{56-57} + 0.106 \bar{T}_r$ $dW = 1.62$
       (1.61) (0.81)

[40] $M_{42} = -0.850 + 0.006[Y_4 - \overline{\Delta BI_4}] + 1.121 \dfrac{\bar{P}_w^x}{\bar{P}_2^x}$ $\bar{R}^2 = 0.861$
      (-1.24) (9.21) (1.66) $F = 44.5$
                                 $dW = 1.46$

[41] $M_{43} = -3.618 + 0.049[Y_4 - \overline{\Delta BI_4}] + 2.050 \dfrac{\bar{P}_w^x}{\bar{P}_3^x}$ $\bar{R}^2 = 0.861$
      (-0.33) (1.40) (0.19) $F = 191.9$

     $+ 0.376 \bar{T}_r$ $dW = 0.89$
       (1.69)

TABLE 11.3 (*contd.*)

[42] $\quad M_{45} = -2 \cdot 207 + 0 \cdot 016 [Y_4 - \overline{\Delta BI_4}] + 0 \cdot 847 \dfrac{\bar{P}^x_w}{\bar{P}^x_5} \qquad \bar{R}^2 = 0 \cdot 962$

$\qquad (-3 \cdot 42) \quad (4 \cdot 39) \qquad\qquad\quad (1 \cdot 44) \qquad\qquad F = 118 \cdot 7$

$\qquad - 0 \cdot 059 \bar{T}_r \qquad\qquad\qquad\qquad\qquad\qquad\qquad dW = 1 \cdot 09$

$\qquad (-2 \cdot 27)$

[43] $\quad M_{46} = 0 \cdot 193 + 0 \cdot 003 [Y_4 - \overline{\Delta BI_4}] + 0 \cdot 430 \dfrac{\bar{P}_4}{\bar{r}_4 \bar{P}^x_6} \qquad \bar{R}^2 = 0 \cdot 963$

$\qquad (0 \cdot 35) \quad (0 \cdot 80) \qquad\qquad\quad (1 \cdot 08) \qquad\qquad F = 92 \cdot 9$

$\qquad + 0 \cdot 096 DV_{56-57} + 0 \cdot 018 \bar{T}_r \qquad\qquad\qquad dW = 2 \cdot 84$

$\qquad (2 \cdot 48) \qquad\qquad\quad (0 \cdot 50)$

[44] $\quad M_{47} = -3 \cdot 016 + 0 \cdot 010 [Y_4 - \overline{\Delta BI_4}] \qquad\qquad \bar{R}^2 = 0 \cdot 974$

$\qquad (-4 \cdot 28) \quad (1 \cdot 92) \qquad\qquad\qquad\qquad F = 178 \cdot 0$

$\qquad\qquad\qquad\qquad\qquad\qquad\qquad\qquad\qquad dW = 2 \cdot 45$

$\qquad + 2 \cdot 884 \dfrac{\bar{P}_4}{\bar{r}_4 \bar{P}^x_7} - 0 \cdot 049 \bar{T}_r$

$\qquad (4 \cdot 18) \qquad\quad (-1 \cdot 31)$

[45] $\quad M_{48} = -0 \cdot 027 + 0 \cdot 011 [Y_4 - \overline{\Delta BI_4}] + 0 \cdot 172 \dfrac{\bar{P}^{xp}_w}{\bar{P}^x_8} \qquad \bar{R}^2 = 0 \cdot 862$

$\qquad (0 \cdot 06) \qquad (2 \cdot 88) \qquad\qquad\quad (0 \cdot 47) \qquad\qquad F = 30 \cdot 14$

$\qquad - 0 \cdot 043 \bar{T}_r \qquad\qquad\qquad\qquad\qquad\qquad\qquad dW = 1 \cdot 47$

$\qquad (-1 \cdot 74)$

[46] $\quad M_{49} = -3 \cdot 035 + 0 \cdot 009 [Y_4 - \overline{\Delta BI_4}] + 3 \cdot 487 \dfrac{\bar{P}^{xp}_w}{\bar{P}^x_9} \qquad \bar{R}^2 = 0 \cdot 909$

$\qquad (-2 \cdot 00) \quad (1 \cdot 41) \qquad\qquad\quad (2 \cdot 99) \qquad\qquad F = 47 \cdot 6$

$\qquad - 0 \cdot 027 \bar{T}_r \qquad\qquad\qquad\qquad\qquad\qquad\qquad dW = 1 \cdot 47$

$\qquad (-0 \cdot 60)$

[47] $\quad M_{410} = 1 \cdot 589 + 0 \cdot 003 [Y_4 - \overline{\Delta BI_4}] - 0 \cdot 925 \dfrac{\bar{P}^{xp}_w}{\bar{P}^x_{10}} \qquad \bar{R}^2 = 0 \cdot 550$

$\qquad (1 \cdot 27) \quad (3 \cdot 26) \qquad\qquad\quad (-0 \cdot 77) \qquad\qquad F = 9 \cdot 40$

$\qquad\qquad\qquad\qquad\qquad\qquad\qquad\qquad\qquad dW = 1 \cdot 02$

[48] $\quad Y_5 = C_5 + \bar{I}_5 + \bar{G}_5 + M_{15} + M_{25} + M_{35} + M_{45}$

$\qquad + M_{65} + M_{75} + M_{95} + M_{105} - M_{51} - M_{52}$

$\qquad - M_{53} - M_{54} - M_{56} - M_{57} - M_{58} - M_{59}$

$\qquad - M_{510} + \bar{B}^{8,11}_5 + \bar{B}^r_5$

[49] $\quad C_5 = 3 \cdot 835 + 0 \cdot 366 Y_5 + 0 \cdot 585 \bar{T}_r \qquad\qquad \bar{R}^2 = 0 \cdot 997$

$\qquad (7 \cdot 27) \quad (8 \cdot 44) \quad (3 \cdot 21) \qquad\qquad\qquad F = 2265 \cdot 6$

$\qquad\qquad\qquad\qquad\qquad\qquad\qquad\qquad\qquad dW = 1 \cdot 76$

TABLE 11.3 (*contd.*)

[50] $\quad M_{51} = 0.035[Y_5 - \overline{\Delta BI_5}] + 0.011\dfrac{\bar{P}^x_w}{\bar{P}^x_1}$ $\qquad \bar{R}^2 = 0.967$
$\qquad\qquad$ (21·73) $\qquad\qquad\qquad$ (0·15) $\qquad\qquad\qquad$ $F = 137.2$
$\qquad\qquad$ $- 0.265\overline{DV}_{58,59,62,67}$ $\qquad\qquad\qquad$ $dW = 1.84$
$\qquad\qquad$ (−3·87)

[51] $\quad M_{52} = -0.290 + 0.011[Y_5 - \overline{\Delta BI_5}] + 0.226\dfrac{\bar{P}_5}{\bar{r}_5\bar{P}^x_2}$ $\quad \bar{R}^2 = 0.975$
$\qquad\qquad$ (−3·19) $\quad$ (3·29) $\qquad\qquad\qquad$ (1·75) $\qquad$ $F = 82.8$
$\qquad\qquad$ $-0.024\bar{T}_r$ $\qquad\qquad\qquad\qquad\qquad$ $dW = 2.91$
$\qquad\qquad$ (−2·26)

[52] $\quad M_{53} = 0.067[Y_5 - \overline{\Delta BI_5}] - 0.201\dfrac{\bar{P}_5}{\bar{r}_5\bar{P}^x_3} - 0.271\bar{T}_r$ $\quad \bar{R}^2 = 0.434$
$\qquad\qquad$ (2·81) $\qquad\qquad$ (−0·67) $\quad$ (−3·14) $\qquad$ $F = 4.24$
$\qquad\qquad\qquad\qquad\qquad\qquad\qquad\qquad\qquad\qquad$ $dW = 1.44$

[53] $\quad M_{54} = -0.189 + 0.011[Y_5 - \overline{\Delta BI_5}]$ $\qquad\qquad$ $\bar{R}^2 = 0.979$
$\qquad\qquad$ (−1·41) $\quad$ (3·32) $\qquad\qquad\qquad\qquad\qquad$ $F = 219.6$
$\qquad\qquad$ $+ 0.099\dfrac{\bar{P}_5}{\bar{r}_5\bar{p}^x_4} - 0.021\bar{T}_r$ $\qquad\qquad$ $dW = 3.02$
$\qquad\qquad$ (0·58) $\qquad\qquad$ (−2·16)

[54] $\quad M_{56} = 0.010[Y_5 - \overline{\Delta BI_5}] + 0.002\dfrac{\bar{P}^{xp}_w}{\bar{P}^x_6}$ $\qquad \bar{R}^2 = 0.839$
$\qquad\qquad$ (7·81) $\qquad\qquad\qquad$ (0·04) $\qquad\qquad$ $F = 25.1$
$\qquad\qquad$ $- 0.112\overline{DV}_{58,59,62,67}$ $\qquad\qquad\qquad$ $dW = 1.94$
$\qquad\qquad$ (−2·57)

[55] $\quad M_{57} = -1.856 + 0.025[Y_5 - \overline{\Delta BI_5}] + 1.274\dfrac{\bar{P}^{xp}_w}{\bar{P}^x_7}$ $\quad \bar{R}^2 = 0.922$
$\qquad\qquad$ (−1·69) $\quad$ (12·58) $\qquad\qquad\qquad$ (1·29) $\qquad$ $F = 56.2$
$\qquad\qquad$ $- 0.043\overline{DV}_{58,59,62}$ $\qquad\qquad\qquad\qquad$ $dW = 0.68$
$\qquad\qquad$ (−0·39)

[56] $\quad M_{58} = -0.300 + 0.020[Y_5 - \overline{\Delta BI_5}] + 0.133\dfrac{\bar{P}_5}{\bar{r}_5\bar{P}^x_8}$ $\quad \bar{R}^2 = 0.970$
$\qquad\qquad$ (1·79) $\quad$ (4·16) $\qquad\qquad\qquad$ (0·52) $\qquad$ $F = 159.2$
$\qquad\qquad$ $- 0.027\bar{T}_r$ $\qquad\qquad\qquad\qquad\qquad$ $dW = 2.14$
$\qquad\qquad$ (−1·55)

TABLE 11.3 (*contd.*)

[57] $M_{59} = 0.424 + 0.0123[Y_5 - \overline{\Delta BI_5}] - 0.605 \dfrac{\bar{p}_w^{xp}}{\bar{P}_9^x}$ $\bar{R}^2 = 0.944$

     (1.07)   (4.18)   (−1.56) $F = 60.3$

     $- 0.024\overline{DV}_{58,59,62} - 0.023\bar{T}_r$ $dW = 1.58$

     (−1.13)   (−1.80)

[58] $M_{510} = -2.291 + 0.038[Y_5 - \overline{\Delta BI_5}] + 2.141 \dfrac{\bar{p}_w^{xp}}{\bar{P}_{10}^x}$ $\bar{R}^2 = 0.932$

     (−1.68)   (3.99)   (1.57) $F = 49.2$

     $- 0.111 DV_{58,59,62,67} - 0.064\bar{T}_r$ $dW = 2.26$

     (−1.82)   (−1.64)

[59] $M_{61} = -9.095 + 0.312\left[\bar{R}_6 + \sum\limits_{j=1}^{5} M_{j6} + M_{r6} \right]$ $\bar{R}^2 = 0.680$

     (−2.83)   (3.77) $_{-1}$ $F = 10.3$

                                        $dW = 1.43$

     $+ 7.438 \dfrac{\bar{P}_w^x}{\bar{P}_1^x} + 0.484\bar{M}_{61}$

     (2.97)   (3.03) $_{-1}$

[60] $M_{62} = -0.890 + 0.025\left[\bar{R}_6 + \sum\limits_{j=1}^{5} M_{j6} + \bar{M}_{r6} \right]$ $\bar{R}^2 = 0.920$

     (−4.72)   (4.13) $_{-1}$ $F = 52.0$

                                        $dW = 2.74$

     $+ 0.783 \dfrac{\bar{P}_w^x}{\bar{P}_2^x} + 0.007\bar{T}_r$

     (4.72)   (4.66)

[61] $M_{63} = -1.543 - 0.065\left[\bar{R}_6 + \sum\limits_{j=1}^{5} M_{j6} + \bar{M}_{r6} \right]$ $\bar{R}^2 = 0.850$

     (−1.16)   (2.56) $_{-1}$ $F = 26.2$

                                        $dW = 2.08$

     $+ 2.240 \dfrac{\bar{P}_w^x}{\bar{F}_3^x} + 0.730\bar{M}_{63}$

     (1.03)   (6.68) $_{-1}$

[62] $M_{64} = 0.022 + 0.053\left[\bar{R}_6 + \sum\limits_{j=1}^{5} M_{j6} + \bar{M}_{r6} \right]$ $\bar{R}^2 = 0.770$

     (0.15)   (3.84) $_{-1}$ $F = 22.4$

                                        $dW = 2.15$

     $+ 0.369\bar{M}_{64}$

               $_{-1}$

     (2.80)

[63] $M_{65} = -0.334 + 0.001\left[\bar{R}_6 + \sum\limits_{j=1}^{5} M_{j6} + \bar{M}_{r6} \right]$ $\bar{R}^2 = 0.90$

     (−0.82)   (0.05) $_{-1}$ $F = 41.5$

                                        $dW = 0.78$

     $+ 0.460 \dfrac{\bar{P}_w^x}{\bar{P}_5^x} + 0.022\bar{T}_r$

     (1.01)   (3.22)

TABLE 11.3 (*contd.*)

[64] $M_{71} = -0.015 + 0.103 \left[\bar{R}_7 + \sum_{j=1}^{5} M_{j7} + \bar{M}_{r7} \right]$ $\bar{R}^2 = 0.78$

$\qquad\quad (-0.11) \quad (1.61)$ $F = 23.8$

$\qquad\quad + 0.085 \bar{M}_{71}$ $dW = 1.40$

$\qquad\quad (0.20) \qquad {}_{-1}$

[65] $M_{72} = -0.001 + 0.004 \left[\bar{R}_7 + \sum_{j=1}^{5} M_{j7} + \bar{M}_{r7} \right]$ $\bar{R}^2 = 0.61$

$\qquad\quad (-0.16) \quad (3.06)$ $F = 11.3$

$\qquad\quad + 0.042 \bar{M}_{72}$ $dW = 1.66$

$\qquad\quad (0.17) \qquad {}_{-1}$

[66] $M_{73} = 0.203 + 0.083 \left[\bar{R}_7 + \sum_{j=1}^{5} M_{j7} + \bar{M}_{r7} \right]$ $\bar{R}^2 = 0.69$

$\qquad\quad (1.21) \quad (1.31)$ $F = 15.3$

$\qquad\quad + 0.346 \bar{M}_{73}$ $dW = 2.03$

$\qquad\quad (1.00) \qquad {}_{-1}$

[67] $M_{74}^{*} = 0.218 \left[0.016 + 0.498 \left\{ \bar{R}_7 + \sum_{j=1}^{5} M_{j7} \, \bar{M}_{r7} \right\} \right.$ $\bar{R}^2 = 0.99$

$\qquad\qquad\quad (0.10) \qquad (4.20)$ $F = 471.5$

$\qquad\qquad\qquad\qquad\qquad\qquad\qquad\qquad\qquad\quad dW = 1.36$

$\qquad\quad \left. + 0.298 \sum_{j=1}^{10} \bar{M}_{7j} \right]$

$\qquad\qquad\qquad\qquad {}_{-1}$

$\qquad\quad (1.71)$

[68] $M_{75} = -0.490 + 0.028 \left[\bar{R}_7 + \sum_{j=1}^{5} M_{j7} + \bar{M}_{r7} \right]$ $\bar{R}^2 = 0.95$

$\qquad\quad (-2.25) \quad (1.93)$ $dW = 2.14$

$\qquad\quad + 0.493 \dfrac{\bar{P}_w^x}{\bar{p}_5^x} + 0.005 \bar{T}_r$

$\qquad\quad (2.0) \qquad\qquad (0.69)$

[69] $M_{91} = 0.001 + 0.023 \left[\bar{R}_9 + \sum_{j=1}^{5} M_{j9} + \bar{M}_{r9} \right]$ $\bar{R}^2 = 0.60$

$\qquad\quad (0.0004) \ (0.52)$ $F = 10.9$

$\qquad\quad + 0.685 \bar{M}_{91}$ $dW = 1.68$

$\qquad\quad (2.77) \qquad {}_{-1}$

[70] $M_{92}^{*} = 0.015 \left[-1.216 + 0.852 \left\{ \bar{R}_9 + \sum_{j=1}^{5} M_{j9} + \bar{M}_{r9} \right\} \right.$ $\bar{R}^2 = 0.97$

$\qquad\qquad\qquad (-2.88) \quad (6.61)$ $F = 231.9$

$\qquad\qquad\qquad\qquad\qquad\qquad\qquad\qquad\qquad\quad dW = 1.04$

$\qquad\quad \left. + 0.148 \sum_{j=1}^{10} \bar{M}_{9j} \right]$

$\qquad\qquad\qquad\qquad {}_{-1}$

$\qquad\quad (1.11)$

TABLE 11.3 (*contd.*)

[71] $M_{93} = 0.579 + 0.144\left[\bar{R}_{9} + \sum_{j=1}^{5} M_{j9} + \bar{M}_{r9}\right]$ $\bar{R}^2 = 0.740$
        (1.83) (2.19) $F = 16.6$
                                     $dW = 1.50$

        $+ 0.288 \bar{M}_{93}_{-1}$
        (1.34)

[72] $M_{94}^{*} = 0.196\left[-1.216 + 0.852\left\{\bar{R}_{9} + \sum_{j=1}^{5} M_{j9} + \bar{M}_{r9}\right\}\right.$ $\bar{R}^2 = 0.970$
           (-2.88) (6.61) $F = 231.9$
                                     $dW = 1.04$

        $\left. + 0.148 \sum_{j=1}^{10} \bar{M}_{9j}_{-1}\right]$
        (1.11)

[73] $M_{95}^{*} = 0.053\left[-1.216 + 0.852\left\{\bar{R}_{9} + \sum_{j=1}^{5} M_{j9} + \bar{M}_{r9}\right\}\right.$ $\bar{R}^2 = 0.970$
           (-2.88) $F = 231.9$
                                     $dW = 1.04$

        $\left. + 0.148 \sum_{j=1}^{5} \bar{M}_{9j}_{-1}\right]$
        (1.11)

[74] $M_{101} = -9.418 + 0.059\left[\bar{R}_{10} + \sum_{j=1}^{5} M_{j10} + \bar{M}_{r10}\right]$ $\bar{R}^2 = 0.960$
          (-2.43) (1.58) $F = 109.1$
                                    $dW = 1.60$

        $+ 9.239 \dfrac{\bar{P}_{w}^{x}}{\bar{P}_{1}^{x}} + 0.180 \bar{T}_{r}$
        (2.44) (4.35)

[75] $M_{102} = -0.086 + 0.012\left[\bar{R}_{10} + \sum_{j=1}^{5} M_{j10} + \bar{M}_{r10}\right]$ $\bar{R}^2 = 0.780$
          (-2.57) (3.39) $F = 23.6$
                                    $dW = 2.05$

        $+ 0.414 \bar{M}_{102}_{-1}$
        (1.53)

[76] $M_{103} = -0.048 + 0.055\left[\bar{R}_{10} + \sum_{j=1}^{5} M_{j10} + \bar{M}_{r10}\right]$ $\bar{R}^2 = 0.860$
          (0.03) (4.30) $F = 28.0$
                                    $dW = 1.59$

        $+ 0.331 \dfrac{\bar{P}_{w}^{x}}{\bar{P}_{3}^{x}} + 0.146 \bar{M}_{103}_{-1}$
        (0.21) (0.69)

TABLE 11.3 (contd.)

[77] $$M^*_{104} = 0{\cdot}131\Bigg[-2{\cdot}437 + 0{\cdot}712\bigg\{ \bar{R}_{10}_{-1} + \sum_{j=1}^{5} M_{j10} \qquad \begin{aligned}&\bar{R}^2 = 0{\cdot}980\\ &F = 332{\cdot}8\\ &dW = 0{\cdot}81\end{aligned}$$
$$\qquad\quad (-4{\cdot}28)\qquad (6{\cdot}36)$$
$$\qquad + \bar{M}_{r10}\bigg\} + 0{\cdot}308 \sum_{j=1}^{10} \bar{M}_{10j}_{-1} \Bigg]$$
$$\qquad\qquad (2{\cdot}48)$$

[78] $$M_{105} = -2{\cdot}280 + 0{\cdot}125\Bigg[\bar{R}_{10}_{-1} + \sum_{j=1}^{5} M_{j10} + \bar{M}_{r10} \Bigg] \qquad \begin{aligned}&\bar{R}^2 = 0{\cdot}987\\ &F = 338{\cdot}7\\ &dW = 1{\cdot}38\end{aligned}$$
$$\qquad\quad (2{\cdot}74)\qquad (3{\cdot}30)$$
$$\qquad + 1{\cdot}412 \frac{\bar{P}^x_w}{\bar{P}^x_5} + 0{\cdot}525 \bar{M}_{105}_{-1}$$
$$\qquad\quad (1{\cdot}71)\qquad\qquad (2{\cdot}95)$$

---

[79] $$P^x_1 = -0{\cdot}325 + 0{\cdot}013\bar{P}_1 + 0{\cdot}007 \sum_{j=1}^{10} M_{j1} - 0{\cdot}029\bar{T}_r \quad \begin{aligned}&\bar{R}^2 = 0{\cdot}952\end{aligned}$$
$$\quad (-1{\cdot}53)\quad (5{\cdot}60)\qquad (4{\cdot}65)\qquad\quad (-4{\cdot}96) \quad \begin{aligned}&F = 93{\cdot}4\\ &dW = 2{\cdot}30\end{aligned}$$

[80] $$r_2 P^x_3 = 42{\cdot}403 + 0{\cdot}575\bar{P}_2 + 0{\cdot}186\bar{T}_r \qquad\qquad \begin{aligned}&\bar{R}^2 = 0{\cdot}812\\ &F = 31{\cdot}1\\ &dW = 2{\cdot}05\end{aligned}$$
$$\qquad (1{\cdot}77)\quad (2{\cdot}16)\quad (0{\cdot}35)$$

[81] $$r_3 P^x_3 = 61{\cdot}449 + 0{\cdot}392\bar{P}_3 + 0{\cdot}918 \sum_{j=1}^{10} M_{j3} \qquad \begin{aligned}&\bar{R}^2 = 0{\cdot}411\\ &F = 4{\cdot}26\\ &dW = 1{\cdot}16\end{aligned}$$
$$\qquad (1{\cdot}28)\quad (0{\cdot}58)\quad (1{\cdot}63)$$
$$\qquad - 5{\cdot}260\bar{T}_r$$
$$\qquad (-2{\cdot}48)$$

[82] $$r_4 P^x_4 = 0{\cdot}562 + 0{\cdot}004\bar{P}_4 + 0{\cdot}006\bar{T}_r \qquad\qquad \begin{aligned}&\bar{R}^2 = 0{\cdot}908\\ &F = 350{\cdot}7\\ &dW = 1{\cdot}32\end{aligned}$$
$$\qquad (3{\cdot}15)\quad (1{\cdot}79)\quad (0{\cdot}77)$$

[83] $$r_5 P^x_5 = 9{\cdot}893 + 1{\cdot}043\bar{P}^x_w - 1{\cdot}432\bar{T}_r \qquad\qquad \begin{aligned}&\bar{R}^2 = 0{\cdot}794\\ &F = 28{\cdot}1\\ &dW = 2{\cdot}14\end{aligned}$$
$$\qquad (0{\cdot}25)\quad (2{\cdot}60)\qquad (-7{\cdot}15)$$

Canada.[7] In general, the income coefficients of the import functions into non-E.E.C. Western Europe (Region 4) and Japan (Region 5) have relatively high t ratios but the price coefficients are typically not significant.

As was pointed out earlier, the import functions into the developing regions are expressed in terms of the capacity to import of these regions, a relative export price variable and the corresponding lagged endogenous import flows. In a few cases instead of trying to estimate the specific imports into the ith developing region from the jth developed region, directly, total imports into i from the developed world $\left(\sum_{j=1}^{5} M_{ij}\right)$ was estimated instead and the exporting region j's share of the ith importing region's total imports (based on 1962–64 averages) was applied to that total import function.[8]

A review of the import functions into the developing regions (Equations 59–78) shows that, in general, the coefficients of the capacity to import as defined above, are highly significant except perhaps for Region 7 (the Middle-East). The coefficients of the price variable are somewhat less significant but still reasonable considering that about half of the price coefficients have t values of 2·0 or above.

Equations 79–83 represent the export price formation equations for the five developed regions. Even though these equations are not used in the model, as such, it is interesting to note that export prices for the developed world are fairly well explained by the respective G.N.P. price deflators and also for the United States and the E.E.C., by the total value of current exports.

---

[7] It is, however, relatively significant in the E.E.C. import functions from, respectively, non-E.E.C. Western Europe; the Middle East; Australia, New Zealand and South Africa; and Africa.

[8] More specifically, this procedure was followed in five cases, namely with respect to M_{74}^*, M_{92}^*, M_{94}^*, M_{95}^* and M_{104}^*. Thus, M_{ij}^* means imports into i ($i = 6, 7, 9, 10$) from j ($j = 1, 2, \ldots, 5$), based on the estimated equation of total imports $\left(\sum_{j=1}^{5} M_{ij}\right)$ which is placed within brackets in each of the above equations while the coefficient outside the brackets (preceding the brackets) is the exporting region j's share of the ith importing region's total imports, based on 1962–64 averages.

TABLE 11.4. Income and Price Elasticities of Demand for Merchandise Imports Reflected in the Estimated Import Functions*

Imports into U.S.	Income elasticity	Relative price elasticity	Imports into Canada	Income elasticity	Relative price elasticity	Imports into E.E.C.	Income elasticity	Relative price elasticity	Imports into non-E.E.C. Western Europe	Income elasticity	Relative price elasticity	Imports into Japan	Income elasticity	Relative price elasticity
M_{12}	2·80	−1·09	M_{21}	3·15	−0·52	M_{31}	2·99	−1·79‡	M_{41}	1·05	−2·45	M_{51}	1·03	−0·011
M_{13}	3·85	−5·01	M_{23}	1·35	−1·82	M_{32}	1·28	wrong sign	M_{42}	0·79	−1·06	M_{52}	1·91	−1·08
M_{14}	3·87	−3·68	M_{24}	0·72	−1·54	M_{34}	0·95	−1·31	M_{43}	0·83	−0·25	M_{53}	7·49	wrong sign
M_{15}	6·05	−2·36	M_{25}	2·95	−1·53	M_{35}	9·10	−1·47	M_{45}	6·54	−2·41	M_{54}	2·10	−0·56
M_{16}	1·17	−1·12	M_{26}	0·01	−2·13†	M_{36}	1·31	−0·33	M_{46}	0·34	−0·36	M_{56}	1·13	−0·05
M_{17}	1·26	−0·08†	M_{27}	1·40	−1·55	M_{37}	1·81	−2·14†	M_{47}	1·14	−2·60	M_{57}	1·89	−2·54
M_{18}	2·25	−0·81	M_{28}	0·62	wrong sign	M_{38}	1·60	wrong sign	M_{48}	1·16	−0·12	M_{58}	1·90	−0·31
M_{19}	1·05	−1·21†	M_{29}	0·22	−0·25†	M_{39}	0·52	−0·43	M_{49}	0·77	−2·24†	M_{59}	4·27	wrong sign
M_{110}	3·07	−1·04	M_{210}	1·81	wrong sign	M_{310}	3·51	−1·77†	M_{410}	0·37	wrong sign	M_{510}	1·88	−2·49

* All elasticities are measured at the means of the relevant variables.
† The price variable which produced this elasticity estimate is the ratio of the world export price index of primary products to the export price index of the exporting region, i.e. P_w^x / P_j^x.
‡ The price variable which produced this elasticity is the ratio of the world export price index to the export price index of the exporting region, i.e. P_w^x / P_j^x.

The income and price elasticities of demand for merchandise imports corresponding to the estimated import functions in the world trade model were computed for the developed regions. Table 11.4 presents the whole matrix of elasticities measured at the means of the relevant variables.[9] An examination of that table suggests the following observations:

(1) The income elasticities of demand for U.S. imports from the other developed regions are relatively high in contrast to those prevailing for U.S. imports from the developing world (except for Southeast Asia). The same distinction can be made with respect to U.S. price elasticities, with the qualification that the U.S. price elasticity of imports from Canada is relatively low;

(2) the income elasticities of imports into Canada are, in general, lower than the corresponding U.S. elasticities. It is only with respect to imports from the U.S., Japan and South-East Asia that a relatively high income elasticity obtains; likewise the income elasticities into the E.E.C. and into non-E.E.C. Western Europe tend to be relatively low with the exception of imports from the U.S. and Japan;

(3) the magnitudes of the price elasticities of imports into Regions 2–5 indicate a fair degree of responsiveness of imports to prices. It is, of course, true that the confidence which can be attached to these price elasticities is more limited than that with respect to the income elasticities because of the lower statistical significance of the estimated price parameters used to compute the price elasticities.

In general, the magnitudes of both the income and price elasticities obtained in this study are substantially higher than those obtained by Rhomberg. The main reason for this difference would appear to be the much more disaggregative nature of the elasticity coefficients generated by this study as compared to Rhomberg's model.

[9] The same matrix of income price elasticities of demand for imports as contained in Table 4 was also computed on the basis of the coefficients estimated through the Cochrane-Orcutt iterative technique. A fairly close correspondence exists between the matrix in Table 4 and that generated on the basis of the above procedure.

TABLE 11.5. *Impact Multipliers of Selected Variables*

Exogenous variables	Y_1	Y_2	Y_3	Y_4	Y_5	M_{12}	M_{13}	M_{14}	M_{15}	M_{16}	M_{17}	M_{18}	M_{19}	M_{110}
$\bar{G}_1$	2·547	0·054	0·179	0·165	0·056	0·050	0·042	0·038	0·039	0·017	0·002	0·005	0·004	0·020
$\bar{G}_2$	0·924	1·045	0·113	0·109	0·034	0·018	0·015	0·014	0·014	0·006	0·001	0·002	0·001	0·007
$\bar{G}_3$	0·527	0·025	3·186	0·394	0·072	0·010	0·009	0·008	0·008	0·008	—	0·001	0·001	0·004
$\bar{G}_4$	0·308	0·030	0·577	3·447	0·083	0·006	0·005	0·005	0·005	0·002	—	0·001	0·001	0·002
$\bar{G}_5$	0·194	0·020	0·296	0·122	1·180	0·004	0·003	0·003	0·003	0·001	—	—	—	0·001
$\bar{R}_6^{-1}$ & $\bar{M}_{r6}$	0·868	0·046	0·296	0·263	0·029	0·017	0·014	0·013	0·013	0·006	0·001	0·002	0·001	0·007
$\bar{R}_7^{-1}$ & $\bar{M}_{r7}$	0·349	0·016	0·354	0·429	0·054	0·007	0·006	0·005	0·005	0·002	—	0·001	0·001	0·003
$\bar{R}_9^{-1}$ & $\bar{M}_{r9}$	0·203	0·025	0·542	0·640	0·081	0·004	0·003	0·003	0·003	0·001	—	—	—	0·002
$\bar{R}_{10}^{-1}$ & $\bar{M}_{r10}$	0·244	0·022	0·279	0·375	0·163	0·005	0·004	0·004	0·004	0·002	—	—	—	0·002

Exogenous variables	M_{31}	M_{41}	M_{51}	M_{61}	M_{71}	M_{91}	M_{101}	M_{34}	M_{43}	M_{37}	M_{39}	M_{47}	M_{510}
$\bar{G}_1$	0·019	0·003	0·002	0·006	0·001	0·0002	0·002	0·005	0·008	0·003	0·001	0·002	0·002
$\bar{G}_2$	0·365	0·002	0·001	0·003	0·001	—	—	0·003	0·005	0·002	0·001	0·001	0·001
$\bar{G}_3$	0·009	0·008	0·003	0·013	0·007	0·001	0·004	0·090	0·019	0·057	0·022	0·004	0·003
$\bar{G}_4$	0·010	0·067	0·003	0·006	0·005	0·001	0·002	0·016	0·167	0·010	0·004	0·036	0·003
$\bar{G}_5$	0·007	0·002	0·042	0·005	0·004	—	0·003	0·008	0·006	0·005	0·002	0·001	0·045
$\bar{R}_6^{-1}$ & $\bar{M}_{r6}$	0·016	0·005	0·001	0·315	0·001	—	0·001	0·008	0·013	0·005	0·002	0·003	0·001
$\bar{R}_7^{-1}$ & $\bar{M}_{r7}$	0·005	0·008	0·002	0·003	0·104	—	0·001	0·010	0·021	0·006	0·002	0·004	0·002
$\bar{R}_9^{-1}$ & $\bar{M}_{r9}$	0·009	0·013	0·003	0·003	0·002	0·023	0·001	0·015	0·031	0·010	0·004	0·007	0·003
$\bar{R}_{10}^{-1}$ & $\bar{M}_{r10}$	0·008	0·007	0·006	0·002	0·001	—	0·060	0·008	0·018	0·005	0·002	0·004	0·006

It should be noted that given the specification of the model (see Equation (7) of Table 2) the same multipliers apply to both $\bar{R}$ and $\bar{M}_{r_i}$, $i = 6, 7, 9,$ and 10.

3. Test of the Predictive Ability of the Model

It is particularly important with a model as large as the present one to test its predictive ability over the sample period (1953–67). The first step in such a test is to derive the reduced form of the model by expressing the set of endogenous variables exclusively as a function of the set of exogenous variables (including the lagged endogenous variables) and the constant terms.

In symbols, let

A = the coefficient matrix of the endogenous variables,
y = the vector of endogenous variables,
B = the coefficient matrix of the exogenous variables (including the lagged endogenous variables),
x = the vector of exogenous variables,
c = the vector of constant terms

The estimated trade model in Table 3 can be expressed as

$$Ay + Bx + c = 0 \tag{1}$$

The reduced form of this model is

$$y = A^{-1}Bx + A^{-1}c \tag{2}$$

The matrix $A^{-1}B$ is the matrix of impact multipliers linking the exogenous variables to the endogenous variables. Since the world trade model in Table 11.3 consists of seventy-eight endogenous variables and eighty-eight exogenous variables, there are a total of 6864 such multipliers. Table 11.5 presents a sample of these impact multipliers for a selected set of variables, by way of an example.

The second step, after having derived the reduced form, consists of substituting the actual values of the exogenous variables into Equation (2) above and obtaining the predicted values of the set of endogenous variables (the $\hat{y}$'s) for each year of the sample period. The final step is to compare the values of the predicted endogenous variables with the actual observed values of the endogenous variables (the $\hat{y}$'s).

The above procedure was followed and the results are presented in Tables A1–A6 of Appendix A which show the actual and the predicted values of all endogenous variables of

TABLE A.1. Actual and Predicted Values of Endogenous Variables for Region 1 (United States) in billions of U.S. dollars at 1958 prices

		1960	1961	1962	1963	1964	1965	1966	1967
C_1	Actual	316.1	322.5	338.4	353.3	373.7	397.7	418.1	430.3
	Predicted	311.1	327.3	345.8	357.2	371.1	390.7	419.2	443.0
M_{12}	Actual	2.855	3.298	3.798	3.985	4.313	4.881	5.947	6.761
	Predicted	2.933	3.301	3.898	4.109	4.336	4.752	6.248	6.803
M_{13}	Actual	2.304	2.245	2.438	2.515	2.776	3.226	4.005	4.327
	Predicted	2.137	2.242	2.512	2.699	2.761	3.094	3.871	4.597
M_{14}	Actual	1.939	1.817	2.023	2.123	2.236	2.630	3.246	3.250
	Predicted	1.676	1.874	2.152	2.249	2.358	2.531	3.043	3.540
M_{15}	Actual	1.073	1.065	1.381	1.494	1.781	2.489	3.056	2.999
	Predicted	0.772	1.077	1.535	1.624	1.897	2.320	2.922	3.310
M_{16}	Actual	3.680	3.384	3.689	3.599	3.620	3.677	4.057	3.932
	Predicted	3.525	3.639	3.825	3.690	3.653	3.584	3.911	4.128
M_{17}	Actual	0.410	0.422	0.410	0.436	0.492	0.538	0.554	0.444
	Predicted	0.363	0.377	0.399	0.413	0.429	0.449	0.478	0.505
M_{18}	Actual	0.359	0.510	0.661	0.668	0.574	0.617	0.738	0.767
	Predicted	0.420	0.465	0.523	0.531	0.562	0.650	0.723	0.838
M_{19}	Actual	0.871	0.990	1.072	1.123	1.298	1.309	1.406	1.388
	Predicted	0.922	0.996	1.065	1.156	1.229	1.285	1.388	1.412
M_{110}	Actual	1.256	1.208	1.322	1.362	1.500	1.701	1.905	2.058
	Predicted	1.119	1.219	1.350	1.388	1.472	1.625	1.918	2.158
$\sum_{j=1}^{10} M_{1j}$	Actual	14.747	14.939	16.794	17.381	18.590	21.068	24.914	25.926
	Predicted	13.867	15.190	17.259	17.859	18.697	20.290	24.502	27.291
Y_1	Actual	487.7	497.2	529.8	551.0	581.1	617.8	658.1	674.6
	Predicted	482.5	501.5	537.3	555.1	578.4	611.2	659.8	687.5

TABLE A.2. Actual and Predicted Values of Endogenous Variables for Region 2 (Canada) in billions of U.S. dollars at 1958 prices and exchange rates

		1960	1961	1962	1963	1964	1965	1966	1967
C_2	Actual	23·841	24·598	25·746	26·906	28·612	30·347	31·876	33·374
	Predicted	23·392	24·481	26·156	27·272	28·710	30·244	32·377	33·189
M_{21}	Actual	4·005	3·744	3·987	4·102	4·709	5·343	6·133	6·769
	Predicted	3·406	3·599	4·091	4·346	4·977	5·307	6·451	6·717
M_{23}	Actual	0·308	0·317	0·313	0·317	0·368	0·461	0·491	0·563
	Predicted	0·300	0·303	0·321	0·355	0·401	0·439	0·519	0·569
M_{24}	Actual	0·684	0·701	0·624	0·590	0·650	0·706	0·742	0·791
	Predicted	0·621	0·609	0·606	0·633	0·677	0·699	0·772	0·824
M_{25}	Actual	0·109	0·114	0·119	0·122	0·163	0·220	0·241	0·282
	Predicted	0·090	0·108	0·132	0·146	0·178	0·205	0·252	0·269
M_{26}	Actual	0·328	0·346	0·357	0·371	0·408	0·381	0·342	0·394
	Predicted	0·352	0·352	0·361	0·385	0·392	0·361	0·392	0·370
M_{27}	Actual	0·121	0·107	0·101	0·116	0·103	0·104	0·110	0·098
	Predicted	0·079	0·082	0·086	0·093	0·100	0·108	0·124	0·134
M_{28}	Actual	0·057	0·058	0·067	0·081	0·088	0·077	0·085	0·097
	Predicted	0·061	0·066	0·072	0·078	0·085	0·090	0·098	0·102
M_{29}	Actual	0·162	0·170	0·169	0·211	0·228	0·199	0·226	0·241
	Predicted	0·166	0·178	0·187	0·198	0·209	0·218	0·230	0·238
M_{210}	Actual	0·098	0·093	0·108	0·122	0·120	0·138	0·144	0·168
	Predicted	0·091	0·099	0·110	0·116	0·128	0·135	0·155	0·161
$\sum_{j=1}^{10} M_{2j}$	Actual	5·872	5·650	5·845	6·032	6·837	7·629	8·514	9·403
	Predicted	5·166	5·396	5·966	6·360	7·147	7·562	8·993	9·384
Y_2	Actual	36·138	37·043	39·579	41·570	44·260	47·168	50·334	51·733
	Predicted	35·374	37·015	40·070	41·776	44·259	46·974	51·134	52·106

TABLE A.3. *Actual and Predicted Values of Endogenous Variables for Region 3 (E.E.C.) in billions of U.S. dollars at 1958 prices and exchange rates*

		1960	1961	1962	1963	1964	1965	1966	1967
C_3	Actual	114·6	121·6	129·2	136·8	142·9	148·9	156·2	161·2
	Predicted	119·0	128·8	136·3	134·7	149·6	155·0	159·9	168·1
M_{31}	Actual	3·407	3·440	3·553	3·864	4·416	4·919	5·070	5·114
	Predicted	3·045	3·523	3·987	3·929	4·624	4·754	5·136	5·604
M_{32}	Actual	0·445	0·494	0·450	0·471	0·529	0·596	0·571	0·610
	Predicted	0·422	0·462	0·489	0·492	0·541	0·562	0·593	0·630
M_{34}	Actual	5·101	5·713	6·294	6·922	7·448	7·583	7·855	7·730
	Predicted	5·007	5·842	6·354	6·711	7·417	7·679	8·142	7·911
M_{35}	Actual	0·166	0·213	0·281	0·330	0·364	0·500	0·619	0·550
	Predicted	0·150	0·284	0·355	0·300	0·456	0·489	0·549	0·620
M_{36}	Actual	1·624	1·731	2·000	2·149	2·271	2·208	2·337	2·490
	Predicted	1·619	1·828	1·976	1·987	2·198	2·262	2·415	2·568
M_{37}	Actual	1·561	1·567	1·753	2·135	2·489	2·905	3·240	3·514
	Predicted	1·686	1·926	2·131	2·412	2·738	2·880	3·115	3·238
M_{38}	Actual	0·660	0·706	0·748	0·748	0·776	0·801	0·830	0·835
	Predicted	0·632	0·712	0·731	0·729	0·807	0·811	0·845	0·878
M_{39}	Actual	2·559	2·822	2·966	3·033	3·181	3·189	3·283	3·115
	Predicted	2·553	2·768	2·900	2·934	3·085	3·167	3·277	3·369
M_{310}	Actual	0·835	0·800	0·776	0·875	0·951	1·029	1·129	1·010
	Predicted	0·781	0·870	0·915	0·826	1·037	1·034	1·111	1·209
$\sum_{j=1}^{10} M_{3j}$	Actual	16·386	17·486	18·821	20·527	22·425	23·719	24·934	24·968
	Predicted	15·895	18·215	19·838	20·320	22·903	23·649	25·183	26·027
Y_3	Actual	188·7	198·7	209·9	219·0	231·7	242·3	251·0	258·8
	Predicted	188·7	203·0	214·5	215·1	235·5	244·5	252·8	265·1

9 TABLE A.4. *Actual and Predicted Values of Endogenous Variables for Region 4 (Non-E.E.C. Western Europe) in billions of U.S. dollars at 1958 prices and exchange rates*

		1960	1961	1962	1963	1964	1965	1966	1967
C_4	Actual	89·8	93·5	96·2	101·8	106·6	110·6	116·7	128·4
	Predicted	81·9	88·5	89·3	88·5	102·4	108·9	116·4	122·1
M_{41}	Actual	2·817	2·652	2·700	2·900	3·381	3·763	3·993	4·057
	Predicted	2·451	2·585	2·837	3·045	3·368	3·595	3·877	4·109
M_{42}	Actual	1·106	1·086	1·063	1·184	1·344	1·343	1·272	1·257
	Predicted	0·969	1·052	1·109	1·127	1·227	1·287	1·312	1·355
M_{43}	Actual	8·046	8·898	9·320	9·900	11·019	12·135	12·825	13·475
	Predicted	7·699	8·579	9·120	9·578	10·833	11·728	12·568	13·493
M_{45}	Actual	0·286	0·332	0·423	0·395	0·515	0·634	0·722	0·890
	Predicted	0·134	0·267	0·293	0·246	0·504	0·630	0·725	0·816
M_{46}	Actual	1·194	1·247	1·307	1·398	1·479	1·400	1·581	1·591
	Predicted	1·182	1·255	1·312	1·332	1·416	1·462	1·536	1·602
M_{47}	Actual	1·175	1·188	1·415	1·528	1·652	1·625	1·940	2·134
	Predicted	1·295	1·487	1·660	1·731	1·911	2·197	2·174	2·354
M_{48}	Actual	1·282	1·304	1·272	1·297	1·474	1·514	1·518	1·641
	Predicted	1·206	1·279	1·275	1·244	1·399	1·485	1·536	1·626
M_{49}	Actual	1·607	1·677	1·640	1·771	1·851	1·989	2·093	1·923
	Predicted	1·521	1·638	1·631	1·730	1·898	1·923	2·011	1·896
M_{960}	Actual	1·200	1·130	1·275	1·295	1·282	1·216	1·168	1·210
	Predicted	1·093	1·154	1·175	1·170	1·212	1·254	1·266	1·300
$\sum_{j=1}^{10} M_{4j}$	Actual	18·713	19·514	20·415	21·668	23·997	25·619	27·112	28·178
	Predicted	17·550	19·296	20·412	21·203	23·768	25·561	27·005	28·551
Y_4	Actual	135·7	142·3	147·0	155·1	164·1	171·3	177·6	194·4
	Predicted	128·5	138·6	141·6	142·8	161·9	171·8	182·9	192·0

TABLE A.5. *Actual and Predicted Values of Endogenous Variables for Region 5 (Japan) in billions of U.S. dollars at 1958 prices and exchange rates*

		1960	1961	1962	1963	1964	1965	1966	1967
C_5	Actual	22·76	24·99	27·55	30·06	33·08	35·08	37·89	41·60
	Predicted	23·04	26·48	28·12	29·83	33·21	33·90	36·93	41·56
M_{51}	Actual	1·326	1·699	1·397	1·677	1·866	2·260	2·468	2·434
	Predicted	1·354	1·588	1·484	1·823	2·068	2·131	2·343	2·380
M_{52}	Actual	0·180	0·239	0·266	0·332	0·387	0·361	0·438	0·505
	Predicted	0·174	0·246	0·294	0·307	0·364	0·373	0·416	0·497
M_{53}	Actual	0·209	0·308	0·304	0·359	0·386	0·381	0·434	0·563
	Predicted	0·152	0·311	0·337	0·193	0·381	0·219	0·336	0·622
M_{54}	Actual	0·146	0·223	0·216	0·243	0·298	0·313	0·379	0·432
	Predicted	0·149	0·204	0·236	0·242	0·296	0·298	0·342	0·417
M_{56}	Actual	0·249	0·366	0·374	0·441	0·542	0·689	0·768	0·502
	Predicted	0·363	0·425	0·357	0·489	0·554	0·572	0·628	0·597
M_{57}	Actual	0·352	0·422	0·506	0·663	0·804	1·208	1·346	1·546
	Predicted	0·432	0·578	0·649	0·832	0·998	1·043	1·202	1·368
M_{58}	Actual	0·369	0·520	0·505	0·563	0·599	0·692	0·848	0·990
	Predicted	0·365	0·477	0·547	0·556	0·663	0·692	0·782	0·946
M_{59}	Actual	0·080	0·111	0·090	0·120	0·191	0·247	0·306	0·372
	Predicted	0·079	0·129	0·142	0·149	0·205	0·212	0·257	0·372
M_{510}	Actual	0·755	0·755	0·755	1·000	1·059	1·378	1·594	1·520
	Predicted	0·739	0·863	0·843	0·988	1·225	1·213	1·414	1·566
$\sum_{j=1}^{10} M_{5j}$	Actual	3·666	4·643	4·413	5·398	6·131	7·529	8·581	8·864
	Predicted	3·807	4·821	4·889	5·579	6·754	6·753	7·720	8·765
Y_5	Actual	40·17	46·44	49·86	53·74	61·00	63·37	69·46	79·45
	Predicted	39·74	47·56	50·44	53·52	61·15	61·46	68·15	79·21

TABLE A.6. *Actual and Predicted Values of Endogenous Variables for Regions 6 (Latin America), 7 (Middle East), 9 (Africa), and 10 (Southeast Asia), in billions of U.S. dollars at 1958 prices and exchange rates*

		1960	1961	1962	1963	1964	1965	1966	1967
M_{61}	Actual	3·440	3·274	3·137	3·109	3·599	3·563	3·871	3·719
	Predicted	3·481	3·351	3·003	3·184	3·316	3·523	3·785	4·097
M_{62}	Actual	0·190	0·232	0·220	0·263	0·314	0·303	0·330	0·300
	Predicted	0·207	0·242	0·246	0·273	0·303	0·318	0·331	0·342
M_{63}	Actual	1·602	1·738	1·640	1·500	1·578	1·583	1·777	1·913
	Predicted	1·592	1·609	1·615	1·600	1·558	1·637	1·740	1·931
M_{64}	Actual	1·020	1·000	0·980	0·897	0·952	1·000	1·118	1·126
	Predicted	0·946	1·004	0·939	0·958	0·978	1·016		1·164
M_{65}	Actual	0·264	0·317	0·323	0·317	0·405	0·423	0·479	0·490
	Predicted	0·291	0·326	0·360	0·379	0·420	0·452	0·485	0·493
M_{71}	Actual	0·682	0·706	0·873	0·824	0·964	0·922	1·079	0·802
	Predicted	0·653	0·735	0·790	0·857	0·899	0·973	1·007	1·025
M_{72}	Actual	0·024	0·026	0·024	0·029	0·027	0·039	0·040	0·024
	Predicted	0·024	0·027	0·029	0·031	0·033	0·035	0·037	0·037
M_{73}	Actual	1·184	1·136	1·120	1·250	1·353	1·697	1·223	1·301
	Predicted	1·045	1·171	1·197	1·233	1·316	1·401	1·551	1·390
M_{74}	Actual	0·911	0·990	0·990	1·058	1·114	1·824	0·955	0·919
	Predicted	0·903	1·002	1·067	1·138	1·204	1·297	1·376	1·420
M_{75}	Actual	0·170	0·204	0·204	0·241	0·292	0·371	0·345	0·330
	Predicted	0·187	0·227	0·261	0·275	0·313	0·345	0·371	0·361
M_{91}	Actual	0·434	0·702	0·775	0·777	0·919	0·735	0·854	0·665
	Predicted	0·523	0·501	0·678	0·727	0·738	0·843	0·736	0·848
M_{92}	Actual	0·085	0·099	0·102	0·109	0·128	0·043	0·036	0·034
	Predicted	0·121	0·119	0·115	0·114	0·120	0·126	0·138	0·156

Table A.6 (contd)

M_{93}	Actual	2·862	2·712	2·330	2·460	2·559	2·835	2·816	2·874
	Predicted	2·588	2·643	2·563	2·450	2·548	2·620	2·813	2·970
M_{94}	Actual	1·470	1·446	1·382	1·485	1·476	1·454	1·381	1·378
	Predicted	1·463	1·446	1·402	1·386	1·463	1·528	1·671	1·893
M_{95}	Actual	0·205	0·198	0·270	0·382	0·524	0·691	0·608	0·680
	Predicted	0·411	0·406	0·393	0·389	0·410	0·429	0·469	0·531
M_{101}	Actual	1·812	1·815	2·118	2·460	2·628	2·674	2·721	2·960
	Predicted	1·975	1·948	2·233	2·573	2·616	2·694	2·995	3·155
M_{102}	Actual	0·112	0·119	0·093	0·131	0·154	0·146	0·204	0·248
	Predicted	0·107	0·116	0·121	0·121	0·146	0·169	0·188	0·227
M_{103}	Actual	1·168	1·195	0·060	1·130	1·249	1·407	1·495	1·504
	Predicted	1·094	1·167	1·179	1·209	1·263	1·341	1·475	1·555
M_{104}	Actual	1·381	1·475	1·363	1·398	1·381	1·398	1·381	1·288
	Predicted	1·144	1·283	1·322	1·421	1·537	1·662	1·889	2·060
M_{105}	Actual	1·244	1·370	1·494	1·610	1·800	2·268	2·711	2·930
	Predicted	1·054	1·378	1·514	1·669	1·887	2·153	2·666	3·006

the world trade model for each year from 1960–1967.[10] An examination of these tables reveals that the model has a relatively high explanatory power over the sample period – with a large number of computed (predicted) values being close to the observed values for the set of endogenous variables.[11]

The actual and predicted values of each developed region's G.N.P. and total imports over the period 1960–67 were plotted in Figures 11.1–10. It can be seen from these figures that the model predicts relatively well the changes in the above endogenous variables. A more formal test of the forecasting quality of the model, i.e. Theil's inequality coefficient[12] was applied to and computed for the ten endogenous variables graphed in Figures 11.1–10. The ten inequality coefficients corresponding to the ten variables graphed in Figures 11.1–10 came out to be very low (varying between 0·006 and 0·020) reflecting the relatively high forecasting quality of the model over the sample period.

At this stage, it appears relevant to describe the internal logic of the model, and the process through which new equilibrium levels of G.N.P. and imports are attained following changes in the exogenous variables (i.e. as a result of changes in policy instruments or autonomous shocks). A description of this process will also illustrate the possible policy use of this model. Let it be assumed, for instance, that an exogenous shock such as an increase in government expenditures or investment

---

[10] The corresponding figures for the first part of the sample period (1953–59) are not presented here.

[11] It can be seen from Tables A1–A6 that a large number of the calculated (predicted) values of the endogenous variables come within 1 per cent– 2 per cent of the actual (observed) values.

[12] The inequality coefficient which is denoted by U in Figures 1–10 is defined as:

$$U = \frac{\sqrt{\frac{1}{n}\left\{ \Sigma(P_i - A_i)^2 \right\}}}{\sqrt{\left(\frac{1}{n}\Sigma P_i^2\right)} + \sqrt{\left(\frac{1}{n}\Sigma A_i^2\right)}}$$

where P_i and A_i are, respectively, the predicted and actual values of the ith observation and n is the number of observations. The coefficient U can vary between 0, corresponding to the case of perfect forecasts ($P_i = A_i$), to one [11, pp. 31–32].

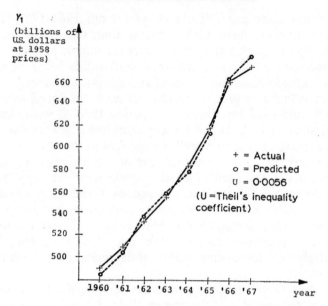

FIG. 11.1 *Actual and Predicted Values of U.S. G.N.P. 1960–67.*

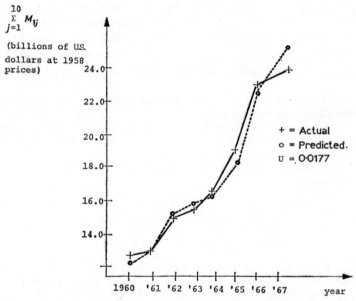

FIG. 11.2 *Actual and Predicted Values of U.S. Total Imports, 1960–67.*

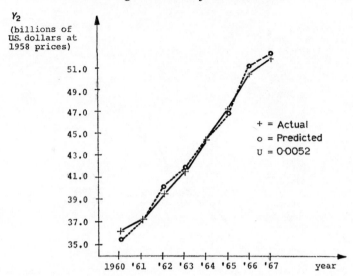

FIG. 11.3 *Actual and Predicted Values of Canada's G.N.P., 1960–67.*

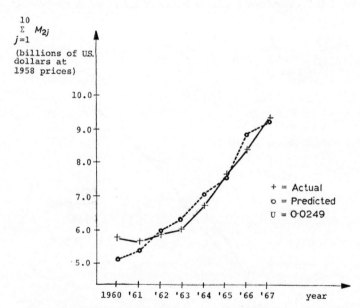

FIG. 11.4 *Actual and Predicted Values of Canada's Total Imports, 1960–67.*

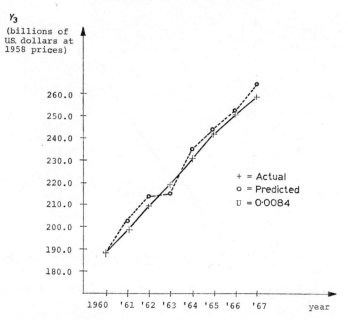

FIG. 11.5 *Actual and Predicted Values of E.E.C.'s G.N.P., 1960–67.*

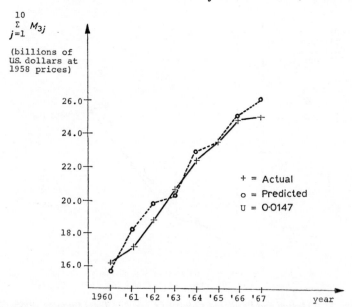

FIG. 11.6 *Actual and Predicted Values of E.E.C.'s Total Imports, 1960–67.*

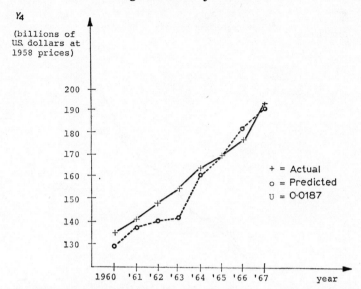

FIG. 11.7 *Actual and Predicted Values of non-E.E.C. Western Europe's G.N.P., 1960–67.*

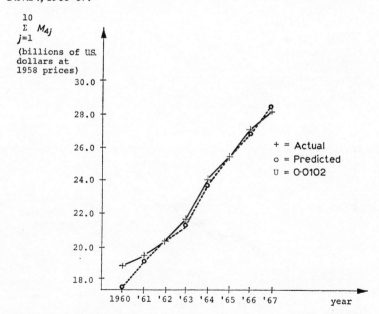

FIG. 11.8 *Actual and Predicted Values of non-E.E.C. Western Europe's Total Imports, 1960–67.*

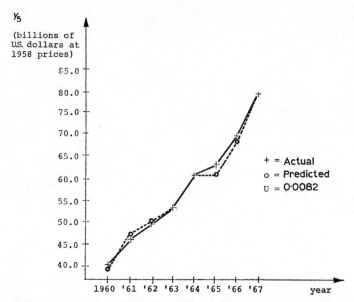

FIG. 11.9 *Actual and Predicted Values of Japan's G.N.P., 1960–67.*

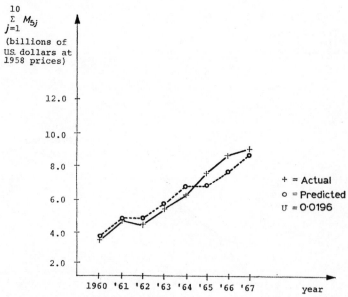

FIG. 11.10 *Actual and Predicted Values of Japan's Total Imports, 1960–67.*

in the United States causes U.S. income to rise. Part of the initial increase in income is used to purchase additional imports from the remaining regions of the world. This increase in U.S. imports is equivalent to a shift in the export schedules of the other regions *vis-à-vis* the U.S. which, through the effect of each region's foreign trade multiplier, leads to correspondingly higher income levels and in turn increased imports. This resulting rise in these regions' imports is transmitted to all other regions including the United States which in the latter case dampens the adverse income effect of the initial increase in imports. The second round growth in U.S. and other regions' G.N.P. resulting from higher exports leads, in turn, to further increases in imports. Ultimately, the system converges to a new equilibrium solution. It should, however, be noted that the income effect described above is further dampened by the price effect. Indeed, as some regions approach the full employment G.N.P. level, their domestic and export price levels will tend to rise which will affect their exports adversely while simultaneously encouraging their imports which have become relatively cheaper.[13]

4. Conclusions

The major purposes of the study were the specification and statistical estimation of a ten-region world trade model over the period 1953–67. Different model specifications and estimation procedures were tried. The model specification which was ultimately selected is discussed in Section 1 and presented in Table 11.2 while the corresponding estimated model is discussed in Section 2 and presented in Table 11.3. Even though the estimated model is by necessity large containing seventy-eight equations in seventy-eight variables and eighty-eight exogenous

---

[13] In the final analysis, all that the model specifies is an equilibrium solution in which each country's output is exactly equal to the demand for that output given the specified structural coefficients. In reality, the path to a new equilibrium specified by the static relationships (the impact multipliers in the reduced form) will depend not only on these multipliers but also on the adjustment processes (time lags) involved. This becomes a problem of economic dynamics which is not considered in this paper except insofar as it is implicitly specified in the import behaviour of the developing region.

variables, the behavioural hypotheses underlying its specification are relatively simple. Imports into the developed regions are assumed to be functions of income and relative prices while imports into the developing regions are supposed to depend mainly on the latter's capacity to import.

In general, the coefficients of the income variables in the import functions were statistically more significant than the coefficients of the price variables.[14] The corresponding income and price elasticities of demand for imports into the developed regions revealed a relatively high degree of responsiveness of imports to income changes and a somewhat lower degree with respect to price changes.

A critical evaluation of the forecasting ability of the model over the sample period, undertaken in Section 3, showed that the model performed relatively accurately in explaining the changes in the endogenous variables over the sample period.

Finally, there would appear to be at least two important areas in which the present model could be extended: (*a*) the addition of a commodity breakdown for imports to the regional breakdown; and (*b*) a more thorough study of the dynamics of the imports adjustment process at least in the developing region.

References

[1] League of Nations, *The Network of World Trade*, Princeton, New Jersey, 1942.

[2] LINNEMAN, H., *An Econometric Study of International Trade Flows*, Amsterdam, North-Holland Publishing Co., 1966.

[3] MAIZELS, A., *Industrial Growth and World Trade*, Cambridge, University Press, 1963.

[4] NEISSER, H., and MODIGLIANI, F., *National Incomes and International Trade: A Quantitative Analysis*, Urbana, Illinois, 1953.

[5] POLAK, J. J., *An International Economic System*, London: George Allen and Unwin, 1954.

---

[14] This last observation, incidentally, is typical of the great majority of econometric trade studies.

[6] PÖYHÖNEN, P., 'A Tentative Model for the Volume of Trade Between Countries', *Weltwirtschaftliches Archiv*, Band XC, 1963.

[7] RHOMBERG, R. R., '*A Short-Term World Trade Model*', Paper presented at the First World Congress of the Econometric Society, Rome, September 9–14, 1965, and summarized in *Econometrica*, XXXIV, Supplement, (1966) 90–1.

[8] RHOMBERG, R. R., and BOISSONEAULT, L., 'Effect of Income and Price Changes on the U.S. Balance of Payments', *International Monetary Fund Staff Papers*, XI, (March 1964) 59–124.

[9] TAPLIN, G. B., 'Models of World Trade', *International Monetary Fund Staff Papers*, XIV, (1967) 433–55.

[10] TINBERGEN, JAN., *Shaping the World Economy: Suggestions for an International Economic Policy*, New York: The Twentieth Century Fund, 1962.

[11] THEIL, H., *Economic Forecast and Policy*, Amsterdam: North-Holland Publishing Company, 1961.

[12] THORBECKE, E., *The Tendency towards Regionalization in International Trade, 1928–1956*, The Hague: Martinus Nijhoff, 1960.

12 Effective Protection and Resource Allocation

JARASLAV VANEK AND
TRENT J. BERTRAND*

ONE of the main topics on the agenda of international trade theorists in recent years has been the problem of effective protection. The concept of the effective rate of protection – the percentage distortion in value added attributable to tariffs on both the final and intermediate products in a production activity – is designed to indicate the degree of protection afforded different activities. As such, it has been used in studying the effect of tariff systems on resource allocation and in designing tariff systems for the achievement of policy goals such as encouraging certain industrial activities in less developed countries. In this paper, we evaluate the usefulness of the concept of effective protection for these purposes. In so doing, this paper establishes certain new results concerning the effect of the tariff system on resource allocation and illustrates a basic result concerning optimal tariff interference.

The assumptions made throughout our paper are as follows. All products are produced using primary factors of production according to a neoclassical production function subject to constant returns to scale. Interindustry flows on the other hand, if any, are subject to fixed coefficients.[1] The economy which we will study is endowed with fixed amounts of primary factors of production which are at all times fully employed. Although our entire analysis is cast in terms of effective protection, the results also pertain to the more conventional case with no interindustry flows and nominal tariffs.

* Professor of Economics, Cornell University; and Associate Professor of Political Economy, Johns Hopkins University.
[1] The model based on this assumption has been analysed by J. Vanek [12] and by T. J. Bertrand and J. Vanek [6].

1. Effective Rate of Protection and Resource Dislocation

The extent to which the effective rate of protection defines resource dislocation from conditions of free trade has been a central issue in recent trade theory. It has been argued that an exact correspondence would exist between a ranking of commodities by effective tariff rates and a ranking by degree of distortion of production levels from the free trade solution.[2] By now, however, the accepted notion is that the effective tariff cannot exactly indicate the so-called resource pull of protection. Or specifically, in an economy producing at least three goods, it is impossible to say that an effective tariff on one good higher than an effective tariff on another will produce a degree of protection more pronounced for the former good than for the latter compared to the free trade solution. The matter is well summarised by Corden: 'The general conclusion then is that the direction of resource pulls does not depend just on effective rates, but depends also on biases in substitution effects and on relative factor intensities' [7, p. 41].

In this section, our purpose is to establish a set of results on resource allocation for a two factor three commodity model of international trade. The dimensions of this basic model are suggested by the usefulness of having a rigorous measure of factor intensity which is relevant for this analysis, which restricts the analysis to two factors, and of having a model where biases in substitution effects can play a role, which requires at least three commodities. The model can then be extended in a straightforward manner to consider the many-commodity case. Furthermore, based on the insights given by the two by three model, it is also possible to discuss in a less rigorous fashion the many-product many-factor model.

The present analysis is carried out with the use of the Lerner factor space diagram. The initial equilibrium solution corresponding to free trade may be defined in Figure 12.1, with V_1 and V_2 denoting the two primary factors of production. The equilibrium condition of zero profits is realised when (with production technique adjusted so that the rate of substitution of primary factors is equated to relative factor prices) the cost

[2] See, for instance: [7a].

of the primary factors of production equals value added generated. The isoquants marked X_1, X_2, X_3 in Figure 12.1 represent equivalent values added; outputs valued at unit values added or net prices denoted as π_1, π_2 and π_3. Thus, if value added per unit of gross output in industry 1 (producing X_1) were twice as high as in industry 2, then the production

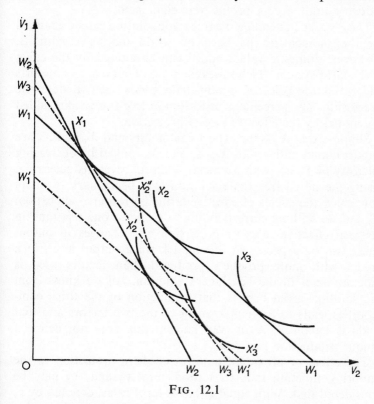

FIG. 12.1

isoquant for X_2 in Figure 12.1 would have to correspond to half the units of output shown for X_1. The cost of the primary factors of production can be denoted by an isocost function W_1W_1, the slope of which defines the relative price of the two factors. Letting this cost correspond to the values added used in deriving the equivalent isoquant, the zero profits condition requires that the three isoquants X_1, X_2 and X_3 be tangent to W_1W_1 as is the case in Figure 12.1. If one of the isoquants were

10

to the north-east of the isocost line, it would mean that the cost of primary factors required would exceed value added and production would not take place. If, on the other hand, the isoquant were to the south-west of the isocost line, the cost of primary factors required would fall short of value added. The excess profits would lead to an expansion in output in this industry until excess profits were eliminated.

The π's used in defining the free trade solution can be assumed for the moment to be fixed by world market conditions. However, domestic values added can be altered by the effect of the tariff system which raises the price of competitive imports and raises the price of intermediate goods used in domestic processing. The percentage distortion in free trade value added is denoted by the effective rate of protection.

Suppose that X_1 is the export commodity and X_2 and X_3 are import commodities with X_1, X_2 and X_3 ranked by decreasing intensity of V_1 use with no factor intensity reversals occurring. Using the initial free trade solution as a benchmark, we may now study the effects of effective tariffs on resource allocation. Of course, nothing corresponding to a one to one relationship between effective rates of protection and changes in output levels can be expected in this model, since output levels in a model with more products produced than factors used is indeterminant in the benchmark solution. All we know from the solution given here is that production of the three commodities leads to full employment of the two factors and that trade is balanced. As is well known, this does not define a unique production pattern.[3]

The effect of providing uniform effective protection to the import competing industries producing X_2 and X_3 may be considered first. With equal effective tariff rates, denoted by z_2 and z_3, the unit values added π_2 and π_3 in the domestic market will initially be raised to $\pi_2(1 + z_2)$ and $\pi_3(1 + z_3)$ respectively and the equal value isoquants for X_2 and X_3 in Figure 12.1 will be given at lower outputs, say X_2' and X_3' with both outputs being reduced by the same percentage.[4] Since values added in

[3] This indeterminacy in production has been discussed in detail by J. Melvin [10] and J. Vanek and T. J. Bertrand [13].

[4] The equivalent percentage change in outputs is reflected by the tangency of X_2' and X_3' to the isocost line $W_1'W_1'$, parallel to W_1W_1.

these industries will exceed factor costs defined by W_1W_1, resources will shift into these industries.

Two solutions are possible with the distinguishing factor whether or not tariffs end up being prohibitive for imports of X_2.[5] If tariffs are not prohibitive for imports of X_2, the domestic unit value added remains fixed at $\pi_2(1 + z_2)$ and the solution is shown in Figure 12.1 where W_2W_2 is the resulting factor price line tangent to both X_1 and X_2'. The shift in production towards the import commodities has raised the relative price of V_2, as is reflected by the slope of the new isocost line W_2W_2. However, this necessarily means that X_3' is north-east of the W_2W_2 line and production of the X_3 commodity is not viable. Uniform effective protection on the import commodities has an extreme bias against the X_3 industry.

The above is not, however, a necessary outcome. If the resulting expansion of X_2 output results in complete import substitution of that commodity, the domestic value added will no longer be fixed at $\pi_2(1 + z_2)$ but may be reduced below this as production expands in the face of a domestic demand that will then have finite elasticity. The elimination of production of X_3 may then not occur, as the fall in the domestic unit value added may result in the equivalent value isoquant for the second commodity shifting to X_2'' which, with the relative factor prices given by the resulting isocost line W_3W_3, makes production of both X_1, X_2 and X_3 once again feasible. Thus, either imports of X_2 or production of X_3 must be eliminated by equivalent effective tariffs on these products.

Recalling that under free international barter exchange the comparative factor intensities of export and import products are a reflection of the relative factor endowments of the country, we can state the conclusion in a more general manner. A country relatively better endowed with V_1 than with V_2 as compared to the rest of the world which imposes a uniform effective duty on its imports will either entirely eliminate production of the import product intensively using the scarce factor V_2 or will eliminate imports of the good whose production uses the abundant factor relatively intensively. Uniform

---

[5] We are assuming that protectionist policies do not go so far as to lead to autarky and that product X_1 continues to be exported.

protection raises value added by a given percentage but protection also raises the relative price of the scarce factor which
biases the protective effect towards the import commodity
using the abundant factor more intensively. Only if imports of
this commodity are eliminated and unit value added reduced by
a decreasing final product price will this bias fail to result in
complete specialisation within the import competing sector.[5a] In
the context of the question of resource pull, it is clear that there
is a bias and that this bias is extreme in the sense that resources
will move into the abundant factor intensive industry of the
import competing sector until either imports are eliminated or
all resources have moved out of the other import competing
industry.

Since it may be argued that a model with very many products
and two basic primary factors, capital and labour, is representative of the real world, it is useful to consider this model with the
product dimension expanded. If the many-product dimension
is interpreted to mean that changes in output in any particular
industry cannot by themselves affect factor prices, the above
analysis leads directly to two similar results. First, positive
effective protection to a single industry would eliminate imports
of that commodity. Second, uniform effective protection to all
import competing industries shifts resources toward these
industries until a final solution is attained with factor prices
changed in favour of the scarce factor, imports of a group of
abundant factor intensive industries eliminated, and production
in scarce factor intensive industries eliminated.

If we attempt to relax the assumptions of the model with
respect to the number of factors, definite results are difficult to
derive. It is not only difficult to define factor intensity but the
clear-cut results on changes in imports or outputs no longer
hold. Thus, in a three-factor three-product model, uniform
protection on the two import goods will not, in general, lead to
either elimination of imports and/or output of any good since
the strong possibility exists that a three dimensional isocost
plane in the three dimensional factor space diagram can remain
tangent to the three equal value isoquants even though domestic

---

[5a] This is assuming that intermediate commodities are traded and that
excess profits cannot be reduced by rising costs of these goods.

value added is defined by free trade value added plus effective tariff.

Nevertheless, as we did for the two primary factor case, we would like to have a theoretical explanation or base for prediction of the direction of the bias of the resource pull of a uniform effective tariff. This explanation no longer can be made absolutely rigorous. However, the above analysis suggests an approximate answer to the question. In the context of pure (Heckscher-Ohlin) theory of international trade, under free trade conditions, the country will normally be a net exporter of factors with which it is relatively abundantly endowed.[6] Uniform effective protection will now put a stronger pressure of demand on the factors which are nationally less abundant, and a comparatively less strong pressure of demand on the nationally abundant factors. Uniform protection of the import competing sector will therefore involve a bias in favour of those industries using the nationally scarce factors less intensively. Of course, we must again stress that this general statement which has a perfectly rigorous meaning in the case of two primary factors becomes only an approximation in the more general situation where there are three primary factors.

The model we have derived our basic results from is characterised by a greater number of commodities than factors. While this permits the above insights to the general model, it may also be argued that it is representative of the real world. One of the difficulties with this model has been that it results in a production possibility set with an efficiency surface characterised by linear segments. If world prices were exogenously given then it might be expected that production of more commodities than the number of factors would not occur. The problem can be understood in terms of Figure 12.1. If all prices are given, so that value added or net prices are uniquely determined, what mechanism assures that more than two equivalent value isoquants are all tangent to the isocost line, the condition defining an equilibrium solution?[7] When tariffs are imposed, there is a

[6] For an analysis of factor service flows in a multiproduct multifactor model, see: [11].

[7] This question has also been studied with respect to the factor price equalisation controversy by A. H. Land [9], T. J. Bertrand [5] and H. G. Johnson [8].

mechanism that leads to a solution with a large number of commodities being produced as discussed above. Thus in Figure 12.1, when the initial imposition of tariffs led to efficient production of only X_1 and X_2, production of X_2 expanded sufficiently in the second case considered to eliminate all imports and then to reduce final product price leading to the north-east shift of the equivalent value isoquant required for efficient production of X_1, X_2 and X_3. Tariffs created a spread between free trade values added and domestic values added within which the required adjustment could occur even if the domestic economy were not of sufficient size to affect world prices.[8] Even without tariffs, the spread between c.i.f. and f.o.b. prices creates a range between values added in export and import competing processing within which the adjustment may occur for non-traded communities.

Another important mechanism by which a multi-product solution may be achieved is through the existence of some market power for the domestic economy with respect to traded commodities. Such market power is likely to be most pronounced with respect to export commodities. For example, in Figure 12.2, consider an initial free trade situation where X_2 is an export commodity and X_3 an import commodity, while it is not efficient to produce X_1. If tariff protection is then given to the import competing industry producing X_3, the domestic value added will increase thereby shifting the equivalent value isoquant to a lower output level, denoted by X_3'. If commodity X_1 was not to be produced, and the price of X_2 was not affected, the new isocost line would be given by W_2W_2. But with the relative primary factor prices defined by the slope of this isocost line, production of X_1 would result in excess profits. Factors of production would therefore shift out of the X_2 industry and would be drawn into the X_1 industry. If all prices remained constant, the final solution would occur with production of only X_1 and X_3, an extreme bias in resource allocation between the export industries having occurred as a result of tariff protection to the import competing sector. However, the shift of resources out of X_2 and the expansion of X_1 output, given market power

---

[8] Changes in product prices will also affect value added in industries using the commodity in question as an intermediate good. These secondary effects are not essential to our analysis and are ignored here.

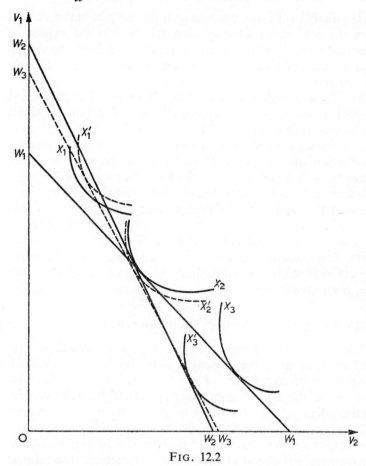

FIG. 12.2

in the export industries, will lead to a rise in the export price of X_2 and a fall in the export price of X_1 which, *ceteris paribus*, will adjust values added towards a solution indicated in Figure 12.2 by the equivalent value added isoquants X'_1, X'_2 and X'_3 tangent to the isocost line W_3W_3, the slope of which defines final factor prices. As far as the resource pull question is concerned, effective protection to the import competing sector has led to a biased shift of resources in the export industries favouring the industry intensively using the now relatively cheaper abundant factor V_1.

The analysis of this section, even if the extreme biases studied here do not occur, suggests that the bias in the degree of protection resulting from factor price changes limits the usefulness of the effective rate of protection for studying resource movements.

Finally, a practical difficulty should be noted in that most protected import competing industries would not be viable under free trade conditions. Thus, an effective rate of protection of, for instance, 80 per cent on an industry whose factor costs of production are 90 per cent above those required to make domestic production viable under free trade will not lead to a resource pull and cannot in any sense define resource flows between this and other industries given the same or different rates of protection. In practical terms this is a major qualification on different grounds than considered here to using effective rates. Empirical evaluations[9] of effective rates indicate many import competing industries that would not be viable under free trade conditions.

2. Designing and Evaluating Tariff Protection

While the results of Section 1 are of interest in themselves, they also are relevant to the discussion in the literature on rationalising the protective effect of the tariff system on various industries in the import competing sector. If the relative protective effect, i.e. the distortion of gross output, were uniquely related to relative levels of effective rates of protection, a uniform protective effect could be achieved by providing uniform rates of effective protection throughout the import competing sector. For the reasons analysed in Section 1 of this paper, in general such a unique correspondence cannot be expected. In fact, in the model with more commodities produced than primary factors, biases in resource pulls tend to be extreme. Nevertheless, this does not necessarily undermine the usefulness of calculating effective tariff rates as the factors leading to a bias in resource pulls, the resulting primary factor price changes and differing factor intensities in different sectors of the economy, can be studied in conjunction with effective rates of protection to yield conclusions on resource allocation.

[9] See, for instance, T. J. Bertrand [4] and B. Balassa [1].

Moreover, there are important areas in which the effective rate of protection can be useful in designing protective tariff structures. It can be shown that uniform rates of protection, although they cannot be expected to yield uniform distortions of production in import competing industries, will nevertheless create distortions which are optimal in the sense of maximising the value of national incomes (valued at world market prices),

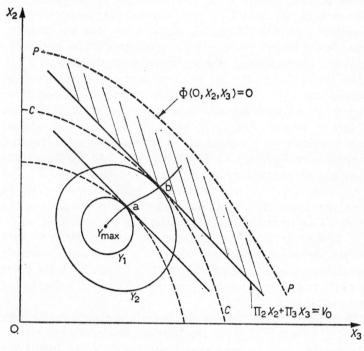

Fig. 12.3

subject to the constraint that a certain amount of value added be generated by a high priority sector of the economy.

This result may be easily demonstrated with reference to Figure 12.3. Suppose that there is a prescribed minimum aggregate value added, V_0, to be produced jointly in the two import competing industries, $V_0 \leq \pi_2 X_2 + \pi_3 X_3$. What is the production mix, and what are the policies which will attain that result with a maximum value of national product or, equivalently, with the maximum consumption possibilities given to the economy? In Figure 12.3, we show the gross output space, $X_2 - X_3$, where PP represents the maximum gross outputs of these two commodities attained when commodity X_1 is not produced. The gross production surface $\Phi(X_1, X_2, X_3) = 0$ may be described in this diagram by two sets of contours. The Y contours represent levels of national income evaluated at world market prices. These are obtained by projecting the intersections between the budget plane and the gross production possibility set into the X_2–X_3 plane. The point of tangency between the budget plane and the gross production possibility set is the unconstrained free trade optimum, denoted as $Y_{\max}$, while the contours Y_1, Y_2, etc. represent decreasing levels of national income. The second set of contours is obtained from projections of the intersection between the gross production possibility set and planes parallel to the X_2–X_3 surface defined by a specified level of output of X_1. The curve PP itself is such a contour corresponding to X_1 equals zero, and CC represents another such contour defined by some positive value of X_1. The constraint that a certain amount of national income V_0 be generated in the X_2 and X_3 industries restricts solutions to the shaded area to the north-east of the line $V_0 = \pi_2 X_2 + \pi_3 X_3$. The highest level of national income will be attained with production on the efficiency surface of the gross production possibility surface corresponding to b in Figure 12.3, the point at which the highest isoincome contour, Y_2, touches the shaded permissible area.

It should be clear that at the point corresponding to b on Φ, say b' (not in the figure), the marginal rate of transformation between X_2 and X_3 must equal the slope of the line $V_0 = \pi_2 X_2 + \pi_3 X_3$, i.e. the ratios of internal values added must equal the corresponding ratio of free trade values added.[10] Consequently, the objective of attaining V_0 with a maximum level of national income will be attained through an equal

[10] Note that at b' the plane $X_1 = $ constant, slicing Φ along CC, and the (slicing) free trade budget plane intersecting along a horizontal line (parallel to the X_2–X_3 plane) tangential to Φ at b' and thus the slicing Y_2 and CC of Φ must be tangential, the slope of CC (by definition) being equal to the marginal rate of transformation X_2 and X_3.

(uniform) effective tariff on X_2 and X_3 which does not distort the internal from the free trade relative unit values added in the import competing sector. This is so because perfect competition with marginal cost pricing leads to the equation of the ratio of domestic unit values added and the marginal rate of transformation along the gross production possibility set.[11]

3. Summary of Results

The main results of this paper may be briefly summarised. First, in a two-factor three-product (Heckscher-Ohlin) model, uniform effective protection to the import competing industries will raise the price of the scarce factor creating a biased resource flow in favour of the import competing industry using the abundant factor more intensively. This will result in either complete specialisation in this industry within the import competing sector or complete substitution for imports of the product of this industry. Second, in a two-factor many commodity model, uniform protection to the import competing sector can be expected to eliminate imports for a range of products intensively using the scarce factor. Third, in the general model with many factors and many commodities, uniform effective protection in the import competing sector will bias resource flows in favour of the import competing industries relatively factor intensive in the relatively abundant factors. Fourth, while uniform effective protection cannot be expected to provide uniform production incentives, it is optimal if the policy objective is to generate a certain amount of value added in these industries in the sense that this will maximise the consumption possibilities open to the community.

References

[1] BALASSA, B. *The Structure of Protection in Developing Countries*. Baltimore, Md: Johns Hopkins University Press, 1971.

[2] BALASSA, B. 'Tariffs, Intermediate Goods, and Domestic

---

[11] This is proved in [6]. A mathematical proof of the proposition discussed in this section is to be found in [3].

Protection: Comment', *American Economic Review*, LX, (December 1970) 959–63.

[3] BERTRAND, T. J. 'Decision Rules for Effective Protection in Less Developed Economies', *American Economic Review*, LXII (September 1972) 743–6.

[4] BERTRAND, T. J. 'The Manufacturing Sector in Nigeria: Recent Developments and the Structure of Industrial Protection', Study prepared for the World Bank, August 1970.

[5] BERTRAND, T. J. 'On Factor Price Equalization when Commodities outnumber Factors: A Note', *Economica*, XXXVII, (February 1970) 86–8.

[6] BERTRAND, T. J. and VANEK, J. 'The Theory of Tariffs, Taxes and Subsidies: Some Aspects of the Second Best', *American Economic Review*, LXI, (September 1971).

[7] CORDEN, W. *The Theory of Protection*. London: Oxford University Press, 1971.

[7A] CORDEN, W. 'The Structure of a Tariff System and the Effective Protective Rate', *Journal of Political Economy*, (June 1966).

[8] JOHNSON, H. G. 'On Factor Price Equalization when Commodities outnumber Factors: A Comment', *Economica*, XXXVII, (February 1970) 89–90.

[9] LAND, A. H. 'Factor Endowments and Factor Prices', *Economica*, XXVI, (May 1959) 137–44.

[10] MELVIN, J. 'Production and Trade with Two Factors and Three Goods', *American Economic Review*, LVIII, (December 1968) 1249–68.

[11] VANEK, J. 'The Factor Proportion Theory: The N-Factor Case', *Kyklos*, XXI, (October 1968) 749–56.

[12] VANEK, J. 'Variable Factor Proportions and Inter-Industry Flows in the Theory of International Trade', *Quarterly Journal of Economics*, LXXVII, (February 1963) 129–42.

[13] VANEK, J. and BERTRAND, T. J. 'Trade and Factor Prices in a Multi-Commodity World', in J. Vanek, J. Bhagwati, R. Mundell, and R. Jones, *Essays in Honor of Charles P. Kindleberger*, Amsterdam: North Holland, 1971.

Appendix: Bibliography of Jan Tinbergen

MANY of Jan Tinbergen's articles were published in Dutch, German, Danish, French and other languages. The selected bibliography in this Festschrift covers only Tinbergen's work originally published in English and some translations from other languages into English. This means that a large number of his important publications will not be listed. The reader can find an extensive bibliography of Jan Tinbergen in his *Selected Papers*, edited by L. H. Klaassen, L. M. Koyck and H. J. Witteveen (Amsterdam: North Holland Publishing Co., 1959). A short supplement to that bibliography was published in *De Economist*, CVII (1959) 798–9, written by J. B. D. Derksen. Finally, J. P. Pronk wrote the most up-to-date bibliography of Jan Tinbergen, covering the period 1959–69 in *De Economist*, CXVIII (1970) 156–73. The selected bibliography presented here is ordered chronologically and includes the following areas: international trade and finance, long-term economic development and planning, econometrics and economic theory. The section on economic theory also includes publications on the theory of economic policy and miscellaneous topics in economics.

1. International Trade

[1] *International Economic Co-operation*, (Amsterdam: Elsevier Economische Bibliotheek, 1945). Translated into English by P. H. Breitenstein and E. Inglis Arkell.

[2] *Some Remarks on the Problem of Dollar Scarcity*, (Washington: Congress Econometric Society, 1946).

[3] 'Unstable Equilibria in the Balance of Payments', in: *Economic Research and the Development of Economic Science and Public Policy*, (New York, 1946).

[4] International Economic Co-operation, *Erasmus Speculum Scientiarum*, Aarau, Switzerland, I, 1 (1947).

[5] 'The Equalization of Factor Prices between Free-Trade Areas', *Metroeconomica*, I, (April 1949) 38–47.

[6] 'Long-Term Foreign Trade Elasticities', *Metroeconomica*, I, (December 1949) 174–85.

[7] 'Some Remarks on the Problem of Dollar Scarcity', *Econometrica*, XVII, (July 1949) Supplement 73–97.

[8] 'The Possibility of Price and Exchange Adaptation', in: *Tracing a New International Balance*, (Leiden: Stenfert Kroese, 1950).

[9] 'On the Theory of Economic Integration', *Les Cahiers de Bruges*, 4 (1952) 292–303.

[10] 'The Relation between Internal Inflation and the Balance of Payments', *Banca Nazionale del Lavoro Quarterly Review*, V, (1952) 187–94.

[11] TINBERGEN, J. and VAN DER WERFF, H. M. A. 'Four Alternative Policies to Restore the Balance of Payments Equilibrium: A Comment and an Extension', *Econometrica*, XXI, (February 1953) 332–5.

[12] 'Customs Unions: Influence of Their Size on Their Effect,' *Zeitschrift für die Gesamte Staatswissenschaft*, CXIII, (1957) 404–14.

[13] 'An International Economic Policy', *Indian Journal of Economics*, XXXVIII, (1957) 11–16.

[14] 'Heavy Industry in the Latin American Common Market', *Economic Bulletin for Latin America*, V, (January1960) 1–5.

[15] 'The Impact of the European Economic Community on Third Countries', in: *Sciences Humaines et Intégration Européenne*, (Leiden: A. W. Sythoff, 1960), 386–98.

[16] TINBERGEN, J., RIJKEN VAN OLST, H., HARTOG, F. *et al.*, *Shaping the World Economy: Suggestions for an International Economic Policy*, (New York: The Twentieth Century Fund, 1962).

[17] 'The European Economic Community: Conservative or Progressive?', in *Wicksell Lectures 1963*. (Stockholm/Gøteborg/Uppsala: Almqvist and Wiksell, 1963), 38ff.

[18] *Lessons from the Past*, (Amsterdam: Elsevier, 1963).

[19] TINBERGEN, J., HART, A. G. and KALDOR, N. *The Case for an International Commodity Reserve Currency;* A memorandum submitted to the United Nations Conference on Trade and Development, 1964.

[20] 'The Evolution in Communist Views on International Trade', *World Justice*, VI, (January 1964) 5–8.

[21] *International Economic Integration*, 2nd revised edition, (Amsterdam/New York: Elsevier, 1965).

[22] 'International, National Regional and Local Industries', in *Trade, Growth and the Balance of Payments; Essays in Honor of Gottfried Haberler on the Occasion of his 65th Birthday*, ed. by R. E. Caves, H. G. Johnson and P. B. Kenen, (Amsterdam: North Holland, 1965), 116–25.

[23] 'Trade between Western and Communist Countries', *Cronache Economiche della CCIA di Torino*, (1965) 266–7.

[24] TINBERGEN, J. *et al. Terms of Trade and the Concept of Import Purchasing Power of the Exports of Developing Countries;* UNCTAD, Trade and Development Board, Permanent Subcommittee on Commodities, First Session (TB/BIC 1/PSC/5), Geneva, 1966.

[25] 'Balance of Payments and Project Appraisal', *Development Planning Problems and Techniques Series*, No. 1, African Institute for Economic Development and Planning, 1967, 5–10.

[26] 'Shaping the World Economy', in: *World Peace Through World Economy*, Youth and Student Division of the World Association of World Federalists, 6th International Study Conference, (Assen, Netherlands: Van Gorcum, 1968).

2. Long-Term Economic Development and Economic Planning

[1] 'Central Planning in the Netherlands', *Review of Economic Studies*, XV, (1947/48) 70–7.

[2] 'The Netherlands' Central Economic Plan for 1947' *Revue Suisse d'Economie Politique et de Statistique*, LXXXIII (January 1947) 19–29.

[3] 'Problems of Central Economic Planning in the Netherlands', *National Økonomisk Tidskrift*, LXXXV, (1947) 96ff.

[4] 'Government Budget and Central Economic Plan', *Public Finance: Openbare Financiën*, XLII, (March 1949) 195–205.

[5] 'Planning for Viability', *The Way Ahead*, II (1949) 38–61.

[6] 'Capital Formation and the Five-Year Plan', *Indian Economic Journal*, I (January 1953) 1–5.

[7] 'Problems Concerning India's Second Five-Year Plan', *Public Finance: Openbare Financiën*, XI, (February 1956) 103–10.

[8] The appraisal of Road Construction, two Calculation Schemes', *Review of Economics and Statistics*, XXXIX, (August 1957) 241–9.

[9] 'The Optimum Choice of Technology', *Pakistan Economic Journal*, VII, (February 1957) 1–7.

[10] 'The Use of a Short-Term Econometric Model for Indian Economic Policy', *Sankhyā; The Indian Journal of Statistics*, XVII, (April 1957) 337–44.

[11] 'Choice of Technology in Industrial Planning', *Industrialization and Productivity; Bulletin of the United Nations*, I, (January 1958) 24–33.

[12] 'International Co-ordination of Stabilization and Development Policies', *Kyklos*, XII, (March 1959) 283–9.

[13] 'Problems of Planning Economic Policy', *UNESCO International Social Science Journal*, XI, (March 1959) 351–60.

[14] 'Fundamental and Derived Aims of Economic Development', *The Punjab University Economist*, I, (February 1960) 1–6.

[15] *Programming Techniques for Economic Development*, (Co-author) (Bangkok: U.N. Economic Commission for Asia and the Far East, 1960).

[16] 'The Appraisal of Investment Projects: the Semi-Input-Output Method', *Industrial India*, 1961, 25–6.

[17] 'Development Theory, and Econometrist's View', in: *Money, Growth and Methodology, and Other Essays in Economics in Honor of Johan Åkerman*, ed. by H. Hegeland, (Lund: Gleerup, 1961, 49–58).

[18] TINBERGEN, J. and BOS, H. C. 'The Global Demand for Higher and Secondary Education in the Underdeveloped Countries in the Next Decade', *Policy Conference on Economic Growth and Investment Education;* Washington, D.C., (O.E.C.D., 1961), Vol. III.

[19] 'The Spatial Dispersion of Production: A Hypothesis', *Schweizerische Zeitschrift für Volkswirtschaft und Statistik*, XCVII, (April 1961) 1–8.

[20] 'Again – The Development Issue', *The Ecumenical Review*, XIX, (February 1962) 226–8.

[21] 'Planning in Stages', *Statsøkonomisk Tidskrift*, (January 1962) 1–20.

[22] TINBERGEN, J. and CORREA, H. 'Quantitative Adaptation of Education to Accelerated Growth' *Kyklos*, xv, (April 1962) 768–86.

[23] TINBERGEN, J. and Bos, H. C. 'The Financing of Higher Education in Africa', *The Development of Higher Education in Africa*, Report of the Conference on the Development of Higher Education in Africa, Tananarive, 3–12 September 1962. (Paris: UNESCO, 1963, 155–212).

[24] 'Project Criteria', in: *Economic Planning*, ed. by L. J. Zimmerman, (The Hague: Mouten, 1963, 7–19).

[25] 'Projections of Economic Data in Development Planning' *Planning for Economic Development in the Caribbean*, (Caribbean Organization, Hato Rey, Puerto Rico, 1963), 26–51.

[26] 'A World Development Policy', *World, Nations and Groups in Development*, (The Hague: Mouten, 1963), 39–55.

[27] *Central Planning*, (New Haven/London: Yale University Press 1964), 1964.

[28] *Development Planning*, (New York, Toronto: McGraw-Hill, 1966).

[29] *Development Planning: The Sector Phase, with Different Gestation Periods* (Nederlands Economisch Instituut, Publication 26/64, Rotterdam, 1964).

[30] 'Educational Assessments', *Economic and Social Aspect of Educational Planning*, (UNESCO, Paris, 1964, 165–222).

[31] *Essays in Regional and World Planning*, (New Delhi: National Council of Applied Economic Research, 1964).

[32] TINBERGEN, J. and Bos, H. C. 'A Planning Model for the Educational Requirements of Economic Development', *The Residual Factor and Economic Growth*, (Paris: O.E.C.D., 1964, 147–69).

[33] 'Possibilities for Application of Operational Research to Problems of Development', *Management Science*, x, (February 1963) 193–6.

[34] 'Project Appraisal: A Traditional Approach', *Essays on Econometrics and Planning, Presented to Professor P. C. Mahalanobis on the Occasion of his 70th Birthday.* (Calcutta: Pergamon, 1964), 295–300.

[35] 'Reply', to T. Balogh, 'Education and Economic Growth', *Kyklos*, xvii, (February 1964) 261–75.

[36] 'Discussion on the Organization of Coexistence', *Review of International Affairs*, XVI, (October 1965) 13–14.

[37] 'Economic Development and Investment Indivisibilities', *Problems of Economic Dynamics and Planning; Essays in Honor of Michal Kalecki*, ed. T. Kowalik, (Warsaw: P.W.N. Polish Scientific, 1965), 455–67.

[38] 'The Economic Framework of Regional Planning', *Semaine d'Etude sur le Rôle de l'Analyse Econométrique dans la Formulation de Plans de Développement*, Pontificiae Academiae Scientarium, Scripta Varia, No. 28, (Rome, 1965), 1233–64.

[39] 'Ideologies and Scientific Development: The Optimal Order', *Review of International Affairs*, XVI, (October 1965) 6–7.

[40] 'Improving International Development Policies', *Review of International Affairs*, XVI, (September 1965) 10–12.

[41] 'Simple Devices for Development Planning', in: *Problems in Economic Development*, ed. by E. A. G. Robinson. (London/New York: Macmillan, 1965).

[42] *Some Principles of Regional Planning*, (Rotterdam: Nederlands Economisch Instituut, Publication 29/65), 1965.

[43] 'The Concept of Unbalanced Growth', in: *Economic Development: Issues and Policies*, Dr P. S. Lokanathan 72nd Birthday, Commemoration Volume, ed. P. H. Butani and P. Singh. (Bombay 1966) 14–17.

[44] 'Economic Growth Plans and Their Impact on Business Management', *United Malayan Banking Corporation Economic Review*, XI, (February 1966) 20–6.

[45] 'International Economic Planning', *Daedalus Journal of the American Academy of Arts and Sciences*, 1966 issue: 'Conditions of World Order', 530–57.

[46] 'Some Refinements of the Semi-Input-Output Method', *Pakistan Development Review*, VI, (February 1966) 243–247.

[47] 'Concluding Remarks', in: *Towards a Strategy for Development Co-operation*, ed. H. B. Chenery *et al.* (Rotterdam: Rotterdam University Press, 1967), 93–101.

[48] 'The Hierarchy Model of the Size Distribution of Centers', *Regional Science Association: Papers*, XX, (1967) 65–68.

[49] 'Links between National Planning and Town and Country Planning', paper presented at the *Symposium on Urbanization of the International Union of Local Authorities*, (The Hague, 1967).

[50] 'Planning in the Common Market', *Sosialøkonomen*, XXI, (June 1967) 14–16.

[51] 'Chenery: Efficient Development Research', *Economisch Statistische Berichten*, LIII, (November 1968) 1013–14.

[52] 'Myrdal's Asian Drama', *Pakistan Development Review*, VIII, (April 1968) 618–25.

[53] 'The Optimal International Division of Labour', *Acta Oeconomica Academiae Scientarium Hungaricae*, III, (March 1968) 257–82.

[54] 'Optimalization – of What?' *Co-Existence*, V, (1968) 1–5.

[55] TINBERGEN, J. and BOUWMEESTER, J. 'The Role of Social Security as Seen by the Development Planner', in: *The Role of Social Security in Economic Development*, ed. E. M. Kassalow. (Washington, 1968), 39–50.

[56] 'The Significance of Science for the Developing Countries', *Higher Education and Research in the Netherlands*, XII, (March 1968) 24–9.

[57] 'Similarities and Differences between the Social Problem and the Development Problem', *Mens en Maatschappij*, XLIII, (January 1968) 120–7.

[58] 'Wanted: A World Development Plan', *International Organization*, XXII, (January 1968) 417–31.

[59] *Gunnar Myrdal on Planning Models*, U.N. Asian Institute for Economic Development and Planning, Institute Monograph No. 11, (Bangkok, 1969), 13ff.

3. Econometrics

[1] *An Econometric Approach to Business Cycles Problems*, (Paris: Hermann and Cie, 1937).

[2] 'Statistical Evidence on the Acceleration Principle', *Economica*, New Series V (1938) 164–76.

[3] *Business Cycles in the United States of America, 1919–1932*, (Geneva: League of Nations, 1939).

[4] 'Econometric Business Cycle Research', *Review of Economic Studies*, (1939/40) 73–90.

[5] *A Method and its Application to Investment Activity*, (Geneva: League of Nations, 1939).

[6] TINBERGEN, J. and DE WOLFF, P. 'A Simplified model of the Causation of Technological Unemployment', *Econometrica*, VII, (July 1939) 193–207.

[7] 'An Acceleration Principle for Commodity Stockholding and a Short Cycle Resulting from It', in: *Studies in Mathematical Economics and Econometrics*, ed. by Lange *et al.*, (Chicago: University of Chicago Press, 1942), 255–267.

[8] 'Some Measurements of Elasticities of Substitution', *Review of Economics and Statistics*, XXVIII, (August 1946) 109–16.

[9] 'The Use of Correlation Analysis in Economic Research', *Ekonomisk Tidskrift*, XLIX, (March 1947) 173–92.

[10] TINBERGEN, J. and DERKSEN, J. B. D. 'Recent Experiments in Social Accounting: Flexible and Dynamic Budgets', in: The Econometric Society Meeting, September 1947, Washington, 1949.

[11] *Business Cycles in the United Kingdom, 1870–1914*, (Amsterdam: North Holland, 1951).

[12] 'Schumpeter and Quantitative Research in Economics', *Review of Economics and Statistics*, XXXIII, (May 1951) 111–19.

[13] 'Some Neglected Points in Demand Research', *Metroeconomica*, III, (February 1951) 49–54.

[14] 'Comments' on: ORCUTT, GUY H. 'Toward Partial Redirection of Econometrics', *Review of Economics and Statistics*, XXXIV, (March 1952) 205ff.

[15] 'Import and Export Elasticities: Some Remarks', *International Statistical Institute, Bulletin*, XXXIII, (1953) 215–26.

[16] 'The Functions of Mathematical Treatment: Mathematics in Economics, Discussion of Mr. Novicks' Article', *Review of Economics and Statistics*, XXXVI, (November 1954) 365–9.

[17] 'Quantitative Economics in the Netherlands Model Building for Economic Policy', *Higher Education and Research in the Netherlands*, II, (March 1958) 3–7.

4. Economic Theory (and Miscellaneous)

[1] 'Annual Survey of Significant Developments in General Economic Theory', *Econometrica*, II, (1934) 13–36.

[2] 'On the Theory of Business Cycle Control', *Econometrica*, VI, (January 1938) 22–39.

[3] 'The Dynamics of Share-Price Formation', *Review of Economics and Statistics*, XXI, (November 1939) 153–60.

[4] 'On a Method of Statistical Business Cycle Research: A Reply', *The Economic Journal*, L, (March 1940) 141–54.

[5] 'Unstable and Indifferent Equilibria in Economic Systems', *Revue de l'Institut International de Statistique*, IX, (1941) 36–50.

[6] 'Critical Remarks on Some Business Cycle Theories', *Econometrica*, X, (April 1942) 129–46.

[7] 'Does Consumption Lag Behind Incomes?', *Review of Economics and Statistics*, XXIV, (February 1942) 1–8.

[8] 'Professor Douglas' Production Function', *Revue de l'Institut International de Statistique*, X, (1942) 37–48.

[9] 'Some Problems in the Explanation of Interest Rates', *Quarterly Journal of Economics*, LXI, (1947) 397–438.

[10] 'The Reformulation of Current Business Cycle Theories as Refutable Hypotheses', in: *Conference on Business Cycles*, National Bureau of Economic Research, 1949.

[11] 'Economic Policy in the Netherlands', *Statsøkonomisk Tidsskrift*, LXIV, (1950) 70–80.

[12] *On the Theory of Economic Policy*, (Amsterdam: North Holland, 1952).

[13] 'The Influence of Productivity on Economic Welfare', *The Economic Journal*, LXII, (1952) 68–86.

[14] 'Financing Social Insurance out of Premiums or out of Income Tax', *Archive of Economic and Social Sciences*, XXXII, (1952) 71–7.

[15] 'Efficiency and Future of Economic Research', *Kyklos*, V, (April 1952) 309–19.

[16] *Centralization and Decentralization in Economic Policy*, (Amsterdam: North Holland, 1954).

[17] *Economic Policy: Principles and Design*, (Amsterdam: North Holland, 1956).

[18] 'On the Theory of Income Distribution', *Weltwirtschaftliches Archiv*, LXXVII, (January 1956) 10–31.

[19] 'The Optimum Rate of Savings', *The Economic Journal*, LXVI, (1956) 603–9.

[20] TINBERGEN, J. *et al.* 'Comments on the Economics of Governor Stevenson's Program Paper: Where is the Money Coming From?', *Review of Economics and Statistics*, (May 1957) 134–42.

[21] 'Welfare Economics and Income Distribution', *American Economic Review, Papers and Proceedings*, XLVII, (February 1957) 490–503.

[22] 'The Economic Principles for an Optimum Use of Space', *Les Cahiers de Bruges*, XI, (1958) 15–18.

[23] 'Should the Income Tax be Among the Means of Economic Policy?', *Festskrift til Frederick Zeuthen*, (København, 1958), 351–62.

[24] *Selected Papers*, (Amsterdam: North Holland, 1959).

[25] 'The Theory of the Optimum Regime', *Selected Papers*, (Amsterdam: North Holland, 1959, 264–304).

[26] 'Economic Models of the Explanation of Inflation', in: *Stabile Preise in Wachsender Wirtschaft. Erich Schneider zum 60 Geburtstag*, ed. by G. Bomback, (Tübingen: J. C. B. Mohr, 1960, 115–24).

[27] 'Optimum Savings and Utility Maximization over Time', *Econometrica*, XXVIII, (February 1960) 481–90.

[28] TINBERGEN, J. and BOS, H. C. *Mathematical Models of Economic Growth*, (New York: McGraw-Hill, 1962).

[29] 'Do Communist and Free Societies Show a Converging Pattern?', *Soviet Studies*, XII, (April 1961) 333–41.

[30] 'The Significance of Welfare Economics for Socialism', *On Political Economy and Econometrics, Essays in Honour of Oskar Lange*, (Warsaw: P.W.N. Polish Scientific Publishers, 1965).

[31] 'On the Optimal Social Order and a World Economic Policy', (A discussion with Professor L. Leontiev), *Oost-West*, V, (October 1966) 242–4.

[32] TINBERGEN, J. and BOS, H. C. 'A Planning Model for the Educational Requirements of Economic Development', *The Residual Factor and Economic Growth*, (Paris: O.E.C.D., 1964, 147–69).

[33] 'A Model for a Flow of Funds Analysis of an Open Country', in *Essays in Honour of Marco Fano*, (Padova, 1966), 688–92.

[34] 'Some Suggestions on a Modern Theory of the Optimum Regime', in *Socialism, Capitalism and Economic Growth, Essays Presented to Maurice Dobb*, ed. by C. H. Feinstein, (London: Cambridge University Press, 1967), 125–32.

[35] TINBERGEN, J., LINNEMANN, H. and PRONK, J. P. 'Convergence of Economic Systems in East and West', in *Disarmament and World Economic Interdependence*, ed. by E. Benoit, (Oslo: Universitetsforlaget, 1967), 246–60.

[36] 'A Few Comments on Professor Lev Leontiev's Answer', *Oost-West*, VI, (May 1967) 49ff.

[37] 'Development Strategy and Welfare Economics', *Co-Existence*, VI, (July 1969) 119–26.

[38] 'Future Relations Between the Countries of Eastern and Western Europe', *Oost-West*, VIII, (May 1969) 165–6.

[39] 'Ideology and Coexistence', *Review of International Affairs*, XX, (1969) 1–2.

Index